DEFINING AUTISM

of related interest

Re-Thinking Autism
Diagnosis, Identity and Equality
Edited by Katherine Runswick-Cole, Rebecca Mallett and Sami Timimi
ISBN 978 1 84905 581 9
eISBN 978 1 78450 027 6

Understanding and Evaluating Autism Theory
Nick Chown
ISBN 978 1 78592 050 9
eISBN 978 1 78450 306 2

The Interbrain
Embodied Connections Versus Common Knowledge
Digby Tantam
ISBN 978 1 84905 476 8
eISBN 978 0 85700 856 5

DEFINING AUTISM

A Guide to Brain, Biology, and Behavior

Emily L. Casanova
and **Manuel F. Casanova**

Jessica Kingsley *Publishers*
London and Philadelphia

First published in 2019
by Jessica Kingsley Publishers
73 Collier Street
London N1 9BE, UK
and
400 Market Street, Suite 400
Philadelphia, PA 19106, USA

www.jkp.com

Front cover image source: Ian Ross.

Library of Congress Cataloging in Publication Data
A CIP catalog record for this book is available from the Library of Congress

British Library Cataloguing in Publication Data
A CIP catalogue record for this book is available from the British Library

ISBN 978 1 78592 722 5
eISBN 978 1 78450 349 9

Printed and bound in Great Britain

MIX
Paper from
responsible sources
FSC
www.fsc.org   FSC® C013056

Contents

To those on the autism spectrum and their families.

To Bram, for our many conversations on science.

Chapter One

KANNER'S CONUNDRUM AND BERNIE'S BIOLOGY

THE BEGINNING

Fortunate to have escaped the ravages of war-torn Europe, by 1924 Jewish-born Chaskel Leib Kanner (Leo Kanner: Figure 1.1) found himself working as a physician in the American Midwest. Born in Klekotow, Austria-Hungary, Kanner had been pursuing a career in medicine at the University of Berlin when his studies were interrupted by the turmoils of World War I. As sometimes occurs with the rise and fall of empires, hundreds of thousands of Austro-Hungarians died in battle or from starvation, and those left alive were further consumed by the Spanish influenza ravaging nations. By 1921, the Austro-Hungarian Empire had lost over one million people to war, hunger, and illness, and malnourishment and poverty would continue to remain a problem for the fallen empire. Raised within the Jewish faith, the young Leo Kanner must surely have looked upon America as a promised land.

Figure 1.1: Leo Kanner

Like Kanner, many Germans and Austrians fled Europe, settling in America. In order to curb the influx of low-skilled immigrants the United States Congress passed laws establishing quotas and requiring literacy tests for those aliens wishing to enter the U.S. These laws favored well-educated Northern Europeans who, like Kanner, emigrated from their homelands eager for a better life.

By the time Kanner had arrived in South Dakota in 1924, the state had been welcoming immigrants in droves for decades. Austrian and German immigrants tended to settle in the Midwest, living inland rather than on the coasts. As continuing incentive, the earlier Homestead Act of 1862 signed by Abraham Lincoln turned over millions of acres at no cost to private citizens, while most of these homestead acquisitions occurred west of the Mississippi River. What's more, the development of the railroads provided an easy means of travel for those enticed by the 1870s gold rush.

Although plenty of land was available west of the Mississippi, the Midwestern Plains were an otherwise undifferentiated landscape with little opportunity for cultural expansion. Though the Plains have an unstructured natural beauty of their own, it's likely the arctic winter blasts and lack of cultural activities weighed heavily on Kanner, prompting him to make his stay in South Dakota a temporary one, *en route* to the metropolitan life that better suited his and his wife's European upbringings.

Nevertheless, South Dakota opened new vistas to the academic career of Kanner in unexpected ways. Originally constructed to house German-Russian immigrants, the South Dakota governor acquired two wooden buildings that were eventually transformed into the Dakota Hospital for the Insane. By the time Kanner arrived, the hospital had been renamed the Yankton State Hospital, in recognition of changing perceptions of the term "insanity," and the fact that patients with other medical conditions, such as epilepsy, were also hospitalized there.

For over a century, the United States lacked regulatory restrictions concerning the practice of medicine. There was an unspoken belief that people in need of medical attention were consumers who had the right to pursue their care, and the government's role was to protect that right. However, by the 1920s, most states had initiated significant restrictions, allowing only medical schools to teach and practice medicine. Nevertheless, a lack of additional oversight still allowed doctors ample latitude within their practices.

Kanner was originally trained in electrocardiography and cardiophonography. And so during his early days at Yankton he surely felt at odds with his surroundings, working in a field in which he had little training. During that period of history, psychiatrists were often known as *alienists*, taken from the French adjective *aliene*, meaning "insane." A cardiologist by training, he likely felt "alien" in his new hospital post. But this was the impetus he needed to reinvent himself as a psychiatrist, which would change the history of autism forever. Ultimately, he would emerge as the father of American child psychiatry.

THE GERMAN SCHOOL

It was not uncommon for polymaths in the 19th and early 20th centuries to play professional musical chairs, changing specialties throughout their careers. In fact, this tradition was long-standing. The father of American psychiatry, Benjamin Rush, was himself a politician, social reformer, and educator. In 1812, he published the textbook *Medical Inquiries and Observations Upon Diseases of the Mind*, in which he advocated for the humane treatment of the mentally ill. However, his humanitarian outlook didn't dissuade him from using patients as guinea pigs, testing treatments such as vinegar-wrapped blankets, mercury rubs, cold baths, and extreme blood-letting. In those days, intentions were good but treatment implementation was based on poorly constructed theory rather than empirically based observations, much to the chagrin of the patients being subjected to these "treatments."

The German-born Alois Alzheimer (1864–1915), a noted pathologist, was also regarded as a psychiatrist, in part due to his close association with Emil Kraepelin (1856–1926), the father of modern psychiatry. Unsurprisingly, this proved to be of mutual influence, since Kraepelin's association with Alzheimer and other neuropathologists impacted his concepts of the biological origin of mental conditions such as schizophrenia. This organic tradition was eventually exported to the United States by Elmer Ernest Southard (1876–1920), a well-known American psychiatrist and neuropathologist, who died tragically young but nevertheless mentored and substantially influenced many prominent thinkers of the day (Casanova, 1995).

A graduate of Harvard Medical School, Southard received his postgraduate education at both the Senckenberg Institute and

Heidelberg University in Germany. After returning to the United States, he interned in the pathology department at Boston City Hospital before becoming the president of both the American Medico-Psychological Association and the Boston Society of Psychiatry and Neurology. He also became the Director of the Massachusetts Psychiatric Institute, devoting much of his time to establishing a new nomenclature of psychiatric illness and working to identify brain abnormalities common to dementia praecox (schizophrenia). Along with Mary Jarrett, he founded the field of social psychiatry, which they applied to the benefit of industrial employees. All of this was accomplished before the ripe old age of 43 when he died suddenly of pneumonia, the likely result of workaholic exhaustion. Had it not been for his untimely death, one can only imagine the many achievements he would have continued to realize. *Death be not proud of dreams destroyed!*

At the beginning of the 20th century, many medical conditions were diagnosed by nonspecific symptoms. These conditions were often systemic in nature and received the descriptive appellation of the "Great Imitators" or "Masqueraders." Various forms of cancers, lupus, multiple sclerosis, and syphilis were all grouped under this rubric. Ultimately, these conditions were diagnosed at autopsy where the pathologist had the final say.

Before the influence of the German School, it was presumed that psychiatric conditions lacked identifiable pathology. Those conditions with distinctive brain pathology were instead thrown into a wastebasket category known as *organic brain syndrome*. As with many European-born psychiatrists of the day, the influence of the German School had a profound effect on how Leo Kanner perceived and treated mental conditions in his professional career. However, another major influence on Kanner would come from the Swiss-born physician, Adolf Meyer (Figure 1.2).

Adolf Meyer was a neurologist who studied under the tutelages of Auguste Forel, John Hughlings Jackson, and Jean-Martin Charcot, all grand names in the annals of psychiatry and neurology (Casanova et al., 2007). Upon arriving in the United States, he practiced pathology before becoming the first psychiatrist-in-chief of the Johns Hopkins Hospital and president of the American Psychiatric Association (APA). Meyer introduced the faculty at Hopkins to Emil Kraepelin's classification of mental disorders, a thesis that laid the foundations for both the World Health Organization's International Classification of Diseases (ICD) and the APA's Diagnostic and Statistical Manual (DSM) (Figure 1.2). (We'll discuss Kraepelin and his thesis further in Chapter 7.)

Figure 1.2: Adolf Meyer (left) and Emil Kraepelin (right)

Also like Kraepelin, Meyer believed psychiatric illness was rooted in biology, gradually setting a course to distance himself from psychoanalytical ruminations. He found clarity in viewing mental conditions from a biopsychosocial perspective, stressing to his students and colleagues the importance of information gathering of major physical, psychological, and social aspects of the patient that could cause or affect their symptoms.

KANNER AT THE CROSSROADS

After four years in South Dakota, Kanner exhibited modest academic proclivity but nothing that truly distinguished himself. He had published on the tertiary stage of syphilis (general paralysis) among Native Americans and had studied the effects of adrenalin on the blood pressure of patients with functional psychosis. Not having much in terms of academic credentials and having traced a confusing career path amongst medical specialties, he interviewed with Adolf Meyer at a congress of the American Academy of Psychiatry in Minneapolis in the hopes of finding a new position.

In spite of Kanner's early lack of distinction, Meyer eventually accepted Kanner into a three-year Commonwealth Fellowship at Hopkins (1928). During this time he had the opportunity to work alongside many distinguished people, including Lauretta Bender, who performed research at the Henry Phipps Psychiatric Clinic, and Paul Schilder, a visiting professor and guest lecturer. After three years as a fellow, however, Kanner's talents were evident. Based on the financial support of the Macy and Rockefeller Foundations, Meyer enlisted Kanner's efforts to establish the Children's Psychiatry Service at the Harriet Lane Home.

The final stage of his academic career began with one small examining room equipped with a washstand and a table. Yet in this new position Kanner would soon transcend his academic role as renowned child psychiatrist to become an even greater social activist on behalf of those with the condition we now know as *autism*.

KANNER'S CONUNDRUM

In 1943, Kanner published his famous thesis—a manuscript describing eleven children and their "*inability to relate themselves* in the ordinary way to people and situations from the beginning of life" (Kanner, 1943, p. 242). He describes the congenital nature of their social challenges: "There is from the start an *extreme autistic aloneness* that, whenever possible, disregards, ignores, shuts out anything that comes to the child from outside" (p. 242). He describes the children's language impairment, often consisting of echolalia, as well as their "*anxiously obsessive desire for the maintenance of sameness* that nobody but the child himself may disrupt on rare occasions" (p. 245).

In future years, Kanner would expand on this work, emphasizing a humanistic approach that rebelled against the prevailing deterministic mentality of the medical profession and the limited accommodations offered by society. Through this, he emphasized the strengths of his patients, proposing new ways in which their potentials could be actualized. He also recognized the clinical heterogeneity amongst his patients, going to great lengths to describe differentiating features across his cases. Like Meyer, he advocated for an integrative approach that included the physical, psychological, and social aspects of each patient. Influenced by the German School, he harshly criticized operant conditioning and the use of aversives (e.g. electric shocks), well before Ivar Lovaas, the father of applied behavioral analysis, rose to fame. Instead, he advocated a variety of approaches in the treatment of autism based upon an individual's needs. However, this propensity often left him conflicted, as his holistic approach clashed with his desire to narrowly define and differentiate autism from other conditions like childhood schizophrenia.

In medicine, it is necessary to establish stringent criteria so that we can begin to conceptualize a condition as a singular entity. Broadening of symptoms sometimes blurs distinguishing features and can falsify diagnostic claims. But as Kanner continued to enumerate more symptoms of autism, the more difficult it became to pinpoint those traits that were truly fundamental to the condition. Meanwhile, his view of autism as a single condition continued to clash with the heterogeneous behaviors he observed amongst his different patients, making the establishment of universal criteria progressively more challenging. Nevertheless, Kanner believed every person should be treated as an individual:

> By this time, it should be—but very likely is not—quite commonplace to state that one of the combined goals of medicine, psychology, social work, and education is to make it possible for children to attain their optimal condition of comfort and smoothness of functioning. No matter how simple this formulation sounds, civilization took a long time to arrive at it, and to many people and in many areas, it still has the ring of novelty. We are, after all, not too far behind from the era of the rod and the dunce cap and the bending of the twig to insure the haphazardly preordained inclination of trees.
>
> ...
>
> Particular emphasis should be placed on the adjective "optimal" contained in the formulation. The optimum which can be reached is, of course, not identical to each individual...[he] can be helped if we examine the specifics of the underlying disharmony of the integrants and work for a better consonance between them. (Kanner, 1971c, p. 134)

It's important to emphasize again that Kanner recognized the existence of a spectrum within autism, although in modern times the definition of that spectrum has continued to broaden. He lauded the children's gifts and called for parents and educators to help them on their paths of personal development so that they could achieve their true potentials. Kanner promoted the civil rights of autistic people and, in a sense, is one of the forefathers of the civil rights movement for "differently-abled" individuals (Casanova, Casanova, & Sokhadze, 2016). The following paragraphs provide a call to action by Kanner:

> In the last few millennia our species has had its gifted and productive thinkers and poets and artists and scientists and explorers. Many of them have advanced our civilization by upsetting deep-seated archaic notions guarded zealously and at times cruelly by mighty autocracies of one kind or another. We are now in a position to spot potential talents at an early age and have the laudable desire to see to it that as many as possible reach their optimum. We can do this only if, as they mature, we as parents, educators, and human engineers can pave their way toward the developments of unhampered automaticity. It is up to us, then, to attenuate the hampering agents, be they organic, emotional, or social, and to encourage rather than crush, spontaneity and self-organization. (Kanner, 1971c, p. 142)

Kanner noted that there is "one other very interesting common denominator in the backgrounds of these children. *They all come of highly intelligent families*" (Kanner, 1943, p. 248). Although he didn't openly speculate that the parents had some form of autism, Kanner did believe that intelligence linked the parents and children. He may have suspected a heritable relationship existed, one which we now refer to as the broader autism phenotype (BAP) (more on this in Chapter 8). He also noted that some children were exposed from "*the beginning to parental coldness, obsessiveness, and a mechanical type of attention to material needs only ... They were left neatly in refrigerators which did not defrost*"—a genuine yet unfortunate observation that was taken up by Bruno Bettelheim as we'll discuss later in the chapter (Kanner, 1949, p. 425). Kanner himself was an intellectually complicated, imperfect man who at times stressed the congenital nature of autism and other times criticized parents for their coldness, the latter a position he officially recanted in 1969 at the first meeting of the Autism Society of America. Unfortunately, he was a product of Freudian times, after all.

Fundamentally, however, Kanner—like the German School— believed that disorders of the mind were rooted in the biology of the brain and therefore autism was a congenital condition, not the result of abnormal parent–child relations. In addition, Kanner abhorred psychoanalytic cogitations and, in spite of his conflicting opinions, criticized the Refrigerator Mother Theory of autism stemming from his original description. It's therefore unfortunate that Kanner failed to identify a broader phenotype[1] in parents, although his early work clearly danced about the idea. Unfortunately, hindsight is 20/20.

> From the start, I was greatly impressed with one observation which stood out prominently: The parents of these patients were, for the most part, strongly preoccupied with abstractions of a scientific, literary, or artistic nature, and limited in genuine interest in people. As time went on and more autistic children were studied, the coincidence of infantile autism and the parents' mechanized forms of living was really startling. This was confirmed by many other observers. I noted then, however: These children's aloneness from the beginning of life makes it difficult to attribute the whole picture exclusively to the type of early parental relationship that they have experienced. (Kanner, 1968, pp. 17–18).

Kanner's book *In Defense of Mothers* was subtitled "How to Bring Up Children in Spite of the More Zealous Psychologists" (Kanner, 1941). Published two years before his case series on autism, Kanner's book urged mothers to "regain that common sense which is yours, which has been yours before you allowed yourselves to be intimidated by would-be omniscient totalitarians." The theme of the book was not psychogenic but focused on explaining abnormal childhood behaviors in a contextual setting, understanding what occurred in the child's life at the time the behaviors began or intensified. Interestingly, Kanner described family dynamics as a democracy in which every member, including children, was an active participant whose voice deserved to be heard.

Later, Kanner would openly criticize and mock Bruno Bettelheim, the psychoanalytic huckster, at the height of Bettelheim's popularity. Kanner's criticisms were highly personal and clearly transcended the usual norms of academic debate. Shortly after Bettelheim's book *The Empty Fortress* was published, Kanner railed:

---

1   "Phenotype" refers to the outward expression of genes. Most often it is used to refer to a physical trait, such as eye color or height; however, in this instance, it refers to a subtler expression of autism known as the "broader autism phenotype."

The futility of such speculation is illustrated by a recent publication, The Empty Fortress, published in 1967. Its intrepid dust jacket promised the reader that it "sheds new light on the nature, origin and treatment of infantile autism," but the author of the book, being perhaps somewhat more hampered by actual fact than the author of the dust jacket, felt called upon to employ such qualifications as "maybe", "perhaps", "probably", "possibly", "as if", "as it were", "seemed to", "suggests", 146 times in 48 pages of the report of the first case, and he cautions his readers further within the text, "This like other interpretations of Laurie's behavior, is highly speculative…" (Kanner, 1968, p. 26)

Kanner championed a humane approach to autism, rather than psychoanalysis:

This modesty, humility and caution must be applied to therapy as well as to etiology, and this is the keynote at certain centers where efforts continue to be made, consistently and patiently, to help these children find their way into a world which may be threatening to them. (Kanner, 1968, p. 26)

At times, Kanner criticized those who joined the common chorus of "Cherchez la mère!" or "Find the mother!"—a refrain derived from the phrase, *cherchez la femme* (find the woman) suggesting that at the root of all men's problems is ultimately a woman. In this instance, Freudians wrongly believed that the root of all the child's problems was the mother. Kanner chastized his psychoanalytic colleagues in defense of his observational methodology: "Poohpoohing description as an obsolete pastime of atavistic nosographers, they started out with interpretations in which the mother–child relationship was put on the pedestal as the only valid etiological consideration" (Kanner, 1965, p. 417). Kanner placed observation before theory, one of the primary tenets of science.

He explained his reasoning for utilizing the term *early infantile autism*, to denote the condition's early manifestation: "We must assume that these children come into the world with an innate inability to form the usual, biologically-provided affective contact with people, just as other children come into the world with innate physical and intellectual handicaps" (Kanner, 1943, p. 250). Kanner did adhere to his diagnostic scheme, believing that dilution of the original concept would lead to an artifactual increase in worldwide prevalence rates that would balloon to include any individual with unusual behaviors. He and others warned about the "abuse of the diagnosis of autism" declaring that it would threaten "to become a fashion" (Kanner, 1965, 1968). He adhered to his criteria in order to make diagnosis "more uniformly reliable" (Kanner, 1965, p. 414).

Contemporary to his writings he noted that other authors had introduced the term *pseudo-autism* for those cases with atypical presentation. Although we now recognize a far broader spectrum of autism than did Kanner, during his time the pseudo-autism classification rapidly expanded to include conditions variously described as "hospitalism," "anaclitic depression,"[2] and "separation anxiety" (Kanner, 1965). As Kanner explained, "An identifying designation appeared to me to be definitely desirable because, as later events proved, there was danger of having this distinct syndrome lumped together with a variety of general categories" (Kanner, 1973, p. 95). He goes on to explain:

> In the early 1950s, Rank created the concept of the "atypical child" as an overall designation for children presenting signs of "ego fragmentation" in close connection with maternal psychopathology. The underlying idea was: Why bother about questions of genetics, organicity, metabolism, or anything else if we can proceed promptly with the psychogenic denominator common to all disturbances of the ego? Thus, a pseudodiagnostic waste basket was set up into which went "all more severe disturbances in early development which have been variously described as Heller's disease, childhood psychosis, childhood schizophrenia, autism, or mental defect." With a perfunctory bow in the direction of "heredity and biology," mother–infant involvement was decreed to be the sole key to everything that goes on within or around the neonate. (Kanner, 1971b, p. 18)

Ironically, Heller's disease, now known as childhood distintegrative disorder, was included under Pervasive Developmental Disorders in both the DSM-IV and DSM-IV-TR but has since been removed in the latest iteration. In addition, it's now recognized that autism occurs alongside many rare genetic syndromes and is more commonly used as a descriptive diagnosis similar to "intellectual disability" rather

---

2   Anaclitic depression is a failure in the development of an infant following his or her separation from its mother.

than as a singular entity unto itself. One therefore may wonder what Kanner would say about our modern usage of the autism diagnosis. In some ways, he would find it foreign and perhaps even be slightly appalled. However, we now recognize the extensive heterogeneity and fundamental biological nature of these conditions, which Kanner probably would have also appreciated.

In support of this notion, we know that Kanner admired Bleuler's conception of schizophrenia, in which Bleuler envisioned schizophrenia not in the singular but as a group of related conditions—*the schizophrenias* (Kanner, 1971b). Kanner similarly mused, "It is well known in medicine that any illness may appear in different degrees of severity, all the way from the so-called *formes frustes* to the most fulminant manifestation. Does this possibly apply also to early infantile autism?" (Kanner, Rodriguez, & Ashenden, 1972, p. 32). Ironically, Kanner frequently dealt with the differential diagnosis of autism as it applied to schizophrenia (Kanner, 1965). And one of his primary opponents in this regard was Lauretta Bender.

Lauretta Bender was an old colleague of Kanner's from Hopkins who had moved to Bellevue Hospital in order to take charge of children services. Bender, who is best known for developing the Bender-Gestalt Visual Motor Test, was married to Paul Schilder, an Austrian psychiatrist and pupil of Freud. Together they composed a towering power couple whose influence surpassed that of Kanner. Indeed, she would publish her experience on hundreds of cases, far more than Kanner would ever study.

Bender and Schilder believed that one of the core features of childhood schizophrenia was anxiety, which could be either biological or environmental in origin. Unfortunately, Bender, much like Benjamin Rush, sometimes instituted aggressive treatments based on subjective bias, ignoring the complaints voiced by her patients. In the end, she administered electroshock and insulin shock therapy to hundreds of children with childhood schizophrenia (inclusive of autism), some younger than three years of age.

Bender thought that autism was an early manifestation of schizophrenia that rarely occurred in "pure" form; that is, "without signs of other developmental disabilities and organic features" (Faretra, 1979, p. 119). In her cases, developmental symptoms anteceded the appearance of psychotic symptoms. She did agree, however, that some cases of autism didn't progress into fullblown schizophrenia and grouped these individuals into a wastebasket category of neurological, environmental, and/or idiopathic causation.

Kanner, for his part, believed childhood schizophrenia was a rare condition, an assertion that casts doubts on Bender's mega series and with which modern clinicians would generally agree. He felt that many of the patients diagnosed with childhood schizophrenia fell into an assortment of neuropathological, progressive, and congenital/acquired anomalies of the central nervous system. Although some cases of childhood schizophrenia manifested a prodromal phase[3] that included autistic symptomology, childhood schizophrenia was ultimately a psychotic disorder with a deteriorating course. Kanner recognized clinical antecedents of autism in the works of Sukhareva in Russia, Lutz and Tramer in Switzerland, and Despert in the U.S. (Kanner, 1965, 1971a), but despite similarities he differentiated these descriptions from his own case studies: "It was deemed essential for the diagnosis in both groups that a period of relative normalcy had preceded the beginning of the illness" (Kanner, 1965, p. 417).

Recognizing the broad spectrum of symptomology, and expressing some frustration with nosological scheme,[4] Kanner nevertheless believed that autism would ultimately fall under the broader classification of schizophrenia. However, he steadfastly maintained that the constellation of symptoms he had described was *sui generis* (unique).

In the end, Kanner believed that the refinement of autism criteria should be guided by autistic people and their families:

> By far the greatest incentive is coming from child patients themselves, not having read those articles and monographs and unconcerned about existing nomenclature present themselves as they are and thus, as individuals, continue inviting further refinements of criteria for differential diagnosis. (Kanner, 1971a, p. 19)

To this date, autism remains a diagnostic conundrum in which autistic individuals and their families have had a growing voice in how it is defined. After all, who knows autism better than those who live with it daily?

---

3   The appearance of an early, lesser phase of symptoms that precedes the onset of schizophrenia.

4   Refers to the classification of diseases.

Kanner was a keen student of human nature, constantly striving to familiarize himself with every quirk and distinguishing trait of his patients. He maintained voluminous correspondence with his patients and at times undertook long train rides in order to keep in touch with them. He fought on behalf of wards of the state and people who had been outcasts of society. In the preamble to World War II, he saved the lives of hundreds of physicians persecuted by the Nazi regime by offering them employment in the United States. Unfortunately, as no good deed goes unpunished, Kanner's place in history has been questioned by some modern authors due to his loose association with the Refrigerator Mother Theory. Nevertheless, Kanner is the father of autism. He provided a comprehensive description of the condition and its heterogeneity and was a fervid advocate for those with the condition and their families. His stream of publications and lectures on the subject spanned several decades, and in the end he molded positive public opinion and fought against institutionalization.

It's difficult to say how the study of autism would have proceeded without the remarkable contributions of Leo Kanner. The identification of autism would have likely been many years delayed, considering Freudian psychology maintained its popularity for several decades to come. Yet Kanner also mentored others who went on to make significant contributions to autism research and advocacy, such as Bernard Rimland, psychologist, researcher, and father to a boy with autism. While Rimland surely would have produced his *magnum opus* with or without Kanner, Kanner reviewed his work and smoothed the way professionally, providing vital support for Rimland's book, which held sway with the medical community of that era.

THE BIOLOGICAL CONUNDRUM

Bernard Rimland earned his PhD in 1953. Shortly afterwards, his son Mark was born. Although Rimland suspected something was different about his child, it was his wife who realized Mark was showing signs of autism, based on case histories she had previously read. In spite of the Freudian views of most medical professionals at the time, Rimland knew that he and his wife hadn't caused their child's autism. Instead, he strongly suspected the roots of autism lay in its biology. With an obsessive focus sometimes characteristic of autism parents, Rimland transformed part of his house into a research headquarters and read all the relevant materials he could get his hands on. Within a few years, he had made himself an autism expert—at least as "autism" was known at the time.

Figure 1.3: Bernard (Bernie) Rimland (left) with Micaela Edelson, daughter of Stephen Edelson, director of the Autism Research Institute. Bernie, Steve, and Micaela (right)

(Images courtesy of Steve and Micaela Edelson)

His original idea was to write an article publicizing his findings. After five years of passionate research, the information he had compiled was far greater than any single article could contain. Instead, his wife suggested he write a book, which was eventually published by Appleton Century Crofts under the title *Infantile Autism: The Syndrome and Its Implications for a Neural Theory of Behavior*.

The foreword to the book was written by Leo Kanner himself, who had exchanged correspondence with Rimland and reviewed a draft of the book. High praise given by Kanner lent the book credibility and helped to publicize it. It won the prestigious Century Psychology Series Award, and has recently been republished (2014)—edited by Dr. Stephen Edelson, Rimland's longtime mentee and dear friend. Emphasis on the historical importance of Rimland's contributions are detailed in the foreword of the new book, written by Temple Grandin and Margaret Bauman, and in the afterword written by Sidney Baker.

From his years of study, Rimland was able to pinpoint and detail major patterns in the literature that provided evidence against the psychogenic view and support for the biological view of autism.

He specifies that the first five points of the following list were identified by Kanner himself, and used as a basis for further study.

> ### Rimland's case for the biological causation of autism (Rimland, 1964, p. 74)
>
> — Some clearly autistic children are born of parents who do not fit the autistic parent personality pattern (i.e. "refrigerator mother").
>
> — Parents who do fit the description of the supposedly pathogenic parent almost invariably have normal, non-autistic children.
>
> — With very few exceptions, the siblings of autistic children are normal.
>
> — Autistic children are behaviorally unusual "from the moment of birth."
>
> — There is a consistent ratio of three or four boys to one girl.
>
> — Virtually all cases of twins reported in the literature have been identical, with both twins afflicted.
>
> — Autism can occur or be closely simulated in children with known organic brain damage.
>
> — The symptomatology is highly unique and specific.
>
> — There is an absence of gradations of infantile autism which would create "blends" from normal to severely afflicted.

In general, Rimland's synthesis indicated that the personality of the parents was not a strict determinant of the child's autism. He also highlighted the congenital nature of most cases of autism—although current research now acknowledges that a minority of cases has near-normal development prior to regression (see Chapter 5). He discussed the lop-sided gender ratio of three to four boys to every girl, a ratio virtually unchanged today. And he discussed high rates of heritability amongst identical twins, yet also the possibility that environmental exigencies can trigger autism, research that will be discussed further in Chapters 3 and 4 in this book.

Rimland goes on to discuss each of these nine points in detail, providing irrefutable evidence against psychogenic theory, citation after citation—sounding the death knell for the era of Bruno

Bettelheim's "refrigerator mother." Kanner helped to publicize the book, but Bernie Rimland's tenacity and doggedness summarized the massive amounts of data that were spread piecemeal throughout the literature. It was sheer persistence and innovation that turned the psychogenic tides.

Bernard Rimland went on to become a founding member of the Autism Research Institute and the Autism Society of America. He remained steadfast against the prevailing mores of the psycho-analytically minded medical establishment, helping to change the way we view autism. Every autism stakeholder, practitioner, and researcher in the field has invariably been touched by his efforts—as the following chapter, "The Brain in Autism," attests. Without Rimland, Freudian psychology would have dominated the study of autism for much longer than it did, and our biological understanding of the heterogeneous condition would be severely delayed.

Both Leo Kanner's and Bernard Rimland's careers have been touched by controversy, which has unfortunately tarnished some of our perceptions of these men. However, in spite of that controversy, they are giants in the field of autism research upon whose shoulders all of us—stakeholder, health professional, and scientist alike—stand. Much like the recent controversy that has arisen over Hans Asperger's role within the Nazi regime (Donvan & Zuker, 2016), most of autism's founding fathers are flawed yet performed truly groundbreaking work. And it is for this reason we humbly acknowledge their contributions.

Chapter Two

THE BRAIN IN AUTISM

Autism is defined as a neurodevelopmental condition, a term that indicates an impairment in the normal development and/or growth of the brain. Many neurodevelopmental conditions are nonspecific, lacking an obvious single underlying cause, and are grouped together by symptoms into broad categories like "intellectual disability," "motor disorders," and "autism spectrum conditions."

Autism makes its presence known early in life and tends to carve a course without remission, although severity of symptoms may improve with age. In order to understand the nature of autism as a neurodevelopmental condition it behooves us to examine key issues about the tightly orchestrated development of the brain and how they bear clinical relevance to the condition. Therefore, we will start by describing the complexity of the brain and some of the many steps that can go wrong during brain development.

It has often been said that the brain has more cells than the Milky Way has stars. While that claim is an exaggeration (the brain has approximately 100 billion neurons and our galaxy has two to four times as many stars), the number of neurons in the brain is nevertheless amazingly large. In fact, that number pales by comparison when considering that each neuron makes 1000 to 10,000 cell-to-cell connections, each expressing one of approximately 50 different neurotransmitters. Seen from this perspective the staggering array of possibilities makes the brain an especially complex organ. This is all the more apparent when tracing the brain's development from a few weeks post-conception, when it is part of an almost unrecognizable tube the size of a grain of sand, to the gelatinous mass of the adult human, weighing some three pounds. It is this amazing transformation in terms of size and complexity that has attracted researchers to the various fields of neuroscience.

Total neuronal numbers and connectivity patterns can vary across individuals considerably. In addition, there are two to ten times the number of supporting cells (glia) as there are neurons. Therefore, it is interesting to note that the final outcome of brain development is an organ with a fairly regular shape comprising consistent subsections or modules, regardless of whether we look at its cellular or chemical architecture. In fact, Korbinian Brodmann, a German neurologist working in the late 19th/early 20th century, was able to divide the brain into different regions based on cell types and other aspects of architectural organization (Brodmann, 1909/2006). According to Brodmann's scheme, the brain is divided into approximately 50 areas whose variations in cellular architecture presumably indicate differences in regional functionality. These regions are now referred to as "Brodmann's areas" and are still occasionally used in research and medicine today. Interestingly, however, there are gross deficiencies in Brodmann's mapping because it was based on a single brain hemisphere of a particular patient, failing to take into account asymmetries between the two hemispheres and other minor aspects of brain architecture that vary across people.

BRAIN EVOLUTION

Throughout evolutionary history the brain has increased its complexity by the addition of newer structures to older ones. One popular theory, espoused by Paul MacLean, is called the Triune brain (MacLean, 1990). This theory divides the brain's evolutionary ladder into three steps, the most primitive of which is the reptilian portion, which provides for a survivalist's autopilot and controls our wake–sleep cycle. The second addition came in terms of the limbic system, which controls our emotions, memories, and habits. And the latest addition is the cerebral cortex (neocortex), which provides for the complex representations and processing of our three-dimensional world.

According to this much-debated model, each evolutionary stage complements the others while not being necessarily interdependent. Experiments from the 1930s showed, for instance, that cats who have had their neocortices removed can still walk, feed, and have emotional responses while only using their reptilian and limbic portions of the brain (Magoun & Ranson, 1938). By contrast, humans are more dependent on their cerebral cortex than other animals, and widespread damage to this area causes a person to enter a persistent vegetative state with general lack of awareness of his or her surroundings.

THE CEREBRAL CORTEX

Thomas Henry Huxley, the famous English biologist and "Charles Darwin's bulldog," long pondered the question of questions: What makes us most human? To many neuroscientists and paleoanthropologists alike, the answer is clear: our brains. And in particular, the cerebral cortex, the seat of higher learning and thought, is most responsible for our uniqueness as a species.

The cerebral cortex is the part of the brain that provides for cognitive control of behavior and is responsible for the regulation of attention, working memory, and cognitive flexibility. Since many of these functions are affected in autistic individuals, it is plausible that developmental abnormalities of the cerebral cortex are responsible for some of the symptoms observed in the condition.

Neocortical minicolumns

The germinal matrix is a region of highly vascularized cells that surround the inner cavity of the brain. The cerebral cortex forms when stem cells within this region divide *symmetrically* to establish a pool of additional precursor cells during early gestation. Later during development, the same cells divide *asymmetrically*, one of them remaining behind as the original primitive or mother cell, while the other one migrates radially towards the cortical plate (Mione et al., 1997). These radially migrating neurons, called neuroblasts, differentiate in the developing cerebral cortex into excitatory cells that form the core of larger structures called minicolumns (Figure 2.1).

The cells surrounding the ventricles are often called germinal cells, but this is a confusing designation since they have nothing to do with the sex cells (gametes) within the reproductive organs. In reality, the germinal matrix contains stem cells that have the capacity to reproduce themselves or to provide a progeny that will differentiate into a more specialized type of cell (e.g. an excitatory neuron). Early divisions of these stem cells are of crucial importance for brain development. The number of symmetrical divisions account for the total number of minicolumns in the cerebral cortex, while later asymmetrical divisions are responsible for the total number of cells in each minicolumn (Figure 2.2).

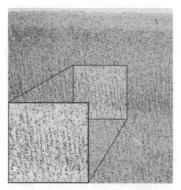

Figure 2.1: Minicolumns within the human brain

Note the vertical arrangement (columns) of these cells that is reminiscent not only of how the neurons had migrated early during embryonic development but also of how the cells wire together and communicate, preferentially, within minicolumns.

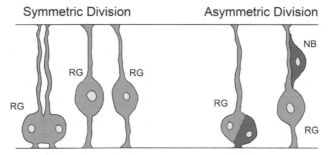

Figure 2.2: Symmetric and asymmetric divisions of radial glial (RG) cells within the developing human cortex

Radial glia are the progenitors of neocortical neurons.

If the switch from symmetrical to asymmetrical divisions occurs too early, the stem cell pool will quickly be depleted, potentially resulting in a smaller brain (e.g. microcephaly). Conversely, if the switch occurs too late, the brain may find itself with a larger pool of cells, resulting in a greater number of minicolumns and a larger brain. Evolution has in fact used this feature to its advantage, preferentially increasing the numbers of minicolumns, the addition of which may increase an organism's cognitive faculties. As an example, when we compare the brains of mice and humans, we find that while there is a threefold increase in cortical thickness between our two species (i.e. an increase in the number of cells within minicolumns), there is a thousandfold increase in total brain surface area (i.e. an increase in minicolumn number). For this reason, humans have a highly convoluted brain with its undulating hills and valleys of gray matter, while the mouse has an especially lissencephalic or smooth brain. Meanwhile, these surface convolutions known as *gyri* are an evolutionary adaptation, allowing us to pack more surface area into a small space.

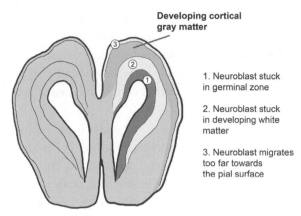

Developing cortical gray matter

1. Neuroblast stuck in germinal zone

2. Neuroblast stuck in developing white matter

3. Neuroblast migrates too far towards the pial surface

Figure 2.3: Processes that can go wrong during early brain development

Minicolumns in autism

Scientists have found significant differences in the organization of minicolumns in the brains of those with autism (Casanova et al., 2002a, 2002b). While we see this effect throughout the cerebral cortex, this is especially the case within the frontal lobes, the seat of important executive functions. However, because the frontal lobes are so large compared to other lobes of the brain, it is possible this may be the result of a statistical artifact, though further research is needed to address this possibility. In general, however, these changes clearly point towards disturbances during early brain development.

To help you better understand, imagine the minicolumn as the microprocessor of your computer. A modern computer usually has two microprocessors—but the human brain has about 600 million microprocessors, aka minicolumns. This huge number of "microprocessors" underlies our capacity for the parallel processing of information. That allows us to acquire and analyze various types of sensory input, coordinate that data, synthesize it, and finally determine and execute an appropriate output. Picture, for instance, how much parallel processing the brain must perform in order to coordinate social interactions, from which we draw huge amounts of incoming data at any given second: the turn of a lip, the flutter of an eye, the angle at which an individual is facing us, the literal meaning of his or her words, the tone of her voice, a hand gesture, and overall context, just to name a few. The sheer amount of simultaneous information is astounding.

Minicolumns are also versatile units that can process different kinds of information depending on how they are trained and how they are connected. In this way, imagine them as an electrical outlet in a wall. Even though you plug different appliances into this outlet, each one requiring somewhat different wattages, the outlet is able to adapt and provide electricity to whatever is connected, be it a tiny nightlight or an electricity-guzzling hair dryer.

Similar to a wall outlet, the minicolumn can perform different functions depending on what is connected to it. For instance, a person who is born blind doesn't have use for a visual cortex. Instead the area that normally would process visual information is appropriated by auditory or tactile fibers. Neuroimaging studies have shown that the visual cortex activates when the blind person reads Braille (Burton, 2003). In a similar way, the auditory cortex of a person born deaf may be co-opted by visual fibers, providing the recipient with superior peripheral visual and motion detection. In either example, be it congenital blindness or deafness, the cortex never goes to waste. Although some people claim this is due to "brain plasticity," it is more accurate to say that the minicolumn is a very versatile unit whose development is guided by the connections it makes in life.

However, even though minicolumns are highly versatile, they are not clone-like elements. There is great variability in minicolumnar organization within and across brain regions, as well as between the brains of different species (e.g. Buxhoeveden et al., 2001). Without some minicolumnar variability, stimuli entering a field of minicolumns would invariably produce the same output as any other field. Although such a clone-like state would make it easier for scientists to study and understand, it would preempt behavioral variability, depriving us of subtleties in our response patterns. Interestingly, studies on autism have shown some reductions in minicolumn variability across brain regions, hinting at one of the reasons why some autistic people may be fond of routine and dislike changes to their environments.

If the reader is not yet convinced that minicolumns play an important role in autism, let me explain in the next few paragraphs how other aspects of brain development and organization give clues to autism's various etiologies.

Anatomists have a long tradition of reductionism (attempting to understand organs and tissues by studying their constituent parts), and neuroanatomists are no exception. In other words, anatomists want to take Humpty Dumpty apart to understand why he keeps falling off that wall. Minicolumns unfortunately have not escaped the reductionistic approach of anatomists. The minicolumn has been partitioned into a central or core compartment and a peripheral compartment. The cellular elements inhabiting the core of the minicolumn are excitatory neurons, the ones that we learned arise from asymmetric divisions of stem cells located below the developing cortical plate. Once these newborn excitatory neurons arrive at the cortex they establish functional relationships with inhibitory cells that have traveled from an even longer distance away from a region called the *ganglionic eminence*. Newly arrived inhibitory cells have to coordinate their function with other cells, primarily the excitatory cells of the core compartment. These anatomical and functional relationships between excitatory and inhibitory cells are called *dyads*. The proper function of the cerebral cortex, including the establishment of an excitatory–inhibitory balance, depends on the finely orchestrated relationship of these dyads. People with autism often experience sensory abnormalities, anxiety, obsessive-compulsiveness, and even seizures, all of which are theoretically related to an excitatory–inhibitory imbalance in the cerebral cortex, suggesting that these dyads have somehow been disrupted.

The inhibitory cells that have migrated into the cortex from the ganglionic eminence usually occupy the periphery or outer portions of the minicolumns. These cells regulate the transmission of information both within and between minicolumns, acting like the brakes on a car. Interestingly, throughout evolution the components of the core of the minicolumn (the excitatory neurons) have been strongly preserved, while the peripheral cell types and arrangements vary more substantially between species (Casanova, Trippe, et al., 2009). Among many species studied, humans seem to have the largest variability in overall minicolumnar width.

While in real life a damaged shower curtain allows water to spill out of the shower onto the floor, in the same way damaged or impaired inhibitory cells allow information to seep outside the core of the column. If a large number of peripheral compartments are impaired, this can result in a cascading effect, with excitation seeping from one minicolumn to the next. In some types of syndromic autism, for instance, especially those that manifest seizures (e.g. tuberous sclerosis), treating the runaway cascade of excitation can reduce autism symptoms (Jambaque et al., 2000).

Connectivity

The masterplan for the connectome or connectivity map of the brain is defined early during development. This map is strongly influenced by the relative concentrations of two key proteins known as EMX2 and PAX6. PAX6 is primarily released from the embryonic anterior or frontal pole of the brain, while EMX2 is released from the posterior regions. When the *EMX2* gene is mutated and fails to produce a functioning protein, this results in an expansion in the size of frontal regions such as the motor area (M1) and the somatosensory cortex (S1) and a diminution of the visual cortex at the back of the brain (V1). When a mutation occurs in the *PAX6* gene, instead the visual cortex is grossly overdeveloped while the motor and somatosensory areas are much smaller than normal (Stiles, 2008) (see Figure 2.4).

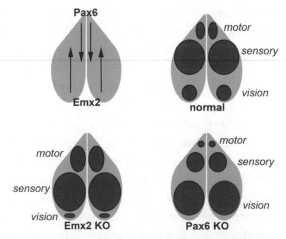

Figure 2.4: Diagram of the mouse brain illustrating how inappropriate expression of *PAX6* or *EMX2* can alter how the motor, sensory, and visual areas of the brain develop

Because of these mutation events, cells within the expanded cortical regions take on characteristics relative to their functions rather than the region in which they were supposed to have been. In *EMX2* mutants, cells that should have been part of the anterior portion of the normal somatosensory cortex now are large and express anatomical features of motor cortex. Meanwhile, in the *PAX6* mutant, the opposite is true, and the posterior of the would-be motor cortex instead contains small granular cells characteristic of somatosensory cortex.

Large cells contain the metabolic machinery necessary to transmit signals and substances over long distances, beyond the brain and out into the spinal cord. Some of these projections span several feet in length. Structures that control protein synthesis in these motor neurons (e.g. nucleoli) are also enlarged to support their high metabolic demands. By way of comparison, smaller cells have much shorter connections and would be incapable of sustaining the metabolic machinery required to transport signals and substances over long distances.

The motor regions are ideally suited to connect different areas of the brain, interlinking the cerebral hemispheres, and projecting long distances outside of the brain. Some motor regions act as hubs of transportation, enabling information to be sent anywhere in the central nervous system within just a few short steps. This is referred to as a *small-world network*. In many biological systems, a small-world network offers a certain degree of resilience to impediment. Think of the pony express, for instance: back in the days when mail was carried on horseback, a small-world network would have dramatically expedited its delivery by reducing the number of stops to the final destination.

By way of contrast, the sensory cortex projects to nearby locations. Sometimes their projections go from one neighboring gyrus to the next, forming connections reminiscent of Roman arches. This type of connectivity is ideal when performing multiple levels of processing for a particular piece of information. A prime example occurs in the visual cortex where short connections facilitate a hierarchy of feature extraction that enables us to process edge detection, estimate the relative motion of objects, and perceive differences in color. Without these short connections in the visual cortex, we would have no hope of ever "finding Waldo."

All of the anatomical findings we have discussed so far that bear on the brain's connectivity have significant clinical repercussions.

Some studies have shown that autistic individuals have heightened visual perception. When watching a computer screen, autistic subjects are able to better discern whether two bars popping up together do so at the same time or at closely timed intervals (Falter et al., 2013). These studies suggest that robust visual processing may give rise to increased resolution of visual events.

If we assume that the brains of autistic people preference short connections over long ones, this finding makes perfect sense. And in fact, that is what scientists have found. In a study performed at Massachusetts General Hospital, researchers discovered that autistic individuals and those with developmental language delay had disproportionate enlargement in white matter that was specifically composed of short connections (as opposed to long-range white matter like the corpus callosum) (Herbert et al., 2004).

Recall that the increase in total number of minicolumns leads to increased surface area and the creation of gyri on the surface of the brain. This is what gives our brains a "cauliflower" appearance. The folding of the cerebral cortex also has important implications for connectivity. As the brain has become progressively more convoluted across species over evolutionary time, the white matter connections coming from the neurons contained in those gyri have a smaller and smaller window through which to exit the cortex and enter the communicating structures below. Anatomically, this creates a "pinching effect," which effectively serves to reduce the number of axons that can exit (Figure 2.5).

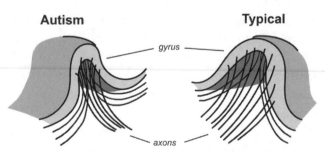

Figure 2.5: An illustration of the gyral window
in the neurotypical and autistic brain

Note how the gyrus is slimmer within the autism example and allows
fewer axons to exit compared to the typically developing gyrus.

Perhaps unsurprisingly, when researchers have measured the size of this "gyral window" in autism, it is significantly diminished in size compared to people without autism. In addition, the corpus callosum, the huge white matter tract that connects both hemispheres of the brain and is composed of large numbers of axons, is also reduced in size in autism (Casanova et al., 2011; Casanova, El-Baz, et al., 2009).

Considering all of this evidence, the brains of autistic people seem to preference shorter neural connections at the expense of longer ones. This is in stark contrast to dyslexia, in which minicolumn width is expanded, the gyral window is wider, and the corpus callosum is larger than in autism (Williams & Casanova, 2010).

It is also interesting to note that these conditions on the whole tend to have contrasting cognitive profiles that echo their respective anatomies. For instance, people with dyslexia are often good synthesizers with a top-down cognitive style that is holistically oriented—the probable result of an emphasis on long connections. Autistic individuals on the other hand have a bottom-up cognitive style, making them detail-oriented and good analyzers, the result of an emphasis on short connections. Therefore, it seems that there is a predisposition for certain cognitive qualities that are acquired early during brain development and that are strongly influenced by the organization of minicolumns and their respective connectivity patterns.

PUTTING IT ALL TOGETHER

When it comes to the brain in autism, the problem isn't that we lack data but that we have too much. In terms of postmortem studies, some of the findings may, unfortunately, have more to do with how a person died rather than whether he or she was autistic. This is often the case when someone dies from blunt trauma or from oxygen deprivation, such as the many cases of drownings in autism (Casanova, 2007). Artifacts in brain tissue, as may occur during tissue collection and storage, can also be mistaken for genuine findings. For this reason, a well-trained neuropathologist should be a requisite for any postmortem brain study. As in the case of autism, it is vital we account for the possibility of numerous types of artifacts so that the science is not misled. More than any other research materials, brain tissue is precious because it represents a remarkable sacrifice by autistic people and their families.

In piecing together this autism puzzle, the researcher must become an anthropologist, who must dig into the brain, looking for telltale footprints of some kind of mechanism. In the case of autism, minicolumnar architecture is altered in a process that appears to take place during early brain development. Yet rarely do such findings occur in a vacuum. Therefore, what other features of the brain may be appended to our minicolumn story? Let us explore.

As I (MFC) was attending an international meeting a few years ago, I heard a well-known researcher claim that there were few significant research findings in the brains of people with autism, with little to separate them from typically developing brains. From this he concluded that autism was an extreme of the human condition.

While this may well be true taken from certain perspectives, in the case of postmortem findings, the autistic brain does seem to have some pretty unique features, of which this individual appeared not to be aware. For instance, many studies have shown that there is often an abundance of neurons residing within the white matter tracts of the brain in autism. We know from many human and animal studies that these neurons should not be there, suggesting that they either got lost along their migratory ways or were once part of an earlier structure called the "subplate," which normally dies off before birth after it has served its function as a way station for incoming nerve fibers, but in the case of autism this clearly hasn't happened efficiently (Hutsler & Avino, 2015). These misplaced neurons are referred to as *heterotopias* (Figure 2.6). These heterotopias are similar to a hernia, which occurs when an organ pushes past a muscle wall and protrudes into a foreign space. Like a hernia, these islands of cells occur in a tissue in which they shouldn't be, a "hernia of neurons." For this reason, scientists don't normally consider these heterotopias "normal," especially when we know that many of these misplaced cells are epileptogenic or prone to the production of seizures.

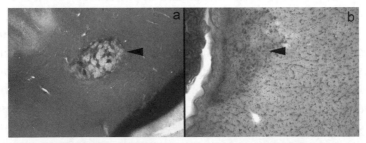

Figure 2.6: Microscopic images showing heterotopias (misplaced clusters of cells) within the hippocampus (left) and cerebellum (right) in cases of autism

(Images courtesy of Dr. Jerzy Wegiel)

Although some heterotopias do occasionally occur in otherwise asymptomatic individuals, they are also often associated with motor problems and even intellectual disability. In autism, heterotopias vary in location and numbers from one individual to another. This provides an important clue to our story: heterotopias that are the result of genetic conditions tend to be widespread, meanwhile autistic individuals without any identifiable genetic conditions tend to have variable "pockets" of heterotopic malformations, suggesting the additional possibility of environmental factors that may increase risk in the condition (see Chapter 4). As an example, prenatal exposure to x-rays can result in clusters of heterotopias within the brain, while the topography of these "herniated neurons" depends on which area of the germinal matrix was originally exposed to radiation (Ferrer et al., 1993).

We know that heterotopias occur in a large number of autistic people (Wegiel et al., 2010). However, the overall prevalence depends on the resolution of the technique being used to investigate them. For instance, neuroimaging studies such as MRI will identify fewer heterotopias than postmortem tissue studies that screen the brain by using a higher-resolution technique (i.e. light microscopy). Yet even with microscopy, the prevalence of heterotopias increases as you dissect more and more brain regions. In summary, postmortem studies that screen serial (consecutive) brain sections will uncover the greatest number of abnormalities. Using this type of technique, it is safe to say that approximately 60 to 80 percent of autistic individuals show some evidence of heterotopias (Wegiel et al., 2010). When we include other cortical malformations, the overall prevalence increases to more than 80 percent (Wegiel et al., 2010; see also Casanova, El-Baz, et al., 2013).

It is possible that an environmental exigency acts in susceptible individuals during particular times of gestation, which disturbs normal neuronal migration, leading to the heterotopias we see in the condition. This triple-hit mechanism (Environment × Risk Factor × Developmental Timing) ultimately leads to poor coordination of excitatory and inhibitory elements within the cerebral cortex (Casanova, 2007; Casanova, Buxhoeveden, & Gomez, 2003). Many studies that have found evidence of a variety of types of neuronal heterotopias and a relative loss of inhibitory cells in the brains of autistic people, indicating that migrational disturbances are a major feature of the condition (Andrews et al., 2017; Avino and Hutsler, 2010; Hashemi et al., 2017).

CLINICAL CONSIDERATIONS

The usefulness of a theoretical mechanism of action lies, in part, on its predictive ability. When considering migrational abnormalities, it's clear that they often co-occur with autism. This can be seen in the prime example, tuberous sclerosis (TSC). This condition is characterized by the growth of noncancerous tumors in numerous organ systems, most especially within the brain, skin, kidneys, and heart. In the brains of people with TSC there is usually a migrational abnormality involving the stem cells surrounding the cerebral ventricles, in which they become waylaid near their places of origin or within the white matter tracts (DiMario, 2004).

In addition, the surrounding cerebral cortex is disorganized by both tumorous growths and other malformations accrued via the underlying migrational abnormality. Many patients with TSC suffer from intractable seizures, attentional deficits, behavioral outbursts, and obsessive-compulsive traits. This constellation of symptoms is highly suggestive of autism and, indeed, this dual diagnosis is given in approximately 50–60 percent of TSC infants by age three (McDonald et al., 2017).

Another example occurs in infants born with congenital cytomegalovirus infection (see Chapter 4). This is a common viral infection that is typically asymptomatic. Often, pregnant women may not even be aware they're infected, yet they may give birth to infants with obvious infection. The most common symptoms are jaundice, hepatosplenomegaly (swollen liver and spleen), and petechiae, which are small purple, red, or brown spots in the skin resultant from small bleeds (Leung et al., 2003). Some infants may also be premature or small for gestational age, and have microcephaly and seizures. In addition, some of these affected infants go on to develop the behavioral phenotype of autism (Yamashita et al., 2003). Interestingly, case studies suggest that children with congenital cytomegalovirus and autism typically exhibit subependymal cysts in the brain, which is a type of migrational disturbance (Yamashita et al., 2003). For readers who are interested in reading more, there are further examples of autistic syndromes with underlying migrational abnormalities that have been reviewed by our research group (Casanova, 2014a, 2014b).

Given what we've learned about these malformations and the excitatory–inhibitory imbalance in autism, this raises the possibility of therapeutic application. For many years, interventions were aimed at treating the symptoms of autism rather than affecting its underlying causes. However, researchers and clinicians in recent years have taken aim at the decreased inhibitory tone of the cerebral cortex. Some scientists have tried to target this excitatory–inhibitory imbalance through the use of certain types of drugs, such as barbiturates, benzodiazepines, and anticonvulsants. Unfortunately, these drugs are often the equivalent of taking a sledgehammer to a small nail, affecting a wide range of neurons throughout the brain.

In the case of autism, it is more useful to implement a degree of specificity. It would be ideal, for instance, if we could directly target those cells involved in maintaining the "shower curtain of inhibition" surrounding minicolumns, which we talked about earlier. This would allow us to rein in excitatory tendencies.

In fact, our laboratory has been able to do exactly that using a technique called *repetitive transcranial magnetic stimulation* (rTMS). To help you understand how this technique works, first you need to know that minicolumns stand perpendicular to the surface of the neocortex, similar to a figure "T." As we discussed earlier, each minicolumn is composed of an inner core of excitatory neurons and an outer core that includes a variety of different inhibitory neurons. One type of inhibitory neuron that is vital in maintaining the shower curtain effect is the double bouquet (DB) cell. Unlike other inhibitory cells, DB cells have long bundled projections reaching both towards and away from the surface of the cortex. They look so much like "horse tails" that is how they are informally known.

When a powerful magnetic force is placed on the surface of the skull (Figure 2.7), anything standing perpendicular to the skull (e.g. minicolumns) may be stimulated. However, in the case of low-frequency rTMS, which is the tool our research group utilizes, the force is weak and preferentially stimulates only larger projections (Sokhadze et al., 2009). In this case, the behaviors of excitatory cells remain largely unaffected and the broad bundled axons of DB cells are stimulated instead. Since activity drives neural plasticity, this stimulation strengthens the DB shower curtain and ultimately improves the excitatory–inhibitory balance.

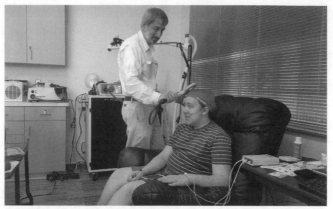

Figure 2.7: A young man with autism receiving low-frequency repetitive transcranial magnetic stimulation (rTMS)

(Image courtesy of Michael)

Since our initial trial, other research groups have used rTMS in autism, reporting similar results (Casanova et al., 2015; Oberman et al., 2016). In fact, an entire book has been written on the topic from the perspective of a patient who received TMS treatment (Robison, 2016). Additional trials of rTMS in autism have shown that it improves functional measures of information processing and behavioral responses, attention, and something known as "error monitoring," which is the way an individual adjusts and adapts to previous mistakes (Casanova et al., 2012; Sokhadze et al., 2012, 2014a). This is usually tested using various kinds of computer programs. Unfortunately, although all of these results are significant, they have shown only modest effects in their outcome measures and are primarily limited to high-functioning individuals who are able to sit still for longer periods of time and follow sets of instructions. For this reason, clinical trials are looking to combine rTMS with other techniques, like neurofeedback, to see if we can impact people's quality of life in more meaningful ways (Sokhadze et al., 2014b).

Chapter Three

THE GENETICS OF AUTISM

THE HISTORY OF GENETICS STUDIES IN AUTISM

Any history of the heritability of autism must begin with Bernard Rimland's seminal 1964 book *Infantile Autism: The Syndrome and Its Implications for a Neural Theory of Behavior*. As we discussed in the introductory chapter of this book, the zeitgeist of the middle 20th century espoused that conditions like autism were psychogenic in origin, rooted in aberrant parent–child relations. However, both as a psychologist and a parent, Bernie Rimland strongly suspected autism's roots were biological. He knew that he and his wife had not caused their son's autism and in fact had done everything in their power to relieve their child's symptoms.[1]

Due to the times but also to limits in methodology, the heredity of autism was not of much interest to early researchers. Prior to *Infantile Autism*, only a handful of twins studies existed, each with somewhat dubious methods, yet all suggesting autism could be a heritable condition (reviewed in Judd & Mandell, 1968, and Rutter, 2000). Unfortunately, these data were largely ignored by the research community until Bernie Rimland's book finally began to draw attention to these studies and provided a soapbox for the topics of genetics and heritability.

It wasn't until 1977, however, that the topic of heritability caught the eye of the broader research community, when Susan Folstein and Michael Rutter published a study on autism concordance rates between identical and fraternal twins (Folstein & Rutter, 1977). Folstein and Rutter discovered that more than a third of their identical twin pairs shared an autism diagnosis, while none of the fraternal twins were

---

1   An excellent book that reviews their story is *In A Different Key: The Story of Autism* by Caren Zucker and John Donvan (2016, Allen Lane).

concordant.[2] This was shocking and strongly indicated that autism was indeed a heritable condition. Because no fraternal twins appeared concordant in the original study, it also suggested at the time that autism could be due to one or a few gene mutations.

However, during this time reports began to arise linking autism with specific prenatal infections, such as rubella and cytomegalovirus (Chess, 1971; Stubbs, 1978) (see Chapter 4). In addition, by the 1980s and '90s scientists found that certain genetic syndromes such as fragile X syndrome and tuberous sclerosis also had high rates of comorbid autism, making it clear that autism wasn't due to a single gene mutation (Gillberg & Wahlström, 1985; Smalley, 1998). Together, this early evidence suggested that the syndrome was far more complex than Folstein and Rutter had originally believed.

Researchers began to grasp autism's genetic complexity starting with two major studies. The first looked at rates of inheritance in first-degree relatives of those with autism (Bolton et al., 1994). Specifically, researchers found that siblings shared a 12–20 percent concordance rate, which depended on the stringency of the criteria used. Approximately 12 percent were concordant for the full autism diagnosis, meanwhile an additional 8 percent expressed a subclinical phenotype, suggesting that autism severity could vary dramatically within the same families.

The other report was a twins study, which, unlike the original Folstein and Rutter investigation, found that fraternal twins exhibited a similar concordance rate for autism as seen amongst non-twin siblings (Bailey et al., 1995). All of these data together suggested that most cases of autism were likely the interaction of multiple heritable factors rather than a single-gene pattern of inheritance. In addition, variations in symptom severity between identical twins suggested that environment also played an important role in the condition.

Although the early twins studies foreshadowed current knowledge of the genetic complexity of autism, at the turn of the millennium geneticists were still hopeful that human genome sequencing would allow us rapidly to identify the causal genes. This was inspired by early linkage studies indicating that multiple genetic loci could act cooperatively to affect risk, such as the long arm of chromosome 7

---

2   In twins studies, "concordance" means that a pair of twins share the same diagnosis; when they do not, they are "discordant."

(Rutter, 2000). However, despite all the hoopla and high hopes, we have since identified *hundreds* of genes significantly involved in autism risk. Some gene mutations, as will be discussed in succeeding sections, confer high risk for autism, and the genes in which they occur are known as *major effect genes*; meanwhile, other mutations confer lower though still measurable risk and are known as *minor effect genes* (see Figure 3.1). Some mutations involve the change of a single nucleotide of DNA. Meanwhile, other variations can span many genes at once, the result of deletions or duplications of large amounts of genetic material.

Although many of these genes share functional overlap, their diversity nevertheless prevents us from identifying a single underlying biology. As a result, to this day, autism is defined by constellations of behaviors, despite the plethora of biological findings. In this respect, it is not unlike related conditions such as intellectual disability.

AUTISM RISK GENES

In genetics, *penetrance* is defined as the proportion of people who carry a particular genetic variation and express an associated trait of interest. To give an example, approximately 80 percent of women who have certain mutations in the *BRCA1* gene will develop breast cancer. That means that the penetrance of these *BRCA1* mutations is 80 percent for the condition. This is a very high penetrance rate, making the *BRCA1* gene a "major effect gene" for breast cancer (Apostolou & Fostira, 2013).

Meanwhile, mutations in genes such as *ATM*, *BRIP1*, *PALB2*, and *CHEK2* have very low penetrance on their own but when they occur in families with a strong history of breast cancer, risk is significantly elevated. These are good examples of "minor effect genes" and probably represent *polygenic* or multigene effects (Byrnes, Southey, & Hopper, 2008). When these genetic variations occur in tandem with other risk factors, overall risk for developing breast cancer can exponentially increase.

Autism is very similar in this way. There is a subset of risk genes that confer very high risk for autism. Most of these are associated with some kind of genetic syndrome and include examples like the *FMR1* gene associated with fragile X syndrome and *TSC2* associated with tuberous sclerosis. However, other genetic variations have minor effects on autism risk and are sometimes seen in unaffected family members and even the general population. Therefore, combinations of major and minor effect variations probably lead to significant variability across autistic individuals and family members with a broader phenotype (Berg & Geschwind, 2012; Girirajan et al., 2012).

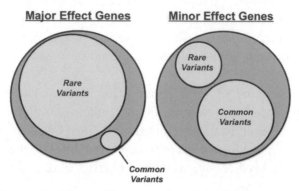

Figure 3.1: Diagram illustrating the relative frequency of rare and common variants in major and minor effect genes

Major effect genes are often affected by rare mutations that have highly deleterious effects. Meanwhile, minor affect genes are more likely the targets of less deleterious rare mutations and common polymorphisms.

A whole lotta genes

There are about 21,000 protein-coding genes in the human genome. Several thousand of these genes have been loosely linked with autism (Xu et al., 2012). Several hundred are considered high-confidence risk factors, and a large minority of these are major effect genes (Casanova, Sharp, et al., 2016). Chromosomal disorders, composed primarily of large deletions and duplications of genetic material, also target multiple genes at once. Oftentimes, each of these genes may be of only minor effect, but in conjunction they confer significant autism risk. Examples include 16p11.2 deletion, 22q11.2 deletion, and 15q11.2-13.1 duplication syndromes. All of this genetic complexity and variable symptom severity makes it clear that autism is a heterogeneous group of conditions that differ in cause but overlap in behavior.

However, there are common threads that tie these genes together, suggesting autism does indeed share some common biology. In our previous work, we discovered that the majority of major effect genes code for proteins that function within the nucleus of the cell, where DNA is located (Casanova, Sharp, et al., 2016). In particular, they help to regulate the expression of other genes (i.e. they are "epigenetic regulators"). Other researchers have also found similar patterns of enrichment amongst autism risk genes (De Rubeis et al., 2014; Geschwind & State, 2015; Glessner et al., 2009; Iossifov et al., 2014; Krumm et al., 2014).

Epigenetic regulators are key in early development by regulating the timing of events. When these regulators fail to function properly, this can lead to either the suppression or premature maturation of cells, potentially altering the quantity and quality of cells within a particular tissue. When this occurs, it's known as a "heterochrony," which loosely means a "mis-timing of events."

A portion of autism risk genes also code for synaptic proteins within the brain. Common examples include neurexins and their partners, neuroligins; neurotransmitter receptors; and calcium channel proteins. Neurexins, which are cell-adhesion molecules, are involved in regulating cell-to-cell communication by acting as anchors in the creation of physical bridges between cells.

Although neurexins and their partners, the neuroligins, are best understood for their roles within the adult synapse, they're also expressed in newborn neurons long before mature synapses develop. Scientists have found that neurexins are expressed in the prenatal mouse brain as early as day ten of pregnancy, during one of the earliest stages of neuron production within the cortex (Puschel & Betz, 1995). This suggests that neurexins may be involved in processes like cell movement, branching, and other aspects of neuron maturation long before they settle into their mature role at the synapse. Because excitatory input is imperative in guiding the development of newborn neurons, these neurexin–neuroligin pairings may allow them to receive input from a foundational network of cells that helps them to coordinate these efforts (Ben-Ari, 2002).

Because they're expressed very early in development, synaptic proteins may play roles in cell-to-cell communication that drive neuron development long before the neuron sprouts adult dendrites and synapses. Synaptic mutations, therefore, have the potential to divert the production of new neurons, their migrations, and other aspects of early development—findings very similar to gene mutations in epigenetic regulators.

On the other hand, epigenetic regulators also continue to play important roles in adult neurons, regulating aspects of branching and synapse formation. In this way, epigenetic regulators and synaptic proteins overlap across all stages of neuron development and plasticity, although they may target different stages of development to varying degrees.

Scientists' obsession with the synapse

Although some synaptic genes clearly play important roles in autism risk, there has been a scientific obsession with the functional role of the synapse in autism, at times leaving other gene types and cellular structures poorly studied.

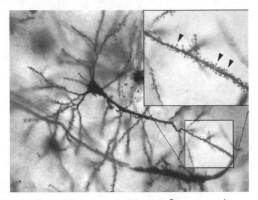

Figure 3.2: Microscopic image of synapses (arrows)

Interest in synapses (Figure 3.2) began following a publication by Thomas Bourgeron and his colleagues, reporting an association of neuroligins 3 and 4 mutations with autism (Jamain et al., 2003). This paper was quickly followed by a hypothesis article by Huda Zoghbi (2003) in which she proposed that autism was a result of "disruption of postnatal or experience-dependent synaptic plasticity" (p. 826). A few years later, enthusiasm for synaptic involvement in autism was further stoked by the identification of other relevant autism-associated mutations in synapse-related genes such as *SHANK3*, *CNTNAP2*, and other risks genes that help to carry out cell signaling, such as the serotonin transporter gene *SLC6A4* (Alarcón et al., 2008; Anderson et al., 2002; Arking et al., 2008; Durand et al., 2006). Since that time, the synapse has been a hot topic in autism research and many researchers have tried to fit new findings into a synapse-focused paradigm, for example:

> ASD may arise from dysregulation of activity-dependent signaling pathways locally at a synapse, including changes in the post-translational modifications of synaptic proteins and the local translation of mRNAs at synapses, as well as from the dysregulation of activity-dependent gene transcription. (Ebert & Greenberg, 2013, p. 328)

Unfortunately, viewing the cell in such a compartmentalized fashion as if its constituent parts were developed in a vacuum is theoretically simplistic. And perhaps more concerning, much of the research has focused on how synapses function in the *adult* neuron, whereas we know little of these mutations' consequences in newborn cells. The autism risk gene *CNTNAP2*, for instance, is not only located within the synapse, its mutation leads to disturbances in neuron migration long before adult synapses are formed. Its mutation results in the formation of heterotopias, which are misplaced clusters of cells that often have the propensity to produce epileptic discharges (Strauss et al., 2006). Ultimately, these data cause us to question what we truly mean when we use the term, "synaptic gene."

Gain-of-function mutations and cell stress

When a gene is severely mutated, failing to produce a viable gene product, this is known as a "loss-of-function mutation." In many instances, no gene product is produced or the product is unstable and breaks down rapidly. However, at other times a protein is produced but is misfolded. When this happens, the protein is retained within a cellular compartment known as the endoplasmic reticulum (ER), an organelle that's vital in identifying and dealing with misfolded proteins either by refolding them or getting rid of them (Figure 3.3). When a large number of misfolded proteins arrive in the ER, this triggers a cascade of signals that slows protein synthesis, upregulates inflammatory pathways, and triggers a general stress response to deal with the backlog.

When this response occurs chronically because of a mutation, this mutation also results in a "gain-of-function," because the cell stress response would not occur normally. This is in contrast to the loss-of-function that results from the loss of the protein product at the site within the cell for which it was intended—at the synapse, for example. Therefore, these mutations result both in a gain and loss of function, respectively.

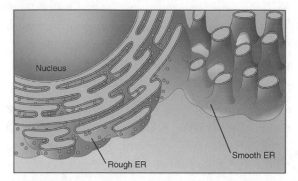

Figure 3.3: The rough and smooth endoplasmic reticula (ER)

The rough ER helps produce proteins within the cell, while the
smooth ER produces fats and steroids (hormones).

(Image adapted from OpenStax Anatomy and Physiology, Version 8.25. Published May 18, 2016)

For reasons not well understood, there are a number of studies that have reported gain-of-function mutations in synaptic genes in autism, all resulting in chronic cell stress responses in the cases they studied (Comoletti et al., 2004; Falivelli et al., 2012; Fujita et al., 2010; Zhang et al., 2009). Is this a reporting bias or are synaptic mutations more likely to cause ER stress? Unfortunately, we don't yet know the answer. But one possible explanation may concern the large, complex structures of synaptic proteins and their propensities for misfolding. (See Chapter 5 for further discussion on processes related to the cell stress response, such as inflammation and oxidation.)

What protein structure tells us about function

> Whether it be the sweeping eagle in his flight, or the open apple-blossom, the toiling work-horse, the blithe swan, the branching oak, the winding stream at its base, the drifting clouds, over all the coursing sun, form ever follows function, and this is the law. Where function does not change, form does not change. (Sullivan, 1896, p. 408)

So wrote the American architect, Louis Sullivan. Sullivan was strongly influenced by the writings of the Roman architect, Marcus Vitruvius Pollio who in his *De Architectura* asserted that a building or structure must be *firmitas, utilitas, venustas*—solid, useful, and beautiful.

Proteins are one of the major building blocks of the cell. Although a protein doesn't need to be solid or beautiful as in the case of a building, its shape certainly helps to determine its function. Even the change of a single amino acid sequence, the building blocks of proteins, has the potential to alter or destroy the function of the entire molecule. The most minute of changes in how a protein folds can mean the difference between a protein being use*ful* or use*less*.

Since there's a relationship between protein shape and its function, the length and complexity of proteins also vary according to their functions. Longer proteins tend to have more functional segments or "domains," while shorter proteins have fewer. What an excellent example of "form ever [following] function." Interestingly, the functions of proteins are also partly reflected in the structure of the genes that code for them. While we would expect this to be the case for the segments of gene that code for the proteins themselves, this trend also includes non-coding sequences within genes, such as introns.

In most genes, the protein blueprint is broken down into segments known as "exons" that are separated from one another by non-coding sequences (i.e. "introns": Figure 3.4). Later on, introns are usually spliced out before RNA is translated into protein. Genes that code for big proteins (such as those found at the synapse) tend to have very long introns. One potential reason for this is that long introns increase the accuracy of gene expression, reducing the number of mutations (Niu & Yang, 2011). The cause of this is biochemically complex, but to put it simply: longer genes compel the cellular machinery to transcribe RNA more *carefully*. This means that long genes may experience fewer mutations than smaller genes. In addition, these long genes are often vital for numerous developmental processes and therefore when a mutation occurs, it's rapidly weeded out (Casanova et al., 2017a; Woolfe & Elgar, 2008).

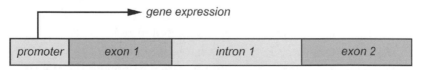

Figure 3.4: Illustration of an intron, which is book-ended by two exons

Normally introns are removed from the gene transcript afterwards and the exons are molecularly "sutured" back together. Although introns don't typically encode for transcripts and proteins, they do, however, contain many regulatory elements that help control gene expression.

Introns also contain many small sequences that help regulate gene expression. In particular, large genes contain a greater density of noncoding regulatory sequences compared to smaller genes. While we won't delve into the complicated ways these sequences regulate genes, just know that they provide vast layers of functional complexity to the genome, which are largely responsible for the evolutionary differences we see between species today. For instance, the proteins that humans and chimpanzees make are virtually identical to one another, yet the differences in our regulatory DNA are much greater.

Regulatory DNA also seems to evolve faster that protein-coding DNA because it's under weaker selection. Imagine that proteins are the building blocks for a city you're designing: you can change the ways in which you combine blocks to make many different designs, but if you change the nature of the building blocks themselves you could endanger the stability of your buildings. Regulatory sequences tell the body the different ways in which it can put proteins together, forever allowing new evolutionary designs to arise, but nature settled on basic protein designs long ago. Therefore, much of genetic evolution over the last several hundred million years has focused on sequences that regulate genes.

Why have we reviewed the relationship between molecular form and its function and what does this have to do with autism? It turns out that because autism risk genes have overlapping functions in areas such as regulation of gene expression and synapse development, their genes and related proteins also tend to share common structural features. For instance, if you compare the length of autism risk genes to the average of all the protein-coding genes in the human genome, you would find that autism risk genes tend to be much longer (Casanova et al., 2017a). In fact, several of these risk genes are among the largest in the human genome, notable examples including *CNTNAP2* and *NRXN1*, both of which are over a million base pairs in length. We, along with other scientists before us, have found that genes strongly associated with the central nervous system tend to be unusually long.

As we noted, these long genes have large numbers of regulatory sequences in their introns that add functional complexity to the gene, allowing it to, for instance, produce different variations of RNA known as *transcripts*. We have also found that autism risk genes tend to produce more transcript variations than other genes on average, making them a nuanced and versatile group of genes, just perfect for building a complex brain (Casanova et al., 2017b). The neurexin genes alone, for instance, produce over 3000 transcript variants!

In summary, the structural features of genes can tell us a lot about their evolutionary histories, how they evolved and adapted over time, and—perhaps most importantly—how these proteins function throughout the different organs of the body, including the brain. As Louis Sullivan so aptly wrote, "form ever follows function," and genes and their proteins are no exception.

RARE MUTATIONS, COMMON VARIATIONS

Most of your genetic makeup is identical to that of any other human being. However, when variation does occur, it's labeled as either "rare" or "common." Common variants, as their name suggests, can be found in a significant proportion of the human population. Most often, these variations occur at a single point within the DNA—however, there are also some examples of common variants that affect large spans of genetic material. These are known as common copy number variations (CNVs), which contrast with rare CNVs often associated with various diseases and syndromes. We'll talk more about CNVs later.

When we refer to "common variants," this typically alludes to differences at a single nucleotide location across individuals. These are also sometimes known as *single nucleotide polymorphisms* (SNP) or simply *polymorphisms*. Polymorphisms comprise a *major allele*, which is a gene variation that occurs in the majority of the population, and one or more *minor alleles*, which occur in anywhere from 5 to 49 percent of the human race.

On the other hand, the definition of rare variations, often colloquially referred to as "mutations," occur anywhere from less than 1 percent up to 5 percent of the human population, depending on the research study.

Now that you have a better grasp of these basic definitions, let's discuss the types of rare variations associated with autism. Cytogenetic abnormalities, for instance, which are major disruptions to the chromosome material, are observed in about 3 percent of all prenatal exams (Park et al., 2001). These chromosomal abnormalities are identified through a method called "karyotyping," in which a sample of amniotic fluid is taken during pregnancy and the DNA from the fetus present in the fluid is tested for major disturbances. About 2 percent of the time, there are entire duplications or deletions of chromosomes, such as we see in trisomy 21, otherwise known as Down syndrome. Another 1 percent of the time, there are structural malformations of one or more of the chromosomes themselves. These tend to involve large deletions, duplications, inversions, or translocations of segments of the DNA.

It's believed that about half of all spontaneous abortions occurring between weeks 5 and 25 of pregnancy are the result of major chromosome abnormalities in the embryo or fetus (Eiben et al., 1990). This doesn't account, however, for spontaneous abortions that occur even earlier in gestation before the mother's aware she's pregnant, which comprise about half of all pregnancies. Therefore, serious genetic mutations are quite common, but the majority are weeded out long before birth. The few infants with major genetic mutations that make it to term may have severe impairment during life but these mutations are comparatively less deadly.

Although the percentage is small compared to the general population, scientists have found that more than 5 percent of those with autism have major chromosome abnormalities (Vorstman et al., 2006). However, not all structural abnormalities can be identified with traditional karyotyping, which may miss smaller genetic mutations that are nevertheless significant. Using newer methods, we now know that CNVs, a type of mutation that karyotyping often misses, occur at a higher-than-expected rate in autism (Sebat et al., 2007). This is especially the case for new CNVs, which arise in either the sperm or egg but are otherwise not present in the parent (see Berg & Geschwind, 2012, for review). Interestingly, however, the rate of inheritance of older CNVs doesn't appear to differ between autistic and typically developing kids.

CNVs are structural variations in the human genome in which segments of DNA, ranging from about one thousand to millions of nucleotides in length, are deleted, duplicated, or translocated in some other fashion. As you might imagine, this can lead to disastrous effects on the genes that are located in or near the CNV, which can ultimately have a cascading effect on many cellular pathways.

Researchers studying autism genetics often separate people with the condition into *simplex* and *multiplex* cases. "Simplex" means that autism occurs only once within a particular family. Meanwhile, "multiplex" means that two or more siblings have the diagnosis (Figure 3.5). While simplex cases of autism have particularly high rates of new CNVs, multiplex families have lower though still significantly elevated rates of these new CNVs as well (Miller et al., 2010; Pinto et al., 2010; Sebat et al., 2007).

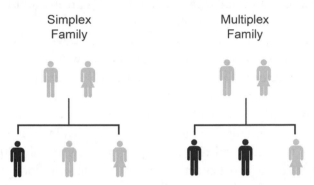

Figure 3.5: Examples of pedigrees of simplex and multiplex families

CNVs only occur in a small minority of those with autism (10%). An additional 10 percent have other smaller genetic variations, such as point mutations, scientifically known as rare *single nucleotide variants* (SNVs) (Jiang et al., 2013). On average, autistic people don't have *more* SNVs than their non-autistic counterparts—in contrast to CNVs associated with autism. Instead, when SNVs occur, they tend to target high-risk autism genes, such as *CHD8*, *ARID1B*, and *SHANK3* (Berg & Geschwind, 2012, for review). From this work, we now know that patterns of gene mutation share strong links with penetrance, a concept we discussed earlier. Genes within CNVs usually have low penetrance but additively confer high risk. Meanwhile, SNVs that target high-risk genes confer significant individual risk and are therefore highly penetrant.

Parents, new mutations, and old mutations

Older paternal age is a known risk factor for sporadic (simplex) cases of autism. This is because males are constantly making new sperm—in contrast to females who are born with their lifelong complement of eggs. As men age, the number of mutations they pass on to each offspring increases (Callaway, 2012). For instance, a 36-year-old father will pass on twice as many new mutations to his child than a father who is the age of 20. Most of these mutations are clinically insignificant, however, the more mutations occur the more likely a harmful one will arise. Men pass on an astounding four times as many mutations to their children compared to women. It's therefore little surprise that increased paternal age is a recognized risk factor in the development of autism and is linked with greater autism severity (Croen et al., 2007; Jiang et al., 2013).

Interestingly, a recent study indicates, however, that advanced paternal age (and the sperm mutations that come with it) may not be the sole driving factor in the correlation between older age and autism risk. Instead, advanced paternal age may explain only about 10–20 percent of increased risk. Meanwhile, scientists have found that fathers with subclinical autism traits are more likely to have children at older ages compared to their "typical" counterparts (Gratten et al., 2016). For instance, mild social deficits may delay at-risk men in finding partners and having children. In addition, fathers with higher levels of education may also elect to postpone parenthood until it's more convenient, including various reasons such as career advancement (Kogan et al., 2009). Therefore, older paternal age in some cases may not be the *cause* of autism but just another symptom of its familial heritability.

But what about mothers? Even though men may pass on *new* mutations to their children at a higher rate, women may be more likely to pass on *old* harmful mutations. This is particularly true in the case of sons, because daughters may be better protected against certain mutations by nature of their sex. Mothers who harbor such mutations may have a subtler phenotype compared to their sons—or no recognizable phenotype at all. Sometimes, this is because the mutation in question is located on the X chromosome. Males typically inherit only a single X from their mothers (except in conditions like Kleinfelter's syndrome, in which the male has an XXY genotype). Therefore, if a gene on the X chromosome is mutated, males have no genetic back-up. Meanwhile, the mother has an extra copy of the X chromosome, subduing the effects of the X-linked mutation.

Other times the mutation in question may lie within one of the "autosomal" or non-sex chromosomes. However, the mother may still not be as severely affected as her son, for reasons poorly understood. While we can only guess as to the mechanisms involved (e.g. hormones), it's possible some of the brain differences between the sexes may exaggerate autism symptoms in males meanwhile attenuating them in females. In this regard, the *extreme male brain theory of autism* may provide a basis for understanding why and how cognition in males (e.g. higher systematizing vs. lower empathizing) overlaps that of autism so considerably (Baron-Cohen, 2002).

Inherited risk for developing mutations

Advanced paternal age is not the only risk factor for developing new mutations in sperm. Not only can mutations be inherited, but the tendency to form new mutations can also be passed on genetically. For instance, Molina et al. (2011) studied genetic deletions and duplications in the sperm of a sample of men. While overall rates of deletions and duplications didn't vary much across the entire genome, there were significant differences between the individual men when looking at two autism- and intellectual disability-risk loci, namely 7q11.23 and 15q11-q13. These differences suggested that the men harbored minor genetic variations in or near these loci that somehow affected the regions' stability, increasing or decreasing risk of mutations in these regions.

Another example of inherited mutation risk is premutations for fragile X syndrome (FXS). The promoter region of the *FMR1* gene contains a CGG triplet repeat[3] and most people have anywhere from 5 to 54 CGG repeats. However, people with 60–230 repeats are carriers for FXS, and these premutations are unstable: the larger the number of repeats, the greater the instability and the greater likelihood they may have children with FXS (Hagerman & Hagerman, 2004). Therefore, not only can mutations be inherited from generation to generation, genetic instability can also be inherited, increasing risk for new mutations in specific genetic loci.

Like attracts like

Another pattern affecting the inheritance of autism risk is "assortative mating." Simply put: *like attracts like*. Recent research suggests that people with risk factors for conditions like autism or schizophrenia are more often attracted to one another, increasing the likelihood that

---

3   The DNA is composed of 4 different nucleotides (A, T, G, and C). CGG triplet repeats are strings of the nucleotides "CGG" repeated within the DNA. In the case of FXS, individuals usually carry 200+ CGG triplet repeats (there's some overlap in genotype with carriers). This ultimately alters how the gene is methylated and therefore how it is expressed.

their children may develop related neurodevelopmental conditions (Nordsletten et al., 2016). This type of mating pattern is probably important in the spread of weak autism risk factors such as common risk variants.

Educational assortative mating (the tendency for people to choose partners with similar educational backgrounds) may also play a minor role in autism risk. Scientists have found that children with autism, especially those with less cognitively impaired forms like Asperger's syndrome or Pervasive Developmental Disorder–Not Otherwise Specified (PDD-NOS), are more likely to have parents with above-average educational attainment (Croen et al., 2007). As you may recall from Chapter 1, this characteristic was well described in Leo Kanner's original manuscript—although his case studies may have represented some ascertainment bias.

Diagnostic gender bias and the female protective effect

On average, males are three times more likely to receive an autism diagnosis than females (Ozonoff et al., 2011). One reason for this discrepancy seems to be a gender-based diagnostic bias. Surprisingly, even when females exhibit similar levels of impairment as males, they are still less likely to receive an autism diagnosis (Russell, Steer, & Golding, 2011). While it's a challenge to understand where this bias comes from, it's clear that much of the foundational work delineating the autism phenotype was performed using male-dominated patient pools, which has presumably influenced our concepts of the stereotype of autism. As an example of the sex-skewed nature of mid-20th-century research, early in his career Hans Asperger didn't even believe autism could occur in females!

Some of the diagnostic skewing may be accounted for by differences between the sexes. For instance, scientists have found that males in general, regardless of whether they are on the autism spectrum, display more repetitive and restricted behaviors than females (Messinger et al., 2015). Autistic and non-autistic males also perform more poorly on certain developmental scales of learning compared to their respective female counterparts, suggesting that some of the characteristics upon which we are basing diagnoses are not necessarily autism-specific but are exacerbated by the condition, particularly in males.

Hereditary research, however, does suggest that males develop autism more often than females. Some cases, for instance, can be accounted for by X-linked mutations, in which females may be asymptomatic or subclinical carriers. But this accounts for only a small portion of familial cases. Instead, sex hormones presumably skew rates of autism occurrence (Gockley et al., 2015).

Family studies have shown that the autistic siblings of females with autism are more severely affected than the siblings of similarly affected males (Robinson et al., 2013, 2014). This indicates that the hereditary load in families with autistic girls is greater, suggesting girls are typically more resilient than the boys. This has been replicated in numerous genetics studies, finding that girls with autism usually have more mutations, and therefore a greater genetic load, than males who are similarly affected (Jacquemont et al., 2014; Sanders et al., 2015; Sebat et al., 2007).

Assuming differences in the hormonal milieu drives the female protective effect, how might the steroid, estrogen, reduce severity of the autism phenotype? One major mechanism of action is the role estrogen and its receptor plays in regulating the expression of genes. Unlike most receptors that are relegated to the outer membrane of the cell, when estrogen binds to the estrogen receptor this complex is able to travel into the nucleus, bind to DNA, and directly regulate gene expression. The receptor is also able to interact with other molecules that bind to and regulate DNA, controlling gene expression through less direct means (Marino, Galluzzo, & Ascenzi, 2006).

Interestingly, genes that are expressed strongly in the male-typical brain significantly overlap those that are abnormally expressed in the brain in autism (Werling, Parikshak, & Geschwind, 2016). This suggests that these genes are targets of sex steroids and female-typical hormones reduce their expressions and thereby alleviate the autism phenotype. Using animal models to test this hypothesis, scientists have discovered that stimulation of the estrogen receptor rescues the effects of certain autism-specific mutations (Hoffman et al., 2016). Additional work needs to be performed, but initial studies indicate that estrogen in particular decreases the severity of autism during certain periods of development.

PHYSICAL FEATURES ASSOCIATED WITH AUTISM

There is ongoing debate whether intellectual disability is as prevalent in autism as standard IQ tests indicate (Nader et al., 2016). While we won't delve into the nitty-gritty of this debate here (see Chapter 9 for further discussion), moderate-to-severe intellectual disability does sometimes co-occur with autism and can have strong genetic roots. When these forms of intellectual disability accompany autism, they are also often associated with multiple congenital anomalies (MCA). People with MCA have physical anomalies in multiple organs of the body, such as malformations of the face, the hands and feet, or heart defects. If these anomalies occur together in a consistent fashion across multiple people, dysmorphologists (professionals who study differences in body structure) define this as a "syndrome." Oftentimes, these syndromes have identifiable causes, such as certain types of mutations or specific environmental insults. Common examples include fragile X and fetal alcohol syndromes, which are genetic and teratogenic (environmental) syndromes respectively.

In recent research, we have found that malformations of the face are particularly common in people with autism and intellectual disability who have rare highly penetrant single-gene mutations. Although people with intellectual disability have higher rates of congenital anomalies in general, those with autism are more likely to have multiple facial malformations for reasons not yet well understood (Casanova et al., 2017a).

On the other hand, people with idiopathic forms of autism don't typically have obvious facial malformations but may have subtler distinctive features. For instance, Aldridge et al. (2011) studied facial features in prepubertal autistic boys using 3D stereographic technology. While the majority of boys in their study appeared not to differ from controls, a large minority of boys with autism (28%) exhibited one of two distinctive facial patterns. The first subgroup had a longer midface, with greater distances longitudinally between the eyes, nose, and mouth, and overall smaller mouths and chins. These boys also tended to be more severely affected, with fewer cases falling within the high-functioning range. Meanwhile, the second subgroup of boys had a shorter midface and a longer upper lip around the area known as the "philtrum." In contrast to the first subgroup, these boys tended to be higher-functioning and also had higher rates of macrocephaly (large heads).

More recently, other researchers have discovered that both prepubertal boys and girls with autism have facial features indicative of increased masculinity, reinforcing the idea that maternal hormones play an important role in autism risk in some cases (Tan et al., 2017). Interestingly, increased masculinity in autism correlates with greater social and communication impairments, suggesting that social ability and secondary sex characteristics share a significant relationship.

Finally, a recent twins study in Sweden discovered that autism twin pairs had significantly more minor physical anomalies (MPAs) compared to ADHD twins and unaffected controls (Myers et al., 2017). These MPAs included hypermobility, flat feet, straight eyebrows, overweight/obesity, vision impairment, long fingers and toes, long eyelashes, and underdevelopment of the external ear (microtia). Some of these features, it should be noted, share overlap with connective tissue disorders such as Ehlers-Danlos and Marfan syndromes.

Ehlers-Danlos syndrome, hypermobility spectrum disorders, and autism

Research is still early, but some studies suggest that Ehlers-Danlos syndrome (EDS) and related hypermobility spectrum disorders (HSDs) share overlap with the autism spectrum (Baeza-Velasco et al., 2015; Casanova et al., 2018; Cederlöf et al., 2016; Eccles et al., 2014; Fehlow et al., 1993; Shetreat-Klein, Shinnar, & Rapin, 2014; Takei et al., 2011). Hypermobility, otherwise known as double-jointedness, can occur in any joint, although it often targets and is most problematic in the major weight-bearing joints like the spine, knees, hips, and shoulders (Figure 3.6). Hypermobility within the hands can also cause significant dexterity issues.

Figure 3.6: A girl with Ehlers-Danlos syndrome illustrating generalized joint hypermobility

(Images courtesy of Lianne Hedden)

While rare forms of EDS are typically associated with collagen mutations, the form known as hypermobile EDS (HEDS) and other HSDs are rarely associated with identifiable genetic mutations, with a few exceptions. This suggests that they are a genetically complex group of associated conditions, not unlike the autism spectrum, whose hereditary underpinnings have so far been challenging to identify.

In some of our recent work, we have found that individuals on the autism spectrum who also have generalized joint hypermobility (GJH), a primary feature of EDS, report high rates of immune-mediated symptoms, such as respiratory, food, and skin allergies, asthma, rhinitis, and autoimmune disorders (Casanova et al., 2018). Our ongoing research, as well as that of others, suggests this is the case for EDS/HSD in general (Casanova, 2017; Cheung & Vadas, 2015).

Similar immune symptoms occur in the related connective tissue disorder, Loeys-Dietz syndrome (LDS), which shares overlap with EDS and Marfan syndrome (MFS), both at the molecular and diagnostic levels. Each of these conditions, for instance, have Marfan-like features, such as hypermobility, long arms, long fingers, chest malformations, poor vision, and crooked teeth (Malfait et al., 2017). While it's uncertain why connective tissue disorders cause immune dysfunction, work on LDS and MFS suggests that the connective tissue surrounding cells is vital in sequestering and inactivating immunostimulatory proteins, such as TFG-β (Frischmeyer-Guerrerio et al., 2013). However, when connective tissue isn't working properly, as in the case of connective tissue disorders, these proteins may be prematurely released, leading to a chronic cascade of local immune activation. Unfortunately, connective tissue is present throughout the body, suggesting that many different organ systems may be affected.

Much work has been performed on the immune system in autism, as we'll discuss in the following chapter. A large subset of those on the autism spectrum exhibit either clinical or metabolic evidence of immune dysregulation (Ahmad et al., 2017; Molloy et al., 2006; Zerbo et al., 2015). It's therefore possible that the immune system may be an important link between autism and connective tissue disorders like EDS/HSD. However, further clinical work is needed to address this possibility, which our laboratory is currently pursuing.

CLINICAL RELEVANCE OF GENETICS

Genetics studies are of great importance in diagnostics and clinical treatment. For those people who have rare syndromic forms of autism with identifiable mutations, knowledge of the causative gene(s) can lead to better understanding of the biological processes that underlie the condition. This knowledge can then foster development of pharmacological or other treatment interventions that reduce symptom severity or even offer a cure for some individuals.

A great example of just such a genetic syndrome is phenylketonuria (PKU). PKU is the result of mutations in the phenylalanine hydroxylase gene, which codes for a protein that helps break down the amino acid phenylalanine into other amino acids the body can use. A large percentage of untreated PKU patients go on to develop symptoms of autism and intellectual disability, which can be prevented by early dietary intervention (Khemir, Halayem, & Azzouz, 2016).

Phelan-McDermid syndrome (PMS) is another genetic syndrome with high rates of intellectual disability and autism. People with PMS have mutations in the *SHANK3* gene, which results in a loss of function. One of *SHANK3*'s primary functions is to form structural bridges at synaptic sites, affecting the function of those synapses. Scientists have found that animals harboring *SHANK3* mutations show dramatic improvement in certain symptoms when treated with insulin-like growth factor-1 (IGF-1), and early pilot studies suggest that children with PMS significantly improve on an IGF-1 drug regime (Kolevzon et al., 2014).

These are just a couple of examples of the roles genetics plays in helping to direct research and treatment into conditions related to autism. But what can genetics studies do for those with autism who don't have rare mutations? Although research is still early, the scientific community is working towards identifying additional rare and common genetic variants that may play important roles in autism's etiologies, as well as medical conditions that sometimes accompany the condition. Once we reach that stage, we will be able to better understand each person's unique biological underpinnings, working towards targeted treatment interventions based on his or her inherited makeup. Although some individuals on the spectrum may prefer to avoid pharmacological intervention for their autism symptoms, genetics studies may nevertheless offer treatment options for other comorbid conditions, such as anxiety and immune disorders. These types of interventions will ultimately improve quality of life for those on the spectrum and are the ultimate goals of Precision Medicine.

Chapter Four

THE ROLES ENVIRONMENT PLAYS IN AUTISM SUSCEPTIBILITY

It's challenging to identify the point at which a living creature ends and the environment surrounding it begins. Our environments don't just surround us, they are in us. You must consume food daily so your cells can break it down into usable molecules, such as sugars, proteins, and minerals. These nutrients become a part of your cells, used as building blocks for numerous structures and processes. For instance, we know that some metal ions, such as zinc and magnesium, bind to DNA and without those tiny metals our DNA wouldn't hold its shape or function properly (Šponer et al., 1998). But your cells don't make zinc or magnesium. Instead, they derive it from the foods you eat. So are these zinc and magnesium ions part of us or part of the environment? There's no simple answer to that question.

You also can't survive without breathing in oxygen, which in turn helps you derive energy from the food you eat. And while we take oxygen levels for granted as if they're an environmental constant (how wrong we are!), they are a foundational variable upon which multicellular life is dependent (see Ward, 2006, for more). So we can't forget the roles that oxygen plays in the way our cells function. We are part of the environment and the environment is an inseparable part of us.

Some of the environmentally induced syndromes we'll be describing in this chapter are complex and are not always due to environment alone. As we'll discuss later in this chapter, approximately 10 percent of infants exposed prenatally to the medication valproic acid develop autism (Moore et al., 2000; Rasalam et al., 2005).

However, another 90 percent do not. While some of this variation may be due to differences in timing of exposure, medication dosage, and length of exposure, it may also be affected by genetic predisposition. Therefore, although we label some syndromes as "genetic" and others as "environmental" or "teratogenic," nature is rarely so simple.

A DISCLAIMER BEFORE WE BEGIN

We have all heard the adage, "Correlation doesn't equal causation." But before we delve into the list of environmental factors that affect autism risk, it is worthwhile reiterating that well-worn phrase. Just because two events coincide does not mean that their relationship is a causal one. In Figure 4.1, we illustrate some of the simple relationship scenarios any two events (A and B) may have, though these illustrations are not exclusive. In the simplest scenario, A may cause B or vice versa. However, in the second scenario we can see that A and B are the result of some other factor (X), leading to a correlation between the two variables. And finally, as shown in the third panel, A may have some complex relationship with factor X, which causes B (or vice versa). In the last two scenarios, A and B may be strongly correlated with one another but they are not related by *causality*. Instead, they are related by more complex means, which is frequently the case when studying biology due to the complicated nature of living systems. In biology, most of the time A does not cause B.

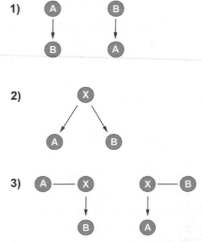

Figure 4.1: Theoretical examples in which correlation does not equate to causation (examples #2 and #3)

This chapter deals largely with the prenatal environment and how different exposures or deprivations can increase autism risk. These range from pharmaceuticals to infections to pesticides. And as you'll glean from these materials, the range of environmental factors is extensive, highlighting once again the heterogeneous nature of the autism spectrum from an environmental perspective.

CHEMICALS
Prescription medications
Anti-seizure medications
Once they're born, infants who were exposed to anti-epileptic drugs (AEDs) in the womb often experience neonatal withdrawal symptoms similar to those seen in adults, such as jitteriness and irritability. Unfortunately, these withdrawal symptoms can cause complications in early infant health, a common concern regarding many types of neonatal drug withdrawal (Hudak et al., 2012).

Infants prenatally exposed to AEDs also have a two-to-three-times increased risk for major congenital malformations, such as neural tube defects like spina bifida (in which the neural tube fails to close properly), cleft palate, urogenital malformations, and heart defects. That risk is even higher with the use of combination therapy, in which two or more AEDs are used in conjunction. Congenital malformations occur in about 14 percent of cases exposed to AED compared to 3 percent in the general population (Dean et al., 2002). Unfortunately, most AEDs afford at least minimal risk for birth defects.

Aside from physical malformations, infants with fetal anti-convulsant syndrome may also have cognitive deficits. The vast majority have either developmental delay or learning difficulties, and language is usually impaired to the extent that most kids require some form of speech and language therapy. Many exposed children also have behavioral challenges like attention-deficit/hyperactivity disorder (ADHD) (Moore et al., 2000; Dean et al., 2002).

Originally, it was hoped that the newer generation of AEDs would be less teratogenic[1] than their older counterparts, but many of these medications such as topiramate and gabapentin instead confer

---

1   A "teratogen" is a foreign agent, such as a chemical or an infectious agent that disrupts prenatal development, often leading to congenital malformations.

measurable risk (Holmes 2002; Hunt et al., 2008; Prakash et al., 2008). An exception appears to be the drug lamotrigine, which due to its low risk is now often prescribed to pregnant women in place of medications like valproic acid (Vajda et al., 2010).

Valproic acid (Depakote)

Valproic acid's mechanism of action isn't well understood, although it does appear to act as an effective sodium channel blocker, helping to suppress the excitability of neurons (McLean & McDonald, 1986). It also has neuroprotective[2] effects because of its role as a histone deacetylase inhibitor, which helps to regulate gene expression and promotes cell growth and repair (Phiel et al., 2001).

Valproic acid is one of the most effective drugs in treating epilepsy. Unfortunately, it is also one of the most teratogenic, an effect that is exacerbated with combination therapy. The incidence of fetal valproate syndrome (FVS) is currently unknown, but it appears to affect males and females in equal numbers. Symptoms can include malformations of the neural tube (spina bifida), the face (epicanthal folds, upturned nose, small mouth), the genitals, the heart, and other parts of the skeleton (ribs, hips, etc.). In addition, eye abnormalities are typically present, including nearsightedness, astigmatism, and strabismus.

Similar to other AEDs, valproic acid also affects the developing brain, and there is considerable risk for behavioral and learning deficits. In addition, about 10 percent of those with FVS also have autism, while an additional 50 percent exhibit autistic features, making autism symptomology a common core to fetal valproate syndrome (Moore et al., 2000; Rasalam et al., 2005).

Following these clinical studies, animal research models have been developed to investigate valproic acid's effects on brain development in relation to autism. Patricia Rodier was one of the first to use valproic acid on rodents prenatally in order to mimic exposure in humans (Rodier et al., 1996). Although she studied the brainstem and not the cortex as is typical in modern autism research, she found significant disturbances to that area of the brain, which she believed linked autism and a brainstem condition known as Moebius syndrome (Figure 4.2). We will discuss more of these links in further sections.

---

2   Able to protect nerve cells against damage.

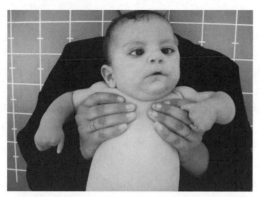

Figure 4.2: An infant with Moebius syndrome
(Reproduced with permission of Al Kaissi et al., 2007)

Following on Rodier's work, Henry Markram and his team studied the microcircuitry of the cortex in rats that had been prenatally exposed to valproic acid (see Markram, Rinaldi, & Markram, 2007, for review). Markram's team found that the excitatory neurons in these animals were both "hyper-reactive" and "hyper-connected" compared to neurons in control rats. As such, a single excitatory neuron had a greater number of neurons with which it was interconnected. Markram proposed that this hyperexcitable, hyperconnected network triggered an exaggerated response to a particular stimulus, mimicking some of the cognitive and behavioral features of autism, such as sensory hypersensitivity. This is the core of the "intense world syndrome" theory of autism.

Antidepressants

Antidepressants work by targeting various combinations of the serotonin, norepinephrine, and dopamine systems. The selective serotonin reuptake inhibitors (SSRI), as the name suggests, block the reuptake of serotonin into the communicating cell, allowing serotonin to remain in the synaptic cleft longer and to continue to activate receptors on the receiving cell. Atypical antidepressants meanwhile function in a variety of ways—some, like Wellbutrin, function as a dopamine and norepinephrine reuptake inhibitors, while others, like Cymbalta, are serotonin and norepinephrine reuptake inhibitors. Unlike the SSRIs and atypicals, tricyclic antidepressants inhibit the reuptake of serotonin, norepinephrine, and partially dopamine and therefore tend to have more side effects. Finally, the monoamine oxidase inhibitors (MAOI) are the oldest class of antidepressant and are typically used as a last line of treatment in depression. They work by inhibiting monoamine oxidase, which is an enzyme that helps to break down many of the neuromodulators like serotonin, norepinephrine, and dopamine, thereby increasing their bioavailability and activity.

Safety studies on the prenatal use of antidepressants have been exceedingly mixed and at times downright confusing. However, most large studies conclude that if risk for congenital malformations is present as a result of prenatal antidepressant use, it is extremely small (e.g. Ross et al., 2013).

There has been considerable interest in the roles serotonin may play in autism risk as well, given reports of hyperserotonemia[3] in the condition. This relationship has therefore inspired interest in prenatal antidepressant exposure in relation to autism. To date, a variety of studies agree that prenatal antidepressant exposure may confer small but measurable risk for autism (Boukhris et al., 2016; Croen, Grether, et al., 2011; King, 2017; Rai et al., 2013; Sujan et al., 2017). Other studies, however, have failed to find a connection, suggesting that differences in methodology may be driving some of the disagreement (Brown et al., 2017; Castro et al., 2016; Hviid, Melbye, & Pasternak, 2013).

However, a recent study has taken the earlier epidemiological research a step further. Scientists studied prenatal antidepressant exposure in patients contained within the Simons Simplex Collection, a database that houses genetic and clinical information on single-incidence autism families. When they studied these simplex cases, they found that individuals with certain genetic mutations who had been prenatally exposed to antidepressants were more severely affected than those who didn't have similar mutations or weren't exposed to antidepressants (Ackerman et al., 2017). As this study suggests, antidepressant exposure superimposed atop a genetic vulnerability may increase the severity of autism. This is akin to the triple hit hypothesis (genetic vulnerability, environmental agent, and timing of exposure) proposed both in autism and other areas of research into complex, partly heritable conditions (Casanova, 2007; Kollodge & Hinkley, 2015).

Research into antidepressant risk in autism will likely be ongoing. Although the evidence is building, the data are not overwhelming and scientists continue to argue as they refine research methodologies.

---

3   "Hyperserotonemia" refers to high levels of serotonin in the blood.

If antidepressants are indeed a risk factor for autism, they appear to be of small risk. Although given their widespread use, even such minor risk may be alarming.

Thalidomide

A clever strategy at rebranding: nowadays it is known as "Immunoprin" and is used in the treatment of cancers and leprosy. Most people, if they're familiar with it, however, know the drug as "thalidomide."

It was developed by the German company, Chemie Grünenthal, in the 1950s and was originally marketed for the treatment of respiratory infections. Eventually, they discovered it was an effective antiemetic and quickly rebranded it for use as a drug to treat morning sickness. At the time, scientists and doctors did not believe that substances the mother consumed could cross the placental barrier and harm the fetus. Therefore, there were no stringent laws on drug development targeting pregnant women. In the meantime, thalidomide was successfully marketed throughout 46 countries.

However, by 1960 there were reports trickling in linking the drug to cases of peripheral neuropathy (Fullerton & Kremer, 1961). And within the following year, reports of major birth defects were already coming to light. Children were being born with shortened limbs (phocomelia), missing limbs (amelia), missing or extra fingers or toes, webbing around the digits, blindness, deafness, cleft palate, facial paralysis (Moebius syndrome), and malformations of the gastrointestinal tract and other organs (Figure 4.3).

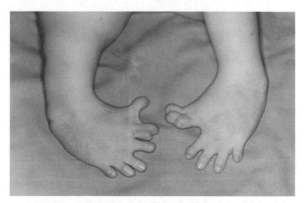

Figure 4.3: Limb and foot malformations in a
case of prenatal thalidomide exposure

*(Reproduced from Wikimedia Commons: Otis Historical Archives
National Museum of Health and Medicine)*

By March of 1962, following horrendous public outcry, the drug was finally removed from the market. However, by that time over 10,000 children with thalidomide-induced deformities had been born worldwide, several thousand of whom died shortly after birth. To the United States' good fortune, only 17 U.S. infants are recognized to have been born with thalidomide-related malformations, even though Chemie Grünenthal managed to distribute samples to approximately 20,000 pregnant women within U.S. borders. It is possible that more thalidomide victims exist that still go unrecognized.

Yet it is a miracle there weren't more. And the heroine of that story is a Canadian woman, Frances Oldham Kelsey.

Kelsey was one of a small number of medical officers who worked for the Food and Drug Administration (FDA) in the late 1950s reviewing drug applications for approval in the U.S. Kelsey, being the officer in charge of thalidomide's review, was already familiar with the reports of neuropathy. She, alongside the pharmacologist and chemist assisting her, was dissatisfied with Chemie Grünenthal's safety studies. They felt that the chronic toxicity studies hadn't been long enough and the manufacturing controls had considerable shortcomings (Bren, 2001). Thus, in spite of extensive pressure from the pharmaceutical company and from her own supervisors at the FDA, she refused to approve the application, repeatedly requiring more data. Before long, reports of limb malformations began popping up worldwide and the drug was banned from market. Thanks to Dr. Kelsey and her assistants, undoubtedly thousands more cases of thalidomide embryopathy were prevented in the U.S. For her service to the country, President John F. Kennedy awarded her the medal for Distinguished Federal Civilian Service in 1962 (Figure 4.4).

But the rest of the world wasn't so lucky. While West Germany itself was hardest hit with approximately 5000 cases reported, Great Britain and Japan had about 700 cases each. In Sweden in particular, approximately 150 cases were reported, although roughly one third died from severe birth defects. This was largely a result of severe organ malformations that were fatal shortly after birth.

In 1994, Kerstin Strömland and her team studied the Swedish cohort of thalidomide victims, investigating Moebius syndrome, the most common condition associated with exposure, which is a brainstem disorder resulting in facial paralysis and various eye motor defects. Interestingly, they also investigated rates of autism in the cohort. Of the one hundred individuals they studied, four fulfilled a diagnosis of autism (4%). (Another individual may have been autistic but was attending a special school for those with mild intellectual disability and was unavailable for examination. Unfortunately, his files were inconclusive.)

Figure 4.4: Frances Oldham Kelsey receiving the medal for Distinguished Federal Civilian Service from President John F. Kennedy in 1962

While 4 percent may seem low, ranging only a few percentage points above the rate seen within the general population (~1%), Rodier et al. (1996) noted that of the 15 individuals who had been exposed to thalidomide on days 20–24 of pregnancy, four (27%) were autistic. All four individuals displayed features indicative of Moebius syndrome, as did a fifth child unavailable for autism screening. Interestingly, no individuals exposed later in pregnancy had any indications of autism. Therefore, when taking into account this time period of vulnerability, thalidomide may promote autism in about 25–30 percent of cases. In those cases, autism is usually accompanied by symptoms of Moebius syndrome. Interestingly, Moebius syndrome occurs alongside autism in other conditions as well (Johansson et al., 2001).

Thalidomide's mechanisms of action are currently unknown, although it seems to have immunomodulatory[4] and antiangiogenic[5]

---

4   "Immunomodulatory" refers to a substance that affects activity of the immune system.

5   "Angiogenic" refers to a substance that stimulates vascular growth; therefore, "antiangiogenic" means that vascular growth is suppressed.

effects, which may explain its usefulness in treating some forms of cancer (Paravar & Lee, 2008). Although the abnormal immune function has been linked with autism, thalidomide-induced autism is more likely the result of suppressed vascular growth. As you will see later in the section on misoprostol, a medication that also causes Moebius syndrome, it triggers ischemia[6] depriving the fetus of adequate blood supply (Dooley et al., 2004). Like thalidomide, it also increases risk for autism, suggesting that first trimester ischemia could be a general risk factor for the condition.

Terbutaline

The drug terbutaline has typically been used as a relief inhaler for asthma and works by stimulating the β_2-adrenergic receptor. It has also been in use off-label as an anti-contraction agent in women who experience premature labor. In February of 2011, the U.S. Food and Drug Administration ordered the placement of a boxed warning on the label, contraindicating its use in pregnant women in the prevention or prolonged treatment of preterm labor as it had led to a number of maternal heart problems and deaths (U.S. Food and Drug Administration, 2011).

Terbutaline is also a risk factor for autism when used for longer durations (two or more days) (Bercum et al., 2015; Connors et al., 2005). Since it was first investigated as a labor repressant in the 1970s (Ingemarsson, 1975), terbutaline has been one of the most commonly used β_2-adrenergic receptor agonists in preterm labor management; the number of cases of autism that go unidentified is therefore probably considerable. This effect seems to be limited to terbutaline in particular and doesn't include other β_2-adrenergic receptor agonists (Croen, Connors, et al., 2011). In future, cases of terbutaline-induced autism will likely decrease due to the new warning label limiting exposure periods. However, researchers may continue to find individual cases of "fetal terbutaline syndrome" in people who were exposed prior to 2011.

Interestingly, some scientists have found that autism risk following prenatal terbutaline exposure is strongest when people have at least one of two particular genetic variants in the gene for the β_2-adrenergic receptor, each of which leads to overstimulation of that receptor

---

6   Reduced, inadequate blood supply.

(Connors et al., 2005). This research has been extended using an animal model, looking at the combined effects of terbutaline and maternal stress on fetal development (Bercum et al., 2015). Combined exposure results in severe disturbances in behavior and high rates of epilepsy (45%). These studies clearly illustrate how genetics and environmental exposures can combine to increase autism risk.

Misoprostol

Misoprostol is used to induce labor, promote abortion, treat postpartum bleeding, and to prevent and treat stomach ulcers. It acts as a synthetic version of a prostaglandin, which is a fat molecule that functions as a hormone in humans.

A small percentage of chemical abortions attempted with misoprostol fail. In those cases when surgical abortion is not attempted or is not an option, the fetus is at risk for developing significant birth defects, particularly if it was exposed during the first trimester of pregnancy. Because surgical abortions are illegal in some countries in South and Central America, many women will use (and misuse) misoprostol, leading to higher rates of drug-induced congenital defects in these regions (Gonzalez et al., 1998).

Birth defects associated with prenatal misoprostol exposure include Moebius syndrome, terminal limb defects in which portions of the limb (e.g. fingers, hands) fail to form, and other malformations like enlargement of the fluid-containing ventricles of the brain (Vauzelle et al., 2013). Misoprostol-induced Moebius syndrome is believed to be related to disruptions in the vascular system, leading to reductions in blood supply that feed developing tissues (Gonzalez et al., 1998).

As we saw with thalidomide, misoprostol increases risk for Moebius syndrome and autism when exposed in the first trimester. In a study performed in Brazil, a group of researchers found that 26 percent of those with Moebius syndrome met criteria for classic autism (Bandim et al., 2003). In addition, another 9 percent who were under the age of two displayed autistic features. Of the seven children with Moebius syndrome and autism or autistic features, 57 percent had been exposed to misoprostol. Once again, this suggests that the causes of Moebius syndrome (e.g. ischemia) are strong risk factors for the development of autism.

Drug abuse
Alcohol

> Behold, thou shalt conceive, and bear a son; and now drink no
> wine or strong drink…

(Judges, 13:7)

Though fetal alcohol syndrome (FAS) wasn't officially identified until
the 1960s, the harm of prenatal alcohol exposure to unborn infants
had long been suspected. There had been isolated case reports strewn
throughout the medical literature for several hundred years:

> [Several] physician groups in England in the late 1700s described
> children of alcoholics as "weak, feeble, and distempered" and "born
> weak and silly…shriveled and old, as though they had numbered
> many years." In 1899, Sullivan described the offspring of alcoholic
> women imprisoned in England. He concluded that these women
> produced children characterized by a pattern of birth defects of
> increasing severity and higher rates of miscarriage… (Hoyme et al.,
> 2005, p. 40)

Linked with the temperance and eugenics movements of the late
19th and early 20th centuries, many people believed that prenatal
exposure could harm the unborn child, leading to a heritable form
of imbecility. It was partly this belief that led to the successful spread
of the temperance movement and to Prohibition in the United States,
which lasted from 1919 until 1933 (O'Neil, 2011).

If you'll recall from the section on thalidomide, before 1962
scientists and doctors didn't believe substances the mother consumed
could cross the placenta and affect the developing infant. After the
thalidomide scare, however, professionals began realizing this wasn't
the case and if thalidomide could cross the placental barrier, other
agents such as alcohol might do so as well.

By 1968, researchers began reporting features of prenatal alcohol
exposure, documenting more than one hundred children born to
women who drank heavily. Scientists noted that these children were
born with physical malformations and eventually developed behavioral
problems (Lemoine et al., 1968). However, it wasn't until 1973 that
the name "fetal alcohol syndrome" (FAS) was officially adopted (Jones
et al., 1973).

FAS occurs on a spectrum and can include physical malformations, as well learning and behavioral issues, the severity of which increases with earlier and extended alcohol exposure. People with FAS may have characteristic facial features (Figure 4.5), small head size, low body weight, hand and foot malformations, problems with the heart or kidneys, learning disabilities, developmental delay, intellectual disability, poor judgment, and even seizures (Centers for Disease Control and Prevention, 2015).

Craniofacial features associated with fetal alcohol syndrome

Facial features of FAS

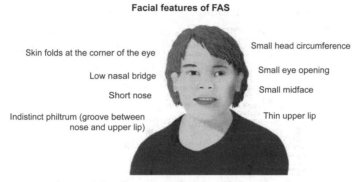

Figure 4.5: The various facial malformations that can occur in fetal alcohol syndrome

People with FAS also have higher rates of autism. Initially, only individual case reports were published, hinting at overlap between the two conditions (Harris, MacKay, & Osborn, 1995; Nanson, 1992). But by the late 1990s, larger studies were being published (Landgren et al., 2010). For instance, one study out of Sweden reported that 13 percent of children with FAS had autism, while an additional 42 percent had ADHD (Aronson, Hagberg, and Gillberg, 1997). Of the FAS children in the study, 25 percent attended school for the intellectually disabled while another 46 percent received some form of special education.

Though you may be unaware, alcohol can be a useful source of energy for the body. In fact, without any alcohol consumption at all, the flora in your gut produce approximately three grams of ethanol per day (Tillonen, 2000). Therefore, you can imagine that alcohol metabolism and the energy derived from it has been an important part of life for a long evolutionary time. Unfortunately, humans have created new ways, namely in the form of wines, beers, and liquors, in which to consume large quantities of alcohol that our bodies are not naturally equipped to handle. And this leads to complications in health.

Alcohol's toxic effects on the body are complex. In the adult, intoxication can disrupt the function of the brain's neurotransmitters. It can alter how the basic building blocks of our cells function. It reduces the immune system's capacity to fight off infection. It impairs the gastrointestinal tract, the liver, and the pancreas. It alters the amount of cortisol the body produces. And it even impairs wound healing (Manzo-Avalos & Saavedra-Molina, 2010).

With the help of the aldehyde dehydrogenase (ALDH) enzyme, the body metabolizes alcohol first into acetaldehyde, a very toxic substance, and finally into the less-damaging acetate. (Acetate, it is believed, is the molecule responsible for headaches during hangovers.) Unfortunately, with excessive or chronic alcohol consumption, the ALDH enzyme becomes "saturated," meaning there is too much acetaldehyde for ALDH to deal with. When this occurs a portion of acetaldehyde escapes into the blood stream. Once it is out in the blood stream, it can travel to many areas of the body, causing damage through its ability to attach to numerous proteins, nucleic acids, fats, and carbohydrates and alter their abilities to function. Acetylaldehyde also forms free radicals that trigger a chain of toxic reactions if not quenched by antioxidants like vitamin C. Its function as a free radical makes acetaldehyde a particularly potent carcinogen (cause of cancer).

Armed with this knowledge, you can easily imagine what far-reaching effects excessive alcohol consumption can have on an unborn child. Under the influence of alcohol, the brain produces fewer neurons and can lead to neuronal death in adult neurons (Hansson et al., 2010; Ikonomidou et al., 2000; Uban et al., 2010). These data help us to understand why small head size (microcephaly) is such a common feature of FAS.

Cocaine

Cocaine is a drug derived from the coca plant, which has both stimulating and anaesthetic properties. Until the early 20th century in the United States, it was sold over the counter as a painkiller and antidepressant and was also an ingredient in the now-popular soft drink Coca Cola. Coca leaves had largely been removed from Coca Cola before the 1914 Harrison Narcotics Tax Act was put into effect, although it took the company another 23 years to perfect the removal of cocaine's psychoactive agent, ecgonine alkaloid, from the drink, which still had trace elements up until 1929 (Hamblin, 2013). In the 1960s, there was an upsurge in popularity of the drug, which led to the Controlled Substances Act of 1970 in which cocaine was re-categorized as a Schedule II controlled substance and the public's access to it became considerably limited. Nevertheless, even today, it is the second most trafficked illegal drug in the world and results in considerable morbidity and mortality. In the United States in 2005 alone, close to half a million emergency department visits were reported involving cocaine use (Foundation for a Drug-free World, 2016).

As mentioned, cocaine is a highly addictive substance that acts by inhibiting the reuptake of certain neurotransmitters (serotonin, norepinephrine, dopamine), which results in their accumulation within the synaptic cleft and prolonged stimulation. Dopamine in particular is a key player in the reward system of the brain, leading to intense addiction.

Unfortunately, the study of prenatal cocaine exposure has been a challenge. One of the biggest confounds is that pregnant mothers who abuse cocaine often abuse other drugs, such as alcohol, cigarettes, and other illegal substances (Lutiger et al., 1991; Mayes et al., 1992). In addition, many coke abusers tend to have poor diets, further complicating the study of infant outcomes. Nevertheless, it's clear that prenatal cocaine exposure leads to higher rates of premature birth. Affected infants also tend to have low birth weight and are small for gestational age (Behnke et al., 2001). Cocaine is known to constrict blood vessels, suggesting infants prenatally exposed do not receive adequate blood supply from their mothers (Ryan, Ehrlich, & Finnegan, 1987). Adverse neurological outcomes, on the other hand, are likely due to reduced blood flow and cocaine's ability to target neurotransmitters systems.

There is also some evidence that prenatal cocaine exposure increases autism risk. One study found that 11 percent of children with documented prenatal cocaine exposure developed autism (Davis et al., 1992). However, almost half of them had been exposed to a combination of cocaine and alcohol, once again highlighting the challenges scientists and doctors face in studying and treating prenatal drug exposures.

NUTRITION
Folate deficiency

Also known as vitamin B_9, folate is an essential B vitamin necessary for DNA synthesis, repair, and methylation. We do not synthesize our own folate and therefore it must be derived from the foods we eat. Because of the vital roles it plays in DNA function, you might imagine its importance in cells that are rapidly growing and dividing.

Dark leafy greens, beans, peas, lentils, citrus fruits, nuts, and seeds all have high folate content. Folate deficiency can occur due to lack of consumption of appropriate foods, an inherited propensity for deficiency (e.g. *MTHFR* polymorphisms, see below), or some combination of the two. When deficiency occurs during pregnancy, this can lead to spontaneous abortion, premature birth, and intrauterine growth restriction of the fetus. It can also increase risk for neural tube defects like anencephaly, which is the absence of a large portion of the brain, the skull, and the scalp and is lethal shortly after birth. There is also increased risk for spina bifida, which is an incomplete closure of the tissues covering the spine and spinal cord.

A common polymorphism in the methylenetetrahydrofolate reductase (*MTHFR*) gene known scientifically as "C677T" occurs in approximately 25 percent of the human population worldwide and may account for up to one quarter of all neural tube defects (Ensembl, 2016; reviewed in Scholl & Johnson, 2000). Functionally, this gene variant reduces the activity of the *MTHFR* protein at high temperatures. When that happens, *MTHFR* can't do its job efficiently, normally helping to detoxify the body of a chemical known as "homocysteine." Homocysteine can wreak havoc on cells, even leading to neurodegeneration within the brain when it isn't cleared properly (Rajagopalan et al., 2012).

When folate metabolism works well, the new folate metabolite converts homocysteine into methionine, which is vital in providing methyl groups for the methylation of DNA, RNA, and proteins. However, when this process doesn't work, such as when a person has one or two copies of the C677T *MTHFR* variant, cells are placed under greater stress and the processes that normally occur smoothly begin to short-circuit. In addition, abnormal DNA methylation can result in disturbances to gene expression. This effect is worsened if the person is not consuming adequate amounts of folate.

Reduced maternal folate consumption is a risk factor for autism (Schmidt et al., 2012). And unsurprisingly, the C677T *MTHFR* variant also increases autism risk, even if the mother is consuming normal amounts of folate. While scientists do not understand precisely how folate deficiency increases risk for autism, one possibility is that folate metabolism affects blood flow. Increased homocysteine levels, for instance, disrupt development of the vasculature, resulting in ischemia (Oosterbaan, Steegers, & Ursem, 2012). This is similar to what we saw with thalidomide and misoprostol.

However, MTHFR is also important in DNA methylation and the regulation of gene expression. If genes are not properly methylated, this can lead to abnormal expression of important neural genes that may dramatically disrupt brain development. A similar issue is seen in Rett syndrome in which loss of function of the *MECP2* gene, which is involved in silencing key neural genes during specific times in development, leads to a syndromic form of autism (Gabel et al., 2015).

Vitamin D

Like estrogen and testosterone, vitamin D is a steroid. Until more recently, its roles in prenatal development have been poorly appreciated and are still little understood. The vitamin D precursor, 7-dehydrocholesterol, is a light-sensitive steroid that is produced in the skin. However, in order to be converted into its vitamin D form and used by the body, it must be exposed to ultraviolet B (UVB) rays. Current research suggests that, in spite of common conceptions, we likely consume adequate amounts of vitamin D and receive enough daily sun exposure to satisfy our basic needs. However, some scientists have found that low vitamin D levels are in fact indicators of other disease processes, such as chronic inflammation (Autier et al., 2014). In which case, if the inflammation is treated, vitamin D levels should also normalize.

As with other hormones, vitamin D receptors are able to bind to DNA, regulating it directly (Eyles, Burne, & McGrath, 2011). For this reason, vitamin D can have dramatic effects on cell biology. For instance, when it is applied to neural stem cells it halts cell division and causes neurons to develop prematurely (Brown et al., 2003). Vitamin D also has antiseizure capacity by blocking uptake of the excitatory ion calcium (Kalueff, Minasyan, & Tuohimaa, 2005).

While reductions in excitation may be good for alleviating seizures, during prenatal development reduced excitability may lead to premature neuronal death since neurons require sufficient excitatory input in order to survive (Yan et al., 1994).

Despite its myriad effects on the brain, vitamin D has been poorly studied in relation to autism. A few retrospective studies have investigated the seasonality of conception and birth in autistic individuals, finding a preponderance of spring births, suggesting winter-associated vitamin D deficiency could play a role (Grant & Soles, 2009; Hebert, Miller, & Joinson, 2010). Links between spring births in schizophrenia and bipolar disorder are more robust, although other factors like wintertime infections may play an added role in these other conditions (Torrey et al., 1997).

A more recent study suggests that low vitamin D levels may be associated with autism (Fernell et al., 2015). A group of Swedish researchers found that autistic siblings had significantly lower neonatal vitamin D levels than their unaffected brothers and sisters. Once again, however, we cannot know whether vitamin D deficiency is itself a risk factor for autism or a symptom of another causal factor, such as inflammation. For instance, inflammatory markers have also been identified in neonates who go on to develop autism (Krakowiak et al., 2015).

On the other hand, specific polymorphisms in the vitamin D receptor (*VDR*) gene may share autism links, suggesting it could be a direct effector in risk. Researchers from the MIND Institute at the University of California at Davis have found that several common gene variants in the *VDR*, including the TaqI and BsmI polymorphisms, are overrepresented in the paternal gene copy of the receptor (Schmidt et al., 2015). Aside from linking *VDR* function and autism risk, these data also suggest that the *VDR* gene may be parentally imprinted, meaning that the gene is expressed differently based on which parent (mother vs. father) it came from.

In summary, vitamin D deficiency does not appear to be a strong risk factor for autism, but it is an excellent candidate worthy of more study. In future, genetic testing for *VDR* polymorphisms may also help obstetricians inform patients what dosages of supplementation they should be taking during pregnancy, potentially reducing the role vitamin D deficiency could play in autism risk.

Iron

Iron is vital for many biological processes. Most people are vaguely familiar with the role it plays in oxygen intake in the lungs. As part of the larger hemoglobin complex, it allows hemoglobin to take a shape that accepts the oxygen molecule, similar to a glove and ball formation. Without the attached iron ion, hemoglobin doesn't form properly, preventing oxygen from attaching to it and being taken up into the body. Oxygen is necessary for helping to turn the food we eat into usable forms of energy.

Iron is also part of the cytochrome structure, a complex molecule that associates with the powerhouses of the cell, the mitochondria, and aids in the generation of cellular energy known as adenosine triphosphate (ATP). As we have seen with hemoglobin, cytochrome doesn't function properly without iron and the mitochondria cannot produce energy efficiently. Iron deficiency can therefore cause very severe problems for the body, depleting it of fundamental resources.

Maternal iron deficiency (a form of anemia) increases risk for premature birth and low infant birth weight. In developing countries in which nutrition is poor and severe anemia is more common, the mother is also at considerable risk for cardiac failure during labor, which is the leading cause of death related to iron deficiency (Allen, 1997).

Like maternal folate deficiency, maternal iron deficiency increases risk for autism, although the mechanisms are not well understood (Schmidt et al., 2014). Functionally, iron shares some overlap with folate since they are both involved in basic cellular metabolism. Both can cause anemia, which is when the blood doesn't manage to carry enough oxygen to the different cells of the body. Anemia can also be caused by bleeding (e.g. menstruation or ulcers); it can be due to decreased red blood cell production; or it can be caused by an increased breakdown in red blood cells. In the case of folate and iron, deficiencies are most typically associated with reduced red blood cell production. The body simply cannot make enough red blood cells to carry oxygen where it needs to go.

In the fetus this can be especially detrimental. Scientists have found that during early brain growth, iron deficiency dramatically alters neuron development and impairs learning and memory well after the deficiency has resolved (Tran et al., 2008). It may also exacerbate the effects of other risk factors, particularly inflammation.

Using animal models, researchers have found that pregnant rats who are iron-deficient produce more inflammatory molecules when exposed to lipopolysaccharide (a bacterial mimic) than mothers who aren't deficient (Harvey & Boksa, 2014). Together, these data indicate that iron deficiency can have some extreme consequences and is a basic substrate to life.

PREMATURITY

Approximately 13 percent of all births are premature, defined as occurring at or before 36 weeks gestation (reviewed in Rais-Bahrami & Short, 2013). The greatest challenge for preterm infants is living in a world for which most of their organs are developmentally unprepared. For instance, because the preemie lungs don't produce enough surfactant, this can lead to significant respiratory distress. Their gastrointestinal tracts may also not receive enough blood supply, leading to a condition called "necrotizing enterocolitis," which is when gastrointestinal tissue start to necrotize or die off. And finally, the brain is also vulnerable to bleeds and ischemia at such a young age. Intraventricular hemorrhage, one of the major types of bleeds, is graded by severity: infants with grades III and IV hemorrhages, which are the most severe, are the most likely to develop cerebral palsy.

Autism seems to share strong links with prematurity. Research has shown that about one quarter of ex-preterm infants who weighed 1500g or less at birth score positively on toddler autism screening tools like the Child Behavior Checklist and the Vineland Adaptive Behavior Scale (Limperopoulos et al., 2008). Other studies confirm these high rates, particularly in extremely preterm infants who are born between 24 and 26 weeks gestation (Kuniewicz et al., 2014).

However, it is not prematurity *per se* that seems to be a risk factor for autism but specific types of brain lesions that are more likely to occur in premature infants. When bleeds and ischemia are so extreme as to cause damage to the tissues surrounding the ventricles, such as the developing white matter and the germinal zone that produces newborn neurons, this can lead to enlargement of the ventricles as cerebrospinal fluid fills the space that these brain tissues once occupied. Infants who are positive for such lesions at birth are almost seven-fold more likely to develop autism than preemies with normal cranial ultrasounds (Movsas et al., 2013). Clearly, early widespread damage to the tissues surrounding the ventricles of the brain is a major risk factor for autism.

THE IMMUNE SYSTEM

The immune system is a most ancient system. Even prokaryotic[7] single-celled organisms like bacteria have the ability to fight off foreign pathogens using various enzymes to break down and degrade invaders. In addition, the ability of some immune cells to phagocytose or "eat" foreign material was derived from eukaryotes' ability to consume other cells or parts of cells as food. And the cells of many invertebrate species, such as amoebas, worms, insects, and sponges, have the ability to bind to other cells, identifying "self" from "non-self." All of these preceding elements compose the foundations of the innate immune system (Buchmann, 2014).

It wasn't until the evolution of jawed fish that the adaptive immune system appeared. While the innate immune system is the first line of defense to invading pathogens, the adaptive immune system is able to *remember* previous infections, mounting an antibody response before the next pathogen has a chance to get a foothold. It is the adaptive immune system that allows vaccinations to work. Insects, for instance, would never benefit from inoculations because they don't have adaptive immune systems!

Although both branches of the immune system are necessary for fighting off infection, they are also integral to processes of growth and repair. Consider for instance if you sprain your ankle: typically the ankle will swell, become red and hot, and you may lose function in the affected area depending on the severity of the sprain. Swelling, redness, hotness, and pain are all indicators that inflammation is working to clear the area of damaged cells and promote growth and repair of tissues.

Interestingly, many proteins involved in inflammatory pathways, like various cytokines and chemokines, also play non-inflammatory roles in the developing brain. They may, for instance, function as growth factors during neurogenesis (birth of neurons) (Borsini et al., 2015). Therefore, although we label them as "inflammatory molecules" and associate them with the immune system, these proteins are truly multifunctional and multisystemic. Unfortunately, however, when an infection occurs during the prenatal period, changes to the levels of cytokines and chemokines can dramatically alter brain development.

---

7   Prokaryotes are single-celled organisms that lack a well-defined nucleus. Meanwhile, eukaryotes are either single-celled or multicellular organisms that have a true nucleus.

Abnormal antibodies may also disrupt brain development. During pregnancy, for instance, IgG antibodies that are produced by the mother can cross the placental barrier. In this way the fetus "borrows" the mother's adaptive immune system, providing the baby with resistance to infections to which the mother has previously become immune. However, a very small portion of IgG is able to sneak past the blood brain barrier and gain access to the developing central nervous system. The area underlying the cortex known as the *periventricular region* seems to be particularly "leaky" for reasons not well understood (Rojko & Price-Schiavi, 2008).

Unfortunately, because the mother shares her antibodies with the developing child, she can also pass on *autoantibodies* (antibodies to self) that may harm fetal development and, depending on the type of autoantibody, even lead to miscarriage. In the case of autism, approximately 12 percent of mothers express autoantibodies that are reactive to fetal brain tissue, suggesting that their presence may have significant effects on brain development and autism risk (Bauman et al., 2013).

Using animal models, scientists have found that when rhesus monkeys are prenatally exposed to IgG autoantibodies derived from mothers of children with autism, after birth these rhesus monkeys show demonstrably abnormal social behavior. Exposed males also tend to have larger-than-normal brains, which is primarily due to an increase in white matter volume, the portions of the brain that make up communicative fibers (Bauman et al., 2013). Surprisingly, however, exposed mothers also display heightened protectiveness and anxiety concerning their "autistic" offspring, suggesting that the adult brain may be vulnerable to autoantibody exposure as well, triggering psychiatric symptoms.

The following section describes various prenatal and, on occasion, postnatal, infections that have been linked with autism. We also describe how immune system activation may lead to autistic regression by triggering pathways related to cell stress and inflammation and ultimately how this process may share links with forms of senile neurodegeneration, such as Alzheimer's disease.

TORCH infections

TORCH stands for "toxoplasmosis, other (syphilis, varicella-zoster, parvovirus B19), rubella, cytomegalovirus (CMV), and herpes" infections.

Pre- and perinatal infections are associated with about 2–3 percent of congenital anomalies worldwide, with TORCH-related infections the most common (Stegmann & Carey, 2002).

Prenatal infections can be dangerous to the developing infant, although they are sometimes an unavoidable part of life. Most congenital infections associated with autism risk are viral as opposed to bacterial. The reasons for this are unclear but may be linked to the body's variable reactions to the different types of infections.

Rubella

Rubella, also known as German measles, is an infection caused by the rubella virus. The virus is spread when an infected person coughs or sneezes. Typically, if a person is symptomatic (many are not) he or she will develop a rash, swollen lymph nodes, and may experience fever, sore throat, joint pain, and fatigue.

According to the World Health Organization (WHO), when a woman is infected with the rubella virus, she has about a 90 percent chance of passing it on to the fetus (WHO, 2016). This is especially dangerous at less than 20 weeks gestation, when there is greatest risk for a miscarriage (Lambert et al., 2015). Fetuses under 20 weeks are also more likely to develop congenital rubella syndrome (CRS).

The classic triad of symptoms that defines CRS is deafness, eye abnormalities (e.g. cataracts), and congenital heart defects. Intellectual disability, developmental delay, learning disabilities, microcephaly, growth retardation, and other organ malformations are also common.

In 1971, a professor at New York University, Dr. Stella Chess, published a paper reporting on the behavioral characteristics of 243 preschool children with CRS. She found that approximately 7 percent of those with CRS in her study had an autistic-like syndrome, more than half fulfilling a full diagnosis of autism. This was a considerable rise compared to the 3 per 10,000 diagnosis rates of the 1970s at the time (Blaxill, 2004). Though additional studies have been few, autism occurrence rates in CRS have tended to hover between 4 and 7 percent (Chess, 1971).

What does the rubella virus do to the developing brain? There is growing evidence that rubella virus triggers cell suicide (apoptosis), leading to high rates of microcephaly in the condition (Duncan et al., 1999). Interestingly, however, immature cells such as neural stem cells are not as vulnerable to the rubella virus and do not typically apoptose.

Instead, mature neurons are targeted leading to a major loss in the adult cell population (Adamo et al., 2008).

Cytomegalovirus

Cytomegalovirus (CMV) is in the same family as herpesvirus and is an extremely common virus spread through contact with bodily fluids. Most adults have antibodies, which are indicative of prior infection. Infected adults are typically asymptomatic, however those with weakened immune systems can develop pneumonia, hepatitis, or even encephalitis. Pregnant mothers can also pass on the infection to their unborn infants, especially if the mother contracts the virus for the first time during her pregnancy (Kenneson & Cannon, 2007). It is estimated that about 40,000 children are born each year with CMV infection, making it the leading cause of birth defects and childhood disabilities in the United States. For perspective, about 4000 children are born each year with Down syndrome and about 5000 are born with fetal alcohol syndrome (Cheeran, Lokensard, & Schleiss, 2009).

According to the Centers for Disease Control and Prevention, about 80 percent of infants born with congenital CMV infection never develop signs of the condition. About 10 percent of infants are, however, symptomatic at birth and present with prematurity, microcephaly, small birth size, seizures, or organ problems and are likely to develop neurological issues such as intellectual disability or developmental delay. Another 10 percent of infants who are initially asymptomatic may eventually develop complications within the first several years of life, displaying signs of gradual hearing loss, vision loss, or other forms of neurological impairment (Centers for Disease Control and Prevention, 2010).

Brain malformations are very common in infants who have symptomatic CMV infection at birth. These malformations include dilation of the ventricles of the brain, calcifications, delayed white matter development, cysts, and various other structural abnormalities, like polymicrogyria (many small gyri) and lissencephaly (smooth brain) (Cheeran et al., 2009).

As early as the 1970s, case reports linking autism and congenital CMV infection began to trickle in (Stubbs, 1978). Unfortunately, the largest study to date investigating these links has contained only seven children, two (29%) of whom fulfilled criteria for autism (Yamashita et al., 2003). With so few data it is impossible to estimate comorbidity between the two conditions.

However, in a more recent retrospective study, a group of scientists looked at rates of CMV infection in blood spot samples and dried umbilical cords from autistic children and found that while active infection was more common in the autism group compared to controls, it was significantly lower (7%) than the earlier study (Sakamoto et al., 2015). However, prior to analysis these scientists weeded out individuals with autism who also had other neurological problems like intellectual disability, the latter which is a hallmark of congenital CMV. It is therefore possible they underestimated prenatal CMV infection in autism. More research is desperately needed in this area in order to determine true prevalence rates.

Herpes

Like cytomegalovirus, herpes simplex virus is part of the Herpesviridae family. When symptomatic, it can cause sores in the affected areas. During these times, affected persons are the most contagious and can spread the illness through exchange of bodily fluids like saliva. In very rare instances, the herpes simplex virus is able to travel into the brain via either the trigeminal or olfactory nerves, leading to a severe form of encephalitis that can involve fever, headaches, seizures, vomiting, long-lasting neurological impairment, and often death. For those who survive the encephalitis, the neurological impairment tends to be permanent.

Although until now we have primarily discussed prenatal infections, postnatal infection by the herpes simplex virus is also a risk factor for autism, although occurrences are rare given the rarity of herpesviral encephalitis. However, the most unusual aspect concerning this form of encephalitis is the age at which it can trigger autistic regression: though regression typically occurs between ages one to three in autism (with rare exceptions in the case of childhood disintegrative disorder), onset of herpesviral encephalitis-related autism has been reported as late as age 31 (Ghaziuddin, Al-Khouri, & Ghaziuddin, 2002; Ghaziuddin et al., 1992; Gillberg, 1986; Gillberg, 1991). Sometimes the autism symptoms remain after recovery, at other times they are transient and resolve with the infection.

The severity with which herpes attacks the brain is dramatic, leading to significant impairment when it occurs. Though the case studies are few, there are other examples of encephalitis-induced autism, such as enterovirus encephalitis, autoimmune-induced encephalitis, and other unidentified types of infection or autoimmunity

(DeLong, Bean, & Brown, 1981; Marques et al., 2014; Scott et al., 2014). Encephalitis, therefore, appears to be a significant risk factor in the development of regressive autism.

Regression following illness or inoculation

In the previous sections, we discussed how prenatal infections can affect the developing infant; and how postnatal infections and other immune challenges, as we saw with herpesviral encephalitis, may trigger an underlying vulnerability and lead to temporary regression or a permanent loss in skills already acquired. But what are the mechanisms that potentially cause this skill loss? Below we will see how both epilepsy and infection can trigger regression.

Fever-inducing factors, epilepsy, and the brain

Autism and epilepsy appear to have much in common. Although most cases of autistic regression do not seem to have an underlying epileptic cause, epilepsy during this critical time period can and does cause regressive symptoms in select cases. A notable example frequently cited is Landau-Kleffner syndrome, in which the child experiences language regression at the onset of his or her epilepsy. Other examples include Dravet syndrome, Angelman syndrome, Phelan-McDermid syndrome, and various types of early infantile and childhood-onset encephalopathies (Carvill et al., 2013; McIntosh et al., 2010; Nava et al., 2014; Soorya et al., 2013; Valente et al., 2006).

While the link between illness and seizure onset is not well understood, it is believed that infection, especially that associated with fever, may increase excitability of neurons in the brain. This can lower the threshold for seizures, which, in a person with a previously unrecognized vulnerability, dramatically increases seizure risk.

One potential mechanism of action is the pro-inflammatory molecule interleukin 1 (IL-1). Originally, scientists believed that fever-associated seizures were due to the fever itself. However, further research has shown that fever-reducers such as Tylenol fail to protect against these kinds of seizures (Uhari et al., 1995). Instead, it is believed that while IL-1 promotes fever, it also targets the brain increasing the excitability of neurons (Vezzani et al., 2011). Further work is still needed to determine whether IL-1 is the primary culprit in fever-related seizures or whether other factors play intermediate roles.

But how do seizures cause regression? Seizures can significantly damage neurons and the cells around them. On the extreme end, severe or chronic seizures can trigger cell death through cytotoxicity. Cytotoxicity is when excessive neuronal activity occurs, leading to huge influxes of calcium and cell damage or even death. On the less severe end, seizures can alter patterns of neural connections, which may lead to an "unwiring" of skills a person has already learned.

A related example with which you may already be familiar is electroconvulsive therapy (ECT). Patients with chronic, medication-resistant depression may be good candidates for ECT. At one time in history, however, ECT electrodes were placed on the temples of the brain overlying the temporal lobes. This tended to result in a loss of memory with chronic ECT use because the parts of the brain that control memory consolidation are located in these regions. Nowadays, however, the electrodes are placed towards the front of the brain, reducing the extent of memory loss.

Illness, inoculation, and cellular stress

Here we will only give a brief introduction to the potential links between immune system challenges, cell stress, and regression, as these will be covered more extensively in the next chapter. For now, however, we will address some of the basics.

When a cell is under stress, whether this is due to an infection, an inoculation, poor nutrition, or a genetic predisposition, it tends to react in a predictable fashion.

During an infection the immune system must rapidly mobilize to deal with the invading pathogen. In order to do so, the cells of the immune system increase their protein production to deal with the acute demand. Whenever a new protein has been produced, it has to go through a system of checks in an organelle of the cell called the endoplasmic reticulum (ER). The ER verifies that the protein has been produced and is folded properly. In the world of biochemistry, shape helps determines function; and if a protein isn't shaped properly, it cannot function in the way it was intended to. So the ER has molecular chaperones that keep an eye out for misfolded proteins and try to reshape them when necessary. If a protein cannot be refolded, it is sent to the trash, otherwise known as endoplasmic reticulum-associated degradation.

When a cell rapidly increases its protein production to deal, for instance, with an acute infection or even an inoculation, it must also increase its number of chaperones in order to accommodate the increased demands (Nakaya et al., 2011). They are part of what is known as the unfolded protein response (UPR), which also includes a sudden decrease in the production of proteins in order to ease the overall flow (Janssens, Pulendran, & Lambrecht, 2014). In an individual who has an impaired or already overworked UPR prior to additional environmental stressors, when they are subjected to an infection this can increase the risk that the UPR will become overwhelmed and will be unable to handle the demand. In such instances, a set of events is triggered that can lead to a stagnation in growth, a regression in growth, or even programmed cell death. This general scenario appears to be the primary mechanism for neurodegenerative conditions like Alzheimer's.

Although research is still early, features of autistic regression are similar to some features of neurodegeneration and may share overlap in their underlying mechanisms (Kern et al., 2013). (For more on this topic, see the next chapter.)

Many of the infections linked with autism risk are viral in nature, as opposed to bacterial or parasitic. Viruses in particular may place greater stress on the ER (He, 2006). Not only does infection disturb the homeostasis of the ER, the cell becomes a protein-producing machine for the invading virus, adding an additional load onto an already strained system. Cell death, on the one hand, may help to slow spread of the infection, but if this occurs in cells in the developing brain the results can be catastrophic.

HORMONES

The immune system is intricately intertwined with the endocrine system, which produces the body's hormones. One practical reason for this is that organisms that use internal fertilization during sexual reproduction must have an immune system that knows not to attack the developing embryo. This is in contrast to organisms that use external fertilization, such as when the egg and sperm are both released into the water in a process known as "spawning."

One of the major ways the immune system knows not to attack a developing embryo is through hormones. Hormones change during pregnancy and effectively tell the immune system to "calm down." Without this crosstalk, internal fertilization would have likely never evolved, dramatically limiting species' evolutionary potential.

But the immune and endocrine systems have continued to refine their crosstalk over hundreds of millions of years, and now cooperate to create biological variability well outside the bounds of pregnancy. In fact, the immune system alters its behavior based simply on sex, irrespective of pregnancy. Consider for instance the high rates of autoimmune disorders in women compared to men (Cooper & Stroehla, 2003). The immune system also alters its activity in response to the presence of stress hormones, such as adrenalin and cortisol, both of which help to suppress inflammation. Unfortunately, chronic stress can leave us vulnerable to infection, which is why we are more likely to get sick following an intense bout of psychological or physical stress. Together, immune and endocrine crosstalk affects organ development and tissue repair, from the birth of the central nervous system to a sprained ankle, and these systems complement each other in numerous ways.

The metabolic syndrome

Given our modern sedentary lifestyles, with refrigerators, cupboards, and vending machines packed full of easily accessible and ready-to-eat high-carbohydrate, high-calorie foods, the obesity epidemic is not shocking. Most of us—perhaps the women amongst us especially—have an inkling that carbohydrates are particularly addictive. Scientists have recently found that the production of insulin, which is part of the lock-and-key mechanism that allows sugars to be taken into the cell, actually amplifies the release of dopamine in areas of the brain that are involved in addiction (Stouffer et al., 2015). This suggests that carbohydrates have an addictive effect, whose intensity may vary by person and even by sex.

Along with obesity come other problems, such as high cholesterol or triglyceride levels, high blood pressure, and insulin resistance or type 2 diabetes. Together these symptoms are known as the *metabolic syndrome*. With the presence of this syndrome comes increased risk for heart disease and stroke, both of which make the top five list of the Centers for Disease Control and Prevention's leading causes of death.

Unfortunately with obesity also comes increased inflammation— fat cells being an active participant in helping to generate numerous cytokines. In addition, macrophages, a type of immune cell, are also drawn to regions of increased fat tissue, compounding the burgeoning problem (Lee & Pratley, 2005). Molecules released by macrophages subsequently disrupt insulin signaling within peripheral tissues and within the pancreas itself, targeting β-cells that produce insulin. This can lead to both insulin resistance, in which insulin fails to activate the insulin receptor, and insulin deficiency (Esser et al., 2014).

Scientists have also found that diabetes and pre-diabetes (insulin resistance) can lead to conditions such as polycystic ovarian syndrome (PCOS) in women. One of the hallmarks of PCOS is a buildup of small cysts on the ovaries. PCOS is the primary cause of female infertility, leading to changes in the menstrual cycle and sometimes an excessive production of male hormones. This latter feature often leads to a condition known as *hirsutism*, which is an unwanted and often embarrassing male-pattern of hair growth, such as the development of thicker facial hair or chest hair.

Recent research has revealed that PCOS, or its underlying metabolic cause, is a significant risk factor in the development of autism. One study found that children of PCOS mothers were considerably more likely to develop autism than those without (Kosidou et al., 2016). What is more, children born to PCOS mothers who were also obese had even higher risk of developing autism, suggesting the severity of these metabolic conditions may also affect the extent of risk.

There have also been a number of studies looking at maternal diabetes and the risk of autism. Most studies suggest that type 2 diabetes increases autism risk at a rate similar to that seen with PCOS (Xu et al., 2015). Given the relationship between PCOS and diabetes 2/insulin resistance in women, it is possible the similar rates of risk are reflective of the same underlying metabolic syndrome, although further research is still needed to address this possibility.

Endocrine disruptors

I [ELC] had a professor back in graduate school who was a renowned biochemist that studied estrogens, their mimics, and how they relate to breast cancer. He was a quirky professor from Texas who had a penchant for wine tasting and whose attire always reminded me of a rough-hewn paleontologist who had spent years in deserts scraping away grit from old fossil bones. In characteristic fashion, he introduced his endocrinology course to us by saying, "Even though my wife hates it when I say this, the estrogen receptor is highly *promiscuous!*" We would all chuckle, and then he'd explain.

The estrogen receptor is in fact highly promiscuous. Compared to most receptors in our bodies, the estrogen receptor not only accepts estrogen as its ligand (a kind of lock-and-key system), but other chemicals can also mimic or block the receptor. These substances are called *xenoestrogens,* "xeno-" meaning "foreign, other, or different in origin." They include plant-derived phytoestrogens, fungally derived mycoestrogens, and a growing list of other man-made estrogen mimics, such as various plastics or pesticides. (Keep in mind that animal products such as meats, eggs, and dairy also contain naturally occurring estrogens. If you are eating food, you are consuming estrogen in some form.)

But other hormone receptors, such as those for androgen, are also at the mercy of these foreign steroid mimics, which can have decidedly unwanted effects on health and development. Man-made xenosteroids, like certain plastics, are of particular concern as they are recent additions to our daily environment, ones that degrade extremely slowly and to which our bodies may not have had time to adapt. In the next several sections, we will review different endocrine disruptors and how exposures to them may increase the risk of autism, all via directly or indirectly activating or antagonizing hormone receptors.

Heavy metal exposure

A condition known as "itai-itai" or "ouch-ouch" disease afflicted post-menopausal women in a small region along the Jintsu River in Japan in the 1940s. Many of these women became bedridden with horribly painful skeletal deformations. Eventually it was discovered that they had been poisoned by high levels of the metal cadmium, which had been deposited into the local river by an upstream mining company (Safe, 2003). These women were exposed to extremely high levels of the metal—however, even low levels have been shown to affect the structure and function of reproductive organs in animals.

A growing body of evidence suggests that specific heavy metals are estrogenic, with the ability to stimulate molecular pathways downstream of the estrogen receptor (Choe et al., 2003). Termed *metalloestrogens*, many of these metals interact directly with the estrogen receptor, exhibiting potency greater than even native estrogen itself (Safe, 2003).

Using animal models, scientists have found that prenatal exposure to various heavy metals, such as cadmium, lead, arsenic, manganese, and mercury, causes various behavioral abnormalities reminiscent of autism. For instance, manganese and arsenic result in repetitive and impulsive behaviors in mice, while lead results in distinctive social abnormalities (Hill et al., 2015). These same exposures lead to changes in epigenetic patterning (and therefore expression) of the *CHD7* gene, whose mutation in humans results in CHARGE syndrome, a genetic condition in which approximately 60 percent of those affected also have autism (Smith et al., 2005).

Other studies have found an increased prevalence of autism births proximal to high environmental concentrations of heavy-metal pollutants, such as near various industrial facilities (Dickerson et al., 2015, 2016). Heavy metals also seem to preferentially target the expression of many autism susceptibility genes, suggesting that they, along with other endocrine disruptors, may significantly increase autism risk by targeting nuclear hormone receptors that help to regulate the activity of these genes (Carter & Blizard, 2016).

Heavy metals, like many of the other xenoestrogens we will be reviewing here, also have effects on the immune system, which is one of the key reasons these metals are so often used as adjuvants and immunostimulants in vaccinations. Unfortunately, this has also led to adjuvant-induced autoimmunity in vulnerable subpopulations, which scientists are actively working to understand and, hopefully, prevent in future (see Guimarães et al., 2015, for a review).

Pesticides

Pesticides are specifically designed to kill living organisms. We have developed them to target insects, plants, and fungi, making things like modern large-scale agriculture possible. We are subsequently exposed to many of these pesticides in foods, household products, home gardens, drift from agriculture, and public health sprayings. In 1961, our agricultural use was about 0.49 kilograms per hectare (kg/ha). However, by 2004, it had quadrupled to 2kg/ha, suggesting our levels of exposure have increased dramatically within a comparatively short period of time (reviewed in Mnif et al., 2011).

Most insecticides are designed to target the nervous system, disrupting activities of various receptors and molecular pathways (Casida, 2009). However, because humans and other animals also have these same pathways and receptors, insecticides have the potential to be poisonous to us when ingested.

By contrast, the mechanisms of action of herbicides and fungicides are often plant- or fungus-specific, targeting pathways involved in photosynthesis, carotenoid synthesis,[8] plant-essential amino acids, and fungal steroids (Casida, 2009). Unfortunately, overuse of pesticides is quickly leading to strains of insects, plants, and fungi that are becoming resistant to whole families of pest-control agents.

Aside from their direct action on the nervous system and synthesis pathways, approximately one hundred pesticides are also recognized as endocrine disruptors, although some of these, such as DDT, are no longer in use but are still present in the environment (Mnif et al., 2011). As with other endocrine disruptors we have reviewed, most of these pesticides interact with hormone receptors, mimicking the activity of native steroids. Some pesticides may also antagonize or block hormone receptors—and others still may disrupt the synthesis, transportation, and elimination of the hormones themselves.

Some pesticides also appear to cause extensive oxidative stress upon exposure, which in turn triggers inflammation (Astiz, de Alaniz, & Marra, 2012). Airborne pesticides can also cause significant inflammation within the lungs, which can damage the bronchial epithelium, leading to symptoms of asthma. This kind of exposure also sensitizes the lungs to other allergens and irritants, worsening the asthmatic condition (Hernández, Parrón, & Alarcón, 2011).

Several studies have raised questions concerning the risk of autism relative to the severity of pesticide exposures. Although organochlorine pesticides like DDT were finally phased out of use in the United States in 2016 (the last-standing pesticide was Endosulfan, whose phase-out began in 2010), many of these pesticides are still present in the environment and may have effects on prenatal development. For instance, women pregnant and living within 500 meters of spray sites in California were several times more likely to have had a child with autism than mothers who lived in regions with the lowest exposure rates (Roberts et al., 2007). It is uncertain, however, whether increased

---

8   The production of red, yellow, and orange pigments in fruits and vegetables.

risk is due to organochlorine pesticides' effects on GABA receptors[9] in the central nervous system, their ability to disrupt the endocrine system, or a combination of both— although GABA receptor antagonism is a more likely cause (Guillette, 2000).

Flame retardants

Prenatal exposure to organophosphates, which are used in building materials, textiles, and electronic appliances due to their low flammability, have been linked with increased risk for autism (Shelton et al., 2014). Excess levels lead to overstimulation of acetylcholine receptors in the nervous system. During acute poisoning, extreme anxiety, convulsions, depressed respiration, and coma can occur (Eddleston et al., 2008). However, organophosphates can also disrupt functions of several types of estrogen receptors, the androgen receptor, and the glucocorticoid receptor (Kojima et al., 2013).

Polychlorinated biphenyls (PCB) and brominated flame retardants also have significant endocrine disrupting properties (Connor et al., 1997; Legler & Brouwer, 2003). In addition, it seems that certain brominated flame retardants trigger an inflammatory response in some autistic children, an effect that is largely unseen in controls (Ashwood et al., 2009). This suggests that in vulnerable subpopulations, chemical flame retardants may have immunostimulatory properties, and that exposure could play a role both in the etiology and presentation of these conditions.

MATERNAL STRESS

Pregnancy is stressful. Parenthood can be stressful. But what if stress is a risk factor for autism? Some studies suggest that mothers who are unusually stressed during pregnancy are more likely to have children with autism (Ronald, Pennell, & Whitehouse, 2010). The greatest risk period seems to span the end of the second and beginning of the third trimesters of pregnancy, for reasons not well understood (Beversdorf et al., 2005).

---

9   "GABA receptors" are receptors for the inhibitory neurotransmitter, gamma-aminobutyric acid (GABA), which helps to regulate and refine excitatory neuron transmission.

However, anxiety disorders are often reported in mothers of those on the autism spectrum, as part of the broader autism phenotype (BAP) (Murphy et al., 2000; Piven et al., 1991). What if anxiety is merely a risk factor in the same way that BAP in parents is a risk factor for autism in their children? A reflection of heredity rather than a cause of autism.

While heredity certainly predisposes towards autism, animal models have also shown that the stress of the mother affects brain development in her offspring. For instance, pregnant mice who are exposed to regular restraint stress tend to have offspring with microscopic brain malformations (Stevens et al., 2013). In particular, newborn inhibitory neurons are especially vulnerable to this stress.

Inhibitory neurons are born in a region of the brain known as the ganglionic eminence and then must travel, sometimes up to several inches, to their final resting places. Maternal stress, depending on the severity, length, and frequency of exposure, disrupts these migrations, preventing inhibitory neurons from reaching their final destinations. This may ultimately result in an excitatory–inhibitory imbalance in the brain, reminiscent of the prevailing theory in autism (Casanova et al., 2003; Rubenstein & Merzenich, 2003). Interestingly, many genetic mouse models of autism show similar deficits in which populations of inhibitory cells are reduced in number within the cortex. This suggests that prenatal stress exposure can mimic the detrimental effects of autism risk genes to some extent.

CLINICAL CONSIDERATIONS

We have covered considerable ground in this chapter, reviewing probable and potential environmental risk factors in the development of autism. We have focused on chemical exposures, such as prescription medications and non-prescription drugs like alcohol, and various endocrine disruptors, such as heavy metals, pesticides, and flame retardants. We have also reviewed nutrition, concerning deprivation of key nutritional elements like folic acid. And we have highlighted how infections, metabolic and hormone disorders like diabetes, and even maternal stress can promote autism risk.

The clinical implications in this chapter are probably the simplest of any of the chapters in this book. In the case of environmental factors that increase risk for autism, the best treatment is prevention by avoiding those substances. Or in the case of nutritional deficiencies, supplementation is strongly advised. But in the case of infections, prevention is decidedly more challenging. Although there are currently no vaccinations for cytomegalovirus, rubella and herpes vaccines are available and it is suggested women get vaccinated prior to pregnancy, provided they don't have a history of adverse reactions to inoculation or are otherwise immunologically compromised. In those instances, women are advised instead to work with their doctors to draw up plans tailored to their individual needs.

Hormonal disorders are also difficult to prevent, especially when there is a hereditary component to many of the conditions associated with the metabolic syndrome. However, a balanced healthy diet and adequate exercise may help significantly to alleviate the severity of these syndromes, decreasing overall risk for autism in the child. Medications targeted to the treatment of diabetes 2/pre-diabetes and PCOS may also be beneficial, such as synthetic insulin and progesterone. In addition, for those who experience a component of food addiction with their weight problems, Wellbutrin may be a useful tool in aiding weight loss prior to pregnancy by targeting the reward systems of the brain and reducing cravings (Billes, Sinnayah, & Cowley, 2014).

In spite of our best efforts, however, there will always be risk factors present in our environments, some of which are inherent to our modern-day lifestyles (e.g. the ingestion of plastics) and others that are simply an unavoidable fact of life (e.g. infections). Yet there are lifestyle changes we can make that may significantly reduce risk for autism and that come from simple awareness of these risk factors.

Autism will always have a major hereditary component—more in some cases than in others. But there are also cases of autism that contain a clear environmental exigency, such as fetal valproate syndrome and congenital rubella. This shows us that although autism is a highly heritable condition, it is not the result of simple heredity.

Chapter Five

REGRESSION IN AUTISM

WHAT IS REGRESSION?

As the following quote from a parent illustrates, observations of regression have been intricately linked with autism from the time of its designation in 1943, when Leo Kanner first published the case histories of eleven children with "autistic disturbances of affective contact."

> I can't be sure just when he stopped the imitation of word sounds. It seems that he has gone backward mentally gradually for the last two years. We have thought that it was because he did not disclose what was in his head, that it was there all right. Now that he is making so many sounds, it is disconcerting because it is now evident that he can't talk. Before, I thought he could if he only would. *He gave the impression of silent wisdom to me.*

(Report from a parent, Kanner, 1943, pp. 225–226)

Although Kanner didn't belabor the point of skills loss in these children, such cases did later inspire him to propose the division of autism into innate and regressive types. Interestingly, as a reflection of concepts of the time, he felt that regressive autism had more in common with childhood schizophrenia than autism *proper*, although nowadays we would differentiate schizophrenia by the presence of psychosis rather than the looser definitions that characterized the condition in the mid-20th century.

Regression in autism usually occurs within the second year of life and can happen either abruptly or gradually. The child experiences a stall in skill acquisition or a measurable loss, which usually occurs in the areas of language and/or social skills, although there are occasional reports of the loss of adaptive and fine motor skills too. Eventually, the regressive period is succeeded by the regaining of skills, although some children may never fully regain the skills they had originally lost (reviewed by Baird et al., 2008).

Anywhere between 10 and 50 percent of children who are diagnosed with autism have experienced regression, with the most common reported figure hovering around one third of cases (Barger, Campbell, & McDonough, 2013; Kurita, 1985). These estimates probably vary because of differences in criteria used to define "regression." Some studies for instance restrict it to extreme forms of language loss, while others include subtler plateaus in language and social skills. However, estimates also probably vary modestly because the primary means for estimating regression in autism is generally parental report. While parents know their children better than anyone else, especially in those early formative years, human memory isn't infallible—particularly if the regressive losses are subtle and the parent is answering a questionnaire ten years after the fact.

Interestingly, regression appears to be largely unique to autism. When comparing autistic toddlers with other children with various intellectual disabilities, scientists have found that language regression occurs in a large minority of those with autism, however, it is rarely seen in those with intellectual disability alone (Baird et al., 2008).

Regression also occurs in some syndromic forms of autism, such as Rett syndrome and childhood disintegrative disorder (CDD) (once known as Heller's syndrome), both of which had previously been grouped under the DSM-IV's autism umbrella, Pervasive Developmental Disorders, but have since been removed.

Most cases of Rett syndrome are linked with loss-of-function mutations involving the *MECP2* gene, which produces a protein that binds to methylated DNA and helps to control gene expression. Almost all cases of Rett syndrome are female due to the lethality of the X-linked mutation in males. When it does occur in males, this is typically due to something known as *somatic mosaicism*, in which the mutation is not present in all cells of the body but only a portion because it has occurred later in embryonic development rather than in the originating germ cells.

Prior to regression, the majority of girls with Rett's present with some type of developmental delay. Regression onset then usually occurs between 12 and 18 months of age, with an average of 16 months, which is slightly younger than the average 20 months in idiopathic autism (Baird et al., 2008; Millichap, 2002). The most prominent feature in Rett syndrome is a decline in motor skills involving the hands, often leading to the characteristic "hand wringing" gesture for which Rett's is known. However, large numbers of girls also lose language, nonverbal communication and play, and other motor skills (Millichap, 2002).

Unlike Rett syndrome, CDD is a poorly studied and understood condition that occurs more often in boys. Currently, there are no known mutations associated with CDD, which may reflect the state of our science but may also suggest that, like autism, it is a heterogeneous disorder. Occasional case studies reporting the occurrence of autism and CDD in the same families suggests the latter may also be true (Zwaigenbaum et al., 2000).

CDD is typified by normal or near-normal development until at least two years of age, after which a regression period begins that may be characterized by high levels of anxiety, followed by a severe decline in skills and the onset of autistic symptomology (Volkmar & Rutter, 1995). Often, language is lost and rarely regained, as are self-help skills such as appropriate use of the toilet or feeding. Unfortunately, most children with CDD develop intellectual disability and are severely affected for the rest of their lives.

A call for research

Despite the prevalence of regressive symptoms in idiopathic autism, there has been little definitive research concerning clinical outcomes, a fact that is both shocking and sad, suggesting the research community and relevant funding agencies have a particular blind spot for this harrowing issue. What few studies that have been performed generally agree that individuals who experience regression are more likely to be diagnosed with intellectual disability than their non-regressive counterparts, they are more likely to experience sleep problems, they tend to develop language more slowly, and their autistic symptoms are more severe (Barger & Campbell, 2014). These studies, however, are preliminary and more research is desperately needed.

ARE AUTISTIC CHILDREN "NORMAL" BEFORE THEY REGRESS?

According to Sally Rogers (2004), autism onset can be grouped into three basic categories:

- Congenital autism—the child's development is atypical from birth.

- Developmental plateau—the child plateaus in developmental milestones in the second year of life.

- Regression—the child loses skills within the second year of life.

Despite this tidy categorization, recent research suggests that symptoms of regression occur in a majority of those with autism and that regression itself falls on a spectrum of timing and severity (Thurm et al., 2014). Though sudden late loss of speech may represent the more severe end of the regressive spectrum and is most obvious and alarming to parents and pediatricians, subtler earlier losses in first words, responding to his or her name, interactive smiling, babbling, and eye contact may represent the lighter end of that same spectrum. Regression may instead be a symptom of autism rather than that of a subset of autism. As the writer Emily Willingham (2014) so poignantly asks:

> ... is regression a universal feature of being autistic but one that occurs at different ages in different people, like walking or puberty or executive function skills? Or are there really truly distinct entities characterized by different onset timing?

Does autistic regression exist?

I [ELC] remember while I was in graduate school, a well-known researcher visited my university and gave a lecture. In it, he showed a video of an autistic child. The video was a compilation of shorts taken from different periods in the young boy's life. The first video was of a boy sitting in a high chair, looking at the videographer who presumably was his mom or dad, and he was smiling and giggling, looking up at the parent. He was completely engaged. But in the next video, he wasn't smiling anymore. He was sitting in his high chair staring off, barely reacting to his name or all the cajoling the parent tried, quiet and almost completely enclosed within himself. I remember how shocked I was to see so drastic a change in such a short period of time in the boy's behaviors—there was such a severe shift in his personality. It was as if he were an entirely different child.

I remember thinking then and there, "Regression is *real*." Before seeing that video, I had waved it away saying, "They were atypical to begin with, the parents just didn't see it." And that may well be true to some extent. But subtle clues don't negate the magnitude of such an extreme shift in how the brain functions. When that loss occurs, it can truly be a monumental one.

Emily Werner and Geraldine Dawson published a landmark study in 2005 that proved to the research community the existence of regression in autism (Werner & Dawson, 2005). The researchers collected videotapes of children's first and second birthdays who had been diagnosed with autistic regression, early-onset autism, or were typically developing. They then used blinded raters (psychologists who do not know the diagnoses of the children) to code the behaviors in the videotapes collected from the two different time points. They found that although children with regressive autism did display some subtle deficits in self-regulation suggestive of some kind of biological vulnerability, their social and communication development did not significantly differ from that of the typically developing kids. In spite of previous assumptions, in no way did these children fulfill the criteria for autism prior to regression.

This sudden regression is illustrated well in a quote from Ron Suskind (2004), a father of an autistic boy who experienced regression at the late age of three:

> In our first year in Washington, our son disappeared. … Just shy of his 3rd birthday, an engaged, chatty child, full of typical speech— "I love you," "Where are my Ninja Turtles?" "Let's get ice cream!"— fell silent. He cried, inconsolably. Didn't sleep. Wouldn't make eye contact. His only word was "juice."

(Suskind, 2014)

WHAT CAUSES REGRESSION?

Some types of autism have variable hereditary patterns. For instance, parents of multiplex (multiple incidence) families often exhibit a broader autism phenotype (BAP) themselves. Meanwhile, parents who have only a single child with autism (simplex cases) are considerably less likely to have autistic features than multiplex parents (Davison et al., 2014). (See Chapter 8.)

Although it may seem surprising given the typical developmental trajectory of children with autistic regression, typified by near-normal development followed by sudden or gradual regression, parents of these children have similar rates of BAP as parents of children without regression (Lainhart et al., 2002). This suggests that regressive autism, on the whole, is as heritable as non-regressive autism.

We know that regressive autism may be partly inherited, but what *causes* it? One of the more popular current theories is the *over-pruning hypothesis* of autistic regression (Thomas et al., 2016). According to this hypothesis, the loss of neural connectivity leading to regression is due to overactive pruning of those connections, which normally starts to occur in toddlerhood and extends throughout childhood. Interestingly, the neurocomputational model used to test this hypothesis does seem to support the idea that regression is due to a loss of connectivity— however, it never proves what causes that loss (e.g. pruning), merely that there is indeed a loss.

In addition, as we covered in Chapter 2, the brain in autism is not typified by generalized underconnectivity and in fact has a wealth of short-range connective fibers. Instead, the larger longer fibers of the brain are preferentially depleted.

Many cases of autistic regression seem to be linked with some kind of stressor or stimulus, as we will review in the following sections. Sometimes, that stressor is the onset of an epileptic disorder. Other times, that stimulus is an illness. Sometimes, it is both. Therefore, we instead suggest that regression is the result of excessive or chronic cellular stress, leading to the rapid or slow loss of synapses, neural connections, and sometimes cells themselves. This loss leads to a subsequent loss in skills, such as language and socialization. Sometimes these skills may be regained, especially in smaller neural networks in which regrowth is possible. However, long-range connections are unlikely ever to be recovered owing to the need for specific developmental cues that lead connections along their arduous paths and that are no longer present in the postnatal brain. In this way, coordination amongst disparate functional modules of the brain will be permanently impaired.

Inflammation and autoimmunity

Links between autism and immune dysregulation have been studied for decades, though the mechanisms of risk are likely complex. Early research identified high prevalence rates of autoimmune disorders in family members of those with autism (Money et al., 1971). Meanwhile, more recent studies have found that mothers, autistic children, and their siblings produce higher numbers of autoantibodies to components of the human brain such as the myelin sheath that covers and insulates axons (Singer et al., 2006). As we discussed in the previous chapter, if mothers produce brain autoantibodies there is concern these molecules may target the developing embryonic brain, increasing autism risk (Warren et al., 1990).

Although it is possible this is a related yet incidental finding of familial immune dysfunction, we do know that maternal IgG antibodies are capable of passing both the placental and fetal blood–brain barriers, suggesting autoantibodies are able to access the embryonic brain (Wills et al., 2007). Primate studies have shown that prenatal exposure to autoantibodies derived from mothers of autistic children leads to socially abnormal behavior in monkeys (Bauman et al., 2013).

Meanwhile, immune factors known as *cytokines* offer another potential avenue for autism risk. Although these molecules were identified because of their associations with the immune system, they are involved in many other processes, including general growth and development. For instance, a number of studies have shown that maternal infection during key periods of pregnancy is significantly linked with increased autism risk (reviewed by Matelski & Van de Water, 2016). During such times as infection, specific cytokines are in abundance, aiding in fever induction and the stimulation of important immune cells that help to fight off the invading pathogen.

While many of these cytokines do not seem to cross the placental barrier in considerable numbers, a few, such as interleukin-6 (IL-6), are able to make it through the placenta (Zaretsky et al., 2004). Interestingly, IL-6 has been shown to alter neuron development both during prenatal development as well as in the adult hippocampus in which neuron production occurs lifelong (Taga & Fukuda, 2005; Vallières et al., 2002). It has been discovered that IL-6 is also vital for the stimulation of certain immune cells involved in triggering autoimmunity within the brain (Samoilova et al., 1998). And so this cytokine may not only alter brain development by stimulating brain cells directly but by priming local immune cells to attack the brain should sufficient autoantibodies be present. This suggests that maternal autoimmunity and infection act in tandem.

In adult forms of dementia, researchers have long recognized the roles that inflammation plays in these various diseases. Although inflammation is a beneficial reaction to an injurious or infectious insult, excessive or prolonged stimulation of inflammatory pathways can lead to major neuronal damage. Likewise, modest inflammatory stimulation superimposed on an already weakened condition (i.e. a predisposition) may also lead to brain damage (reviewed in Cunningham, 2013).

There are indications that a similar process occurs in autistic regression. Scientists have found, for instance, that autistic children who regress are more likely than their non-regressive counterparts to have experienced fever-related illness in the six months prior to their regression. In addition, families of those with regressive autism are also more likely to have autoimmune disorders (33% vs. 12%), suggesting there is a heritable immune component underlying risk for regression (Scott et al., 2017).

A clear-cut case of immune-related regression can be seen in the genetic condition known as Dravet syndrome. Dravet's is a form of epileptic encephalopathy that is almost always accompanied by intellectual disability. In addition, about 25 percent of Dravet syndrome patients have autism (Li et al., 2011). Children with Dravet's typically experience somewhat normal development until the toddler years when they begin to have seizures, which subsequently lead to a regression in psychomotor skills.

Surprisingly, in a large subset of these children seizure onset is closely preceded by either illness or vaccination, suggesting that immune challenge is a key factor in triggering regression in this condition (McIntosh et al., 2010). It should be noted that the clinical outcomes of children with seizure onset following immunological challenge are not significantly different from those who experience no obvious environmental triggers prior to epilepsy onset, with the exception that the former group develops seizures on average a few months earlier (McIntosh et al., 2010). This may be good reason to consider altered vaccine schedules for such a vulnerable population. However, it also comes with the realization that for most children it may only slightly postpone the inevitable. Yet since most individuals with Dravet syndrome harbor mutations in the sodium channel gene *SCN1A*, clinical genotyping in infancy may offer parents and doctors that choice as well as foreknowledge of the condition.

Oxidation

You have probably heard the term, *antioxidant*, in the context of nutrition. We know that many plant-based foods, such as berries or spices like turmeric, tend to be very high in antioxidants. Meanwhile, animal-based foods such as eggs or fish are generally fairly low (Carlsen et al., 2010).

Antioxidants help to neutralize *free radicals*, which are molecules that have unpaired electrons, a state that leaves them chemically unstable. In the case of biological systems, we are usually most interested in oxygen-based free radicals known as *reactive oxygen species* (ROS), because they are a common metabolic byproduct. In order to stabilize, free radicals steal electrons from other molecules around them. However, in doing so, whatever molecule has been robbed of its electron typically becomes a free radical itself. This can lead to a long chain of electron thievery, leaving misshapen and poorly functioning molecules in its wake (Figure 5.1).

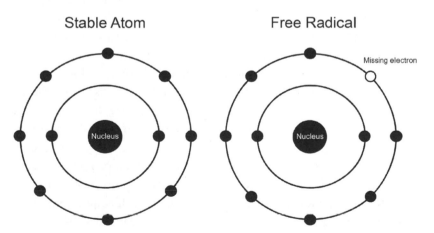

Figure 5.1: A free radical, known for stealing electrons from other molecules thereby creating a chain reaction of free radicals

Thankfully, the body has a supply of antioxidants that shuts down this runaway reaction, either by donating electrons or degrading the free radical itself. As we mentioned, many of the antioxidants in our bodies are derived from the foods we eat, most of which come from fruits and vegetables and include the vitamins, A, C, and E. However, we also produce antioxidants ourselves, such as glutathione.

In fact, the sleep hormone, melatonin, is a very powerful antioxidant (Reiter, 1996). Melatonin is mostly produced by the brain's pineal gland, beginning in the evening hours and reaching its peak at night. Melatonin production is suppressed by exposure to the blue end of the light spectrum, which is why sleep specialists recommend the use of dim yellow lighting in the evenings to mimic effects of the setting sun. Unfortunately, energy-saver bulbs popular in today's houses tend to produce a lot of white light (including blue light), suppressing melatonin and potentially complicating sleep problems. For these reasons, sleep specialists recommend avoiding the use of bright unnatural lighting in later evening.

Mitochondrial dysfunction and reactive oxygen species

Mitochondria (Figure 5.2) are the powerhouses of the cell. Through a complex string of events known as *respiration*, mitochondria take energy from the food we eat (glucose) and the air we breathe (oxygen) and produce the basic energy currency of the cell, adenosine triphosphate (ATP). The cell can then take that ATP and break off phosphate molecules to produce an energy catalyst for processes within the cell.

ROS are major byproducts of cellular respiration. Whenever the cell is overrun by ROS, this leads to oxidative stress, which in turn triggers a host of reactions termed the "oxidative response." In bacteria, this response is fairly straightforward because they tend to live in environments with fluctuating oxygen levels, therefore the presence of ROS can trigger an oxidative response. Eukaryotic organisms such as ourselves, however, live in environments in which oxygen levels are fairly constant. Therefore, the presence of ROS is not necessarily an indicator of impending damage but a normal part of respiration. Thus, it is the quantity of ROS, not their presence, that leads to a complicated cascade of events in mammalian cells that help not only to deal with increased ROS load but also repair damage to cellular structures. In some cases, when extreme, these processes may even lead to apoptosis or cell suicide (Martindale & Holbrook, 2002).

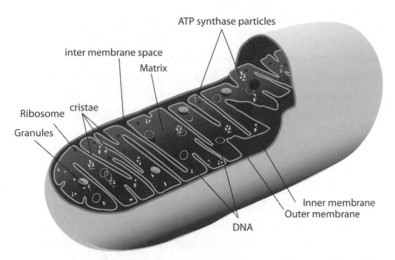

Figure 5.2: Diagram of a mitochondrion, the powerhouse of the cell

Most cells have many mitochondria, which produce ATP as a form of cellular energy.

(*Reproduced from Wikimedia Commons*)

How oxidative stress damages the brain

Because we need oxygen to survive, our cells are constantly bombarded by ROS, leading to perpetual damage of DNA, proteins, and fats that must constantly be repaired. However, ROS are not only byproducts of cellular metabolism, they also play important roles in various molecular pathways, such as inflammation, and therefore we are always in a precarious state of balance between having too much and too little ROS. For this reason, it is important to eat antioxidant-rich foods but also not to take excessive amounts of antioxidant supplements because we need *some* ROS for our cells to work properly (reviewed in Halliwell, 2006).

Unfortunately, as we age the ability of our tissues to repair themselves following ROS damage declines. The brain is especially vulnerable to oxidative damage because of its high oxygen demands, requiring about 20 percent of the body's basal consumption. In addition, many things can go wrong in the brain, leading either to increases in ROS or impairments in the mechanisms that deal with them.

For instance, excessive availability of the excitatory neurotransmitter glutamate can lead to cell damage or death through "excitotoxicity" or the excessive stimulation of neurons. Oxidative stress can damage neurons, leading to a release of glutamate into the surrounding space, triggering an excitotoxic domino effect. This excitotoxic storm is one of the major risks following stroke, as cellular damage from the initial ischemic attack releases excessive glutamate into the extracellular space, overstimulating intact neurons surrounding the original lesion. For this reason, stroke patients need to be treated rapidly with medications that prevent the spread of excitotoxicity to surrounding areas of the brain (Hazell, 2007).

Metal ions, such as iron, can also act as free radicals and are released into the extracellular space following neuronal damage. Unfortunately, because the brain has little iron-binding capacity, the presence of these metal ions can persist for long periods of time, triggering oxidative stress until they are finally flushed from the cerebral spinal fluid.

The fatty membranes of neurons are also common targets of oxidation in a process known as "lipid peroxidation." When lipid peroxidation occurs in excess, the membranes of cells can become more permeable, allowing in toxic agents that damage the cell. The functions of ion channels and receptors within the membrane can also be irreparably damaged, ultimately leading to cell death and many of the processes mentioned above (e.g. release of glutamate and metal ions into the surrounding tissue).

In contrast to much of the rest of the body, antioxidant defense is comparatively modest in the brain (Halliwell, 2001). Considering the communicative roles some ROS play in brain function, such as nitric oxide, this may well be an adaptive evolutionary strategy. However, with such benefits come risks, notably increased oxidative stress over time.

With time also come mutations. Not only do we house DNA within the nucleus of our cells, our mitochondria contain their own small genomes, which, like nuclear DNA, acquire more and more mutations over time that affect the mitochondria's capacity to function properly. Because mitochondria produce a lot of ROS, many of these mutations are likely the result of oxidative damage. Impaired mitochondrial function can lead to excessive ROS production and further oxidative stress, resulting in a positive feedback loop.

Finally, inflammation also drives oxidative stress. Astrocytes, a type of glial (helper) cell, produce inflammatory molecules such as various cytokines. These cytokines then stimulate immune cells within the brain known as microglia. These microglia release more inflamma-tory molecules, as well as various ROS, as part of their inflammatory response (Duncan & Heales, 2005; reviewed in Halliwell, 2006). If this type of reaction occurs chronically, it can lead to progressive damage as seen in some types of neurodegenerative disorders.

There are many more ways in which ROS can damage the cell. However, the majority of these mechanisms feed into one another, leading to progressive damage regardless of which pathway is stimulated first. All of these processes together lead to aging of the brain and, in those vulnerable individuals, play pivotal roles in the development of senile neurodegeneration. However, as we'll discuss in the next section, they may play important roles in neurodevelopmental conditions such as autism as well.

Mitochondrial diseases and dysfunction in autism

More than three decades ago, scientists realized that the mitochondrion, the powerhouse of the cell, may play a role in autism susceptibility (reviewed in Frye & Rossignol, 2011). We now know that mitochondrial disorders occur in roughly 7 percent of the autism spectrum population, making it one of the most common "rare" disorders associated with the condition (Oliveira et al., 2005). However, the vast majority of autistic people may have some kind of mitochondrial dysfunction, although in most cases it may be a secondary symptom of another underlying problem, such as chronic inflammation (Giulivi et al., 2010). It is likely, however, that mitochondria play an integral role in positive feedback loops that maintain this chronicity.

Individuals with certain types of mitochondrial disease are sometimes vulnerable to immunological challenges, such as illness and vaccination, which can trigger cognitive decline, a feature reminiscent of regression in autism (Verity et al., 2009). Surprisingly, about 60 percent of children with both autism and mitochondrial disease experience regression, rates that are twice as high as those seen in the rest of the spectrum (Shoffner et al., 2010; Weissman et al., 2008). What is more, the vast majority (~70%) of these children regress following a fever-related illness or vaccination. However, vaccination does not appear to trigger regression in the absence of fever, suggesting the extent of immunological challenge is the driving factor in disease onset in these cases (Shoffner et al., 2010).

Although true mitochondrial disorders occur in only a small minority of those with autism, genetics research suggests that many autistic children have mitochondrial mutation profiles similar to those seen in older people, indicating significant oxidative damage. Interestingly, the same patterns of oxidative damage are seen in mothers of children with autism, suggesting that damage to the DNA may occur maternally and is then inherited by the child (Napoli, Wong, & Giulivi, 2013).

Because of the mitochondrial DNA's proximity to the production of ROS within the mitochondrion, it is more vulnerable to the effects of free radicals than nuclear DNA. And because we all inherit our mothers' mitochondria, we preferentially inherit our mothers' mitochondrial mutations. Thankfully, women seem to produce far more antioxidants and fewer ROS than males, leading to a four-fold decrease in the comparative rates of mutation, an effect that is largely mediated by the hormone estrogen (Borrás et al., 2003).

Undoubtedly, evolution has taken great strides to protect the mitochondria from harmful mutations in women because of their carrier status, whereas men are effectively mitochondrial dead ends. Unfortunately, this also means that males are more vulnerable to the effects of oxidative damage and mitochondrial dysfunction, which has been suggested as a reason why men on average do not live as long as women. In addition, if mitochondrial dysfunction plays a role in autism susceptibility, it may also help explain the higher prevalence in males.

Epilepsy and regression
Seizures, oxidation, and inflammation
As we discussed earlier, the excitatory neurotransmitter glutamate is toxic to the brain in excessive quantities. It is therefore easy to understand how poorly controlled epilepsy can lead to significant loss in neural connections and cells via excitotoxicity. Oxidative stress seems to play an important role, not in seizure control, but in triggering damage following seizures, which can be prevented with the application of antioxidants like vitamin E and glutathione (Frantseva et al., 2000).

Inflammation and oxidation are interdependent systems, both of which have been implicated in conditions such as diabetes, high blood pressure, cardiovascular disease, neurodegeneration, cancer, and even aging (Biswas, 2016; Salzano et al., 2014). Not only can inflammatory cells trigger a free-radical cascade, oxidation can also increase inflammatory signaling. It is believed, however, that although oxidative stress may increase morbidity in some of the conditions mentioned, chronic inflammation is a major driving factor in these disease states (reviewed in Biswas, 2016).

There is increasing evidence that inflammation may be a crucial element in some cases of epilepsy as well (reviewed in Vezzani et al., 2011). For instance, steroidal and anti-inflammatory drugs are useful in the treatment of some drug-resistant cases, suggesting an immunological underpinning. In addition, febrile seizures and some types of genetic epilepsies, such as Dravet syndrome, are triggered by an immune challenge most typically associated with fever. And finally, epilepsy associates with certain autoimmune disorders for reasons not entirely clear (Vincent & Crino, 2011). In fact, a portion of epilepsies may be autoimmune in origin. Although prevalence is currently unknown, early research suggests that roughly 10–25 percent of cases of the idiopathic condition may be autoimmune disorders and could be treated with immunotherapies in addition to anti-seizure medications (Dubey et al., 2016).

Epilepsy-induced regression

The relationship between epilepsy and autistic regression is a complicated one. There are specific syndromes, collectively known as *epileptic encephalopathies*, whose onset is associated with seizure activity, leading to a decline in cognition, language, and/or behavior that sometimes resembles autism. Perhaps the most classic example is Landau-Kleffner syndrome, a condition typified by language impairment (aphasia) that is the result of seizures in and around the language centers of the brain.

Once scientists realized that seizures could trigger the regressive symptoms of Landau-Kleffner syndrome (a syndromic form of autism), general interest in autistic regression and epilepsy exploded. Since that time, numerous studies have been performed investigating potential links between the onset of seizures and regression. However, it seems that for almost every study that finds a link between the two, there is another study reporting no association (Baird et al., 2006, 2008; Canitano, Luchetti, & Zapella, 2005; Giannotti et al., 2008; Kumar, Devendran, & Devendran, 2017; Oslejsková et al., 2008). This suggests that some of the variability in results may be due to differences in methodology, such as the definition of "regression" used by these studies, the ways in which epileptiform (seizure-like) activity was classed, and what types of patient pools were utilized (e.g. age, IQ).

We know that uncontrolled seizure activity can lead to cell damage and death. In addition, current research suggests that autistic regression is due to a loss in neural connectivity. We also know that Landau-Kleffner syndrome exhibits language regression at the onset of seizure activity—a regression that is not dissimilar to the language loss seen in idiopathic autism. All of these data suggest that epilepsy may trigger regression in some cases of autism. However, scientists are not yet agreed whether that is the case and, if so, how prevalent it might be. Further research will hopefully continue to address these important questions, potentially offering better treatment interventions that ameliorate skill loss and aid in recovery.

Infantile proteopathy

A *proteopathy* is a condition in which the structure of particular proteins is altered, placing stress on the workings of the cell and increasing the likelihood of cell damage and death. Classic examples include some of the adult and senile neurodegenerative conditions like Alzheimer's disease, with its characteristic Tau protein neurofibrillary tangles and plaques; Lewy body dementia, with its Lewy bodies composed of misfolded α-synuclein protein; and Huntington's disease, in which proteins produced from the mutated *HTT* gene contain expanded numbers of the amino acid glutamine, which ultimately leads to misfolding and aggregation of the Huntingtin protein.

Scientists are learning, however, that not all forms of proteopathy are limited to adulthood and senility. Some in fact occur in infancy and early childhood and may be responsible for specific forms of intellectual disability and developmental delay. Unlike their adult counterparts, infantile proteopathies do not necessarily appear like classic cases of progressive neurodegeneration. Instead, given the remarkable biological plasticity of youth, infantile proteopathies may not result in obvious tissue damage as in senile dementia, but they may impair cell function in other ways by affecting cell development (Sarnat & Flores-Sarnat, 2015).

One form of infantile proteopathy—specifically a *tauopathy*— with overlap with autism is tuberous sclerosis (TSC), a condition that is due to mutations in either the *TSC1* or *TSC2* genes. Tuberous sclerosis occurs in no more than five in 10,000 births and is characterized by benign tumor-like growths in organs such as the skin, brain, heart, kidneys, and lungs. *TSC2* mutations are the most common mutation in tuberous sclerosis, composing more than two thirds of that population (Numis et al., 2011). Autism occurs in about 40 percent of people with the condition, although infrequently in the presence of *TSC1* mutations (~3%). Instead, *TSC2* mutations are responsible for about 75 percent of cases of tuberous sclerosis-associated autism.

Down syndrome, like tuberous sclerosis, also shares significant comorbidity with autism, occurring in about 13 percent of that population (Capone et al., 2005). Unfortunately, many people with Down's go on to develop Alzheimer's disease, with prevalence rates at 40 percent by ages 50–59 (Holland et al., 1998). Down's, like classic Alzheimer's, is a tauopathy exhibiting evidence of neurofibrillary tangles and plaques in the brains of those affected (Cárdenas et al., 2012).

Regression is a characteristically autistic phenomenon, regardless of whether it occurs alongside idiopathic autism or is associated with a genetic syndrome. In Down syndrome with comorbid autism, an astounding 50 percent of children experience a loss in language or sociocommunicative skills (Castillo et al., 2008). Different from idiopathic autism, however, regression in these patients is more likely to occur in late childhood. But similar to the idiopathic form, many individuals with Down's do not develop autism until the time of their regression (Worley et al., 2015).

Because Down syndrome is considered partly a tauopathy, it begs the question whether autistic regression in Down's is the result of Tau pathology. Likewise, it also suggests other forms of autistic regression could be the result of infantile proteopathies.

Crossroads at the synapse

Although there has been much emphasis placed on the presence of neurofibrillary tangles and plaques in the advanced Alzheimer's brain, the root of dementia seems to lie within the synapse (reviewed in Krüger & Mandelkow, 2016). Scientists have found, for instance, that laboratory mice that express a mutated form of Tau begin to have memory impairment when their synapses begin to fail, which occurs long before they develop neurofibrillary tangles and plaques

(Van der Jeugd et al., 2012). To confuse matters more, tangles and plaques are also common findings in the brains of elderly who don't experience dementia, suggesting that in low numbers they are part of a normal continuum of aging (Arnold et al., 2013; Mufson et al., 2016).

Alpha-synuclein, a protein known for its involvement in Lewy body dementia, is also responsible for some rarer forms of Alzheimer's disease, Parkinson's, and even multiple system atrophy (Cheng, Vivacqua, & Yu, 2011). Although its cellular functions are not well understood, it is richly expressed at the synapse and may be involved in neurotransmitter release and synaptic plasticity. Similarly, the Huntingtin protein, responsible for Huntington's disease, is also enriched within the synapse, and the early pathology of the disease is characterized by synaptic impairment long before symptoms have become manifest (Milnerwood & Raymond, 2010). All of this work suggests that the synapse is a major seat of vulnerability in some neurodegenerative diseases (Wishart, Parson, & Gillingwater, 2006).

While it is too early to say whether autistic regression is an infantile form of non-progressive neurodegeneration, they do have some features in common, most strikingly a distinctive loss of already acquired skills. Recent research suggests that autistic children who harbor mutations in synaptic genes are more likely to experience regression than children with other types of mutations (Goin-Kochel et al., 2017). In addition, our own recent work indicates that a significant number of different forms of syndromic autism share certain clinical neurodegenerative-like features, such as evidence of brain atrophy and psychomotor dysfunction like spasticity and hyperreflexia (overactive reflexes) (Casanova et al., 2017a). Together, this work provides early yet tantalizing evidence that synaptic dysfunction may be a key player in autistic regression. Meanwhile, epilepsies, illness/autoimmunity, proteopathies, and oxidative stress can all converge on a vulnerable synapse, tipping a precariously balanced scale.

CLINICAL CONSIDERATIONS

The best way to reduce the occurrence of autistic regression is to identify the underlying causes and develop treatments that target these specific vulnerabilities. Ideally, diagnosis occurs before regression happens—however, some metabolic and immune disorders may not be apparent until regression onset. Yet even after the onset of regression, treatment application may alleviate regression severity and ultimately alter its course, providing better outcomes for these children. In order to do this, however, we require more research into the etiologies of regression and the heritable factors that underlie the conditions.

Some types of regression follow certain triggers. Often this comes in the form of an immune challenge, regardless of whether the underlying disorder is metabolic or immunological. In addition, this immune challenge may either be an exposure to wild-type illness (as it occurs in nature) or to inoculation. This unfortunately poses a particular conundrum for healthcare professionals and parents alike, because vaccinations protect against wild-type infections but may also trigger onset of illness. Therefore, to go unvaccinated poses similar risks to those associated with inoculation. What to do in such circumstances?

Although research is poor in this area, there are some possible avenues of further study. First, we know that altered vaccination schedules affect the rates of adverse reactions (e.g. Englund et al., 2005; Nolan et al., 2002). Combining vaccines modestly increases the likelihood of adverse reaction, suggesting that dividing vaccinations may reduce risk, while also providing sufficient protection against wild-type illness and maintaining overall heard immunity.

In addition, should an infant or child experience a significant adverse reaction to a particular vaccination, doctors and parents should discuss whether the vaccine schedule needs to be further altered to reduce the likelihood of reactivity or even discontinued altogether. This should be on a case-by-case basis. Before vaccination, doctors also need to discuss with parents the differences between what is considered a *significant adverse reaction* and a *typical reaction*, as many vaccines trigger a mild immune response that is normally of little risk to the child.

Finally, it is important that doctors take a full history not only of the child but also of first-degree relatives. Familial symptoms and disorders indicative of immune and/or metabolic dysregulation should be suspect, informing the doctor that an altered vaccination schedule may be wise. In taking these precautions, we may reduce the number of serious adverse reactions children have following inoculation while also protecting them and others around them from significant, potentially life-threatening, illness.

Chapter Six

AUTISM AND EPILEPSY

THE HISTORY OF EPILEPSY

According to the Grecian physician, Hippocrates, now known as the Father of Medicine, the cause of epilepsy lay within the brain.

> The popular superstition, the magicians, the wizards and charlatans, who named the disease sacred, are being attacked. The alleged divine character is only a shelter for ignorance and fraudulent practices. The assumption of the gods being its cause reveals those people as fundamentally impious, for the gods do not make men's bodies unclean, as the magicians would have them believe. ... [Epilepsy's] cause lies in the brain, the releasing factors of the seizures are cold, sun and winds which change the consistency of the brain. Therefore, epilepsy can and must be treated not by magic, but by diet and drugs.
>
> (Hippocrates, cited in Temkin, 1994)

Prior to his work, the ancient Greeks believed that illness, regardless of its symptoms, was a disease that was sent by the gods or spirits and affected the entirety of the human body. Epilepsy, in particular, was a sickness of the soul and could be attributed to different deities depending upon the specific epileptic symptoms present. The ill would, therefore, often seek sanctuary and healing from magico-religious physics who set up practice near mountains or natural springs, and who in turn would provide proper diet, exercise, and baths for the sick—often for considerable fees (Haykin, 2012).

The *Hippocratic Corpus*, which is a collection of medical texts associated with the works and teachings of Hippocrates, established a rational scientific interpretation of "the sacred illness" as a sickness of the body with a specific, natural cause. For this rational approach,

Hippocrates' work was lauded by the post-Socratic Greek philosophers Plato and Aristotle.

Unfortunately, with the rise of early Christianity in Europe came a revival of superstitions surrounding epilepsy. No longer was the epileptic deemed afflicted by the gods, as in Grecian times—the epileptic was instead possessed by the Devil or demons. And worse still, people with epilepsy were viewed as demonically contagious, resulting in considerable stigmatization and their isolation. As one 15th-century professor instructed, "Therefore, neither talk nor bathe with him, since by their mere breath they infect people" (cited in Temkin, 1945). Sadly, even by the 18th century, epilepsy was still viewed as infectious.

With the rise of the philosophical Enlightenment in Europe in the 17th century, philosopher-intellectuals slowly sought to demystify the roots of human illness, including epilepsy, seeking explanation in natural rather than spiritual causes. In particular, the works of William Cullen (1710–1790) and Samuel-Auguste Tissot (1728–1797) set the stage for the future of epileptology, in which they outlined and studied several types of epilepsy (Magiorkinis et al., 2014).

The study of epilepsy spread throughout France, driven by notable physicians such as Maisonneuve, Calmeil, and Esquirol. However, it was work by the English neurologist John Hughlings Jackson (Figure 6.1) that turned the tides of epileptology and gave the condition its first true physiologic definition. He wrote: "Epilepsy is the name for occasional, sudden, excessive, rapid and local discharges of grey matter" (reviewed in Magiorkinis et al., 2014, p. 2). As you will see, this definition is very similar to the one we utilize today.

Much of Jackson's work was based on lesion studies, in which localized damage or some other type of structural disturbance to the brain correlated with the seat of epilepsy.

Around the same time, two German physicians, Gustav Fritsch and Eduard Hitzig, performed a series of experiments that laid additional groundwork for Jackson's theory. The two German physicians experimented on dogs—utilizing methods that are thankfully considered unethical by today's research standards—by exposing the brain and stimulating it with current from a battery. This led to muscle contractions that varied depending upon the motor region of the brain that was stimulated. In addition, it also showed that symptoms of a seizure could be replicated through excitatory stimulation, lending credence to Jackson's theory of gray matter "discharges" (Magiorkinis et al., 2014).

Figure 6.1: The famous neurologist John Hughlings Jackson, who is well known for his research on epilepsy

Work on epilepsy exploded in the 20th century and was buoyed by the invention and application of the electroencephalogram (EEG), which is used to measure the electrical activity of the brain and is a common tool for diagnosis today. This work was furthered by the invention of the patch-clamp technique by Erwin Neher in 1944 that allowed the research scientist to measure the flow of current through individual ion channels of the cell, leading to the discovery of the importance of calcium channels in epileptogenesis. Neher and his colleague Bert Sakmann went on to win the Nobel Prize in 1992 for their invention (Magiorkinis et al., 2014).

Epilepsy in autism

Epilepsy in autism became a focus of scientific inquiry during the 1960s. By the 1970s, several observations further linked the two conditions, notably the frequent co-occurrence of infantile spasms and autism, as well as high occurrence rates of autism in the condition known as tuberous sclerosis, which itself is known for high rates of epilepsy comorbidity (reviewed by Tuchmann, Moshé, & Rapin, 2009).

Since that time, scientists have argued over the frequency of epilepsy in autism, reporting as little as 5 percent to as much as 46 percent of sample populations (Spence & Schneider, 2009). However, this also does not include a large minority of people with autism who exhibit abnormal EEG activity but have no apparent behavioral manifestations of seizures. Therefore, the number of people on the autism spectrum with EEG abnormalities, with or without epilepsy, is substantial.

Of interest, there are ongoing trials to treat individuals with autism and abnormal EEG activity who do not manifest apparent seizures, in the hope that some of the severity of autism may also be alleviated. This work will further help to address where precisely the dividing line lies between autism and epilepsy, whether they are simply different but overlapping conditions or, at least in some cases, may be one and the same.

WHAT IS A SEIZURE?

Most readers are probably somewhat familiar with the terms "epilepsy" and "seizure." Thankfully, at least one benefit of our television- and internet-oriented culture is that people tend to have a greater familiarity with medicalese, even if we are that much more likely to misuse it. As the 18th-century poet Alexander Pope wrote, "A little learning is a dangerous thing." But in this case, these types of resources have familiarized us with a variety of medical terms, including "epilepsy."

According to the International League Against Epilepsy (ILAE), a worldwide group of physicians and health professionals vested in the study and treatment of epilepsy, an epileptic seizure is defined as, "a transient occurrence of signs and/or symptoms due to abnormal excessive and synchronous neuronal activity in the brain" (reviewed in Engel, 2013, p. 4). (We will delve later into what is meant by the terms "excessive" and "synchronous.")

Subclinical or non-convulsive seizures can also occur even when there is no recognizable change in cognition or behavior but the EEG shows abnormal brainwave activity, consisting of spike or spike-and-wave discharges (Tuchman et al., 2009). Therefore, the person may look and feel relatively normal but their brainwave activity in fact indicates that they are having a seizure. In contrast, there are also times when changes to cognition or behaviors characteristic of seizure activity happen but are not accompanied by an abnormal EEG reading. In these instances, a diagnosis is made primarily based on the symptom history of the patient. Still, this can sometimes be a challenge since some types of seizures may have ambiguous symptom presentations, such as absence seizures that can be mistaken simply for inattentiveness or day-dreaming.

When looked at over a lifetime, about 4 percent of people will develop epilepsy (Epilepsy Foundation, 2016). However, this includes not only people who experience epilepsy because of developmental factors such as we'll be discussing in further sections, it also includes people who develop seizures following head trauma, like traumatic brain injury or stroke, or as a result of brain tumors, certain types of dementia, and infections of the central nervous system (Centers for Disease Control and Prevention, 2016b; Kotila & Waltimo, 1992; Palop & Mucke, 2009; Yeh et al., 2013). In addition, about 5 percent of infants and young toddlers will experience a fever-associated (febrile) seizure during illness or following vaccination, although this in itself is not considered epilepsy (Stafstrom, 2002). After experiencing a febrile seizure, the majority of children will not have any further seizures nor go on to develop epilepsy proper.

When we look at the prevalence of seizure history in children at any one time, we see that epilepsy occurs in about 1 percent of the population, which is roughly the occurrence rate of autism (1–2%) (Centers for Disease Control and Prevention, 2016a, 2016b). Autism and epilepsy co-occur with one another about 30 percent of the time, respectively (reviewed in Tuchman et al., 2009). Meanwhile, an additional 20 percent of individuals with autism have epileptic-like discharges but do not appear to show any identifiable cognitive or behavioral changes during these discharges (Hughes & Melyn, 2005). In autistic children without intellectual disability, rates of epilepsy hover around 8 percent (Amiet et al., 2008; McCue et al., 2016). Rates of epilepsy further increase with the onset of puberty (Rossi, Posar, & Parmeggiani, 2000).

Although there is a significant relationship between autism and epilepsy, the major risk factor for developing epilepsy in autism is the presence of intellectual disability. Individuals with both autism and intellectual disability are almost seven times more likely to experience seizures, affecting about 40 percent of that subpopulation. Meanwhile, autistic individuals without intellectual disability or other epilepsy-related familial risk factors, such as close relatives with a seizure disorder, share a similar rate of epilepsy to that seen in children with language impairment without autism (reviewed in Tuchman et al., 2009). While that rate is dramatically lower than we see in autism with intellectual disability, it is still six times more common than in the general population.

What's going on in the brain during a seizure?

During a seizure, excitatory neurons begin to fire excessively. Inhibitory cells that normally work to control these excitatory neurons, for various reasons, are not able to keep up with the demand and the excitation grows out of control. During that time, more and more neurons are recruited into the seizure, causing them to fire synchronously and allowing the seizure activity to spread to adjacent or distant-but-connected regions. Sometimes, as in the case of a generalized seizure, this activity can spread throughout the brain and cause a loss of consciousness and major muscle contractions (grand mal). The excessive, synchronous firing gives rise to the classic "spike and wave" formation seen on an EEG during a seizure, in which the term "spike" refers to the high-amplitude excitatory waveform (the hills), meanwhile, "waves" are the small valleys in between the spikes that reflect a brief drop in excitation (Engel, 2013) (Figure 6.2).

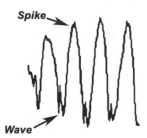

Figure 6.2: Diagram of the spike and wave formation that is often seen on EEG during a seizure

BRAIN MALFORMATIONS UNDERLYING EPILEPSY

It is usually easier to understand what triggers epilepsy when seizures follow an acute event, like head trauma or a tumor. However, when it comes to identifying the roots of developmental or "idiopathic" epilepsy the picture becomes decidedly muddier.

About 15 percent of childhood epilepsies are refractory (resistant) to pharmacologic treatment. In approximately 40 percent of those cases, clinicians are able to identify some type of cortical malformation (Barkovich, Dobyns, & Guerrini, 2015). Of these treatment-resistant malformations, focal cortical dysplasias (FCD), a type of lesion we discussed in Chapter 2, make up a significant portion.

To refresh the reader's memory, FCD refers to a localized area of the brain in which neurons have failed to develop properly (Figure 6.3). In some cases, this may be due to failed migration of neurons, but in other instances neurons may have reached their targets but do not have the structural features common to those regions. They may, for instance, appear disoriented in space, failing to form the neat rows and columns of excitatory cells characteristic of cortex. In other cases, some excitatory cells may have grown abnormally large, known as *hypertrophic* neurons. In addition, these areas may contain unusually high numbers of glial (helper) cells and activated microglia, probably a reflection of the stress that epileptic activity puts on these regions, requiring help to repair frequent cellular damage (Sisodiya et al., 2009).

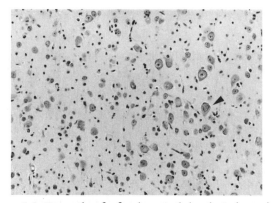

Figure 6.3: Example of a focal cortical dysplasia (arrow) in a portion of epileptic tissue that has been surgically removed
(Image based on Sisodiya et al., 2009)

On brain imaging, FCD often appear as thickening or thinning of focal regions of the cortex. In addition, there is sometimes visible blurring of the junction between the gray and white matter, suggesting some cells have failed to fully migrate into the gray matter region (Kabat & Król, 2012). Interestingly, both of these features have been found in autism, once again highlighting the causal overlap in autism and epilepsy (Avino & Hutsler, 2010; Casanova, El-Baz, et al., 2013).

The brain is such a complex organ. Although it has considerable potential for plasticity and healing, it is also sensitive to changes in developmental timing. Scientists have theorized that the evolution of the human brain is not only rooted in the aggregation of larger quantities of gray matter, but in small variations in developmental timing between brain regions (Deacon, 2000). These differences in timing are known as "heterochronies" or literally "other time." Most typically, the term "heterochrony" is used by biologists when comparing organ structures across different species, such as the difference in forearm structure between a mouse and a bat. However, it is also a useful term to describe how small changes in the timing of developmental events can lead to premature or delayed maturation of cells that results in structural and functional changes in that brain region. It is likely that regional mis-timing is a significant risk factor in the development of FCD, whether it is the result of gene mutations or environmental factors.

THE GENETICS OF EPILEPSY

Similar to autism, the genetic risk for epilepsy is complex. In the early days of epilepsy research, scientists focused mainly on "channelopathies." Channelopathies are caused by impaired function in ion channels within the central nervous system and are typically either genetic or autoimmune in origin. Ions are charged particles, such as sodium and calcium, which are major players in cellular communication. Ion channels regulate the flow of charged ions into and out of the cell, dynamically changing the capacity of that cell to communicate with other cells. For instance, there are several sodium channel subunit genes that, when mutated, are strong risk factors for both epilepsy and autism, including *SCN1A*, *SCN1B*, and *SCN2A*. *SCN1A* mutations often lead to a condition known as Dravet syndrome, which we discussed in the previous chapter, in which the mutation results in a persistent inward current of sodium into the cell, leading to excessive excitation. Mutations in subunits of the GABA receptor, which are important inhibitory mechanisms of the cell, are also involved both in epilepsy and autism (reviewed in Poduri & Lowenstein, 2011).

Scientists initially over-focused on channelopathies, primarily because the pathology in relation to epilepsy was more easily understood. Ion channels help control excitation; therefore, in a condition that is partly defined by excess excitation, defects in those channels are a logical place to look.

Although scientists initially focused on channelopathies because of their simplicity, we now realize that channelopathies are only the tip of the iceberg and make up a minority of heritable epilepsies. There are epilepsies, for instance, that are associated with mutations in genes that control early development. These conditions typically have congenital malformations as an associated feature. Meanwhile, there are other forms of epilepsy that do not tend to have related physical features but have neurodegenerative traits such as mild brain atrophy or various movement disorders. These conditions tend to be associated with mutations in genes that code for aspects of cell metabolism, like enzyme functions and transporter activities (Casanova et al., 2016). Similar to autism, epilepsies associated with rare gene mutations tend to have cognitive impairment. On the other hand, we know comparatively little about genetic risk for epilepsy in those with average or above-average IQs.

Epilepsy researchers have also come to realize that some heritable forms of epilepsy are associated with copy number variants (CNV) that comprise multiple genes. As with many CNVs in autism, there is no single major effect gene but multiple genes acting in concert (reviewed in Poduri & Lowenstein, 2011).

LOW SEIZURE THRESHOLD IN THE INFANT AND TODDLER BRAIN

Infant and toddler brains are hyper-excitable compared with the adult brain and are particularly prone to seizure activity. Ironically, they have a lower risk for developing epilepsy because the brain at this young age is poorly interconnected compared with older children and adults, which prevents seizures from spreading and gaining a pathological foothold. In contrast, the older child and adult brains are comparatively less excitable, but if seizures do occur they spread more easily into adjacent regions, triggering the classic cognitive and behavioral manifestations of epilepsy.

One major reason for the early excitatory–inhibitory imbalance in the infant and toddler brain is the delayed development of cells known as "glia." These cells act as supports for neurons—however, in the young brain they are still underdeveloped. In the mature brain, glial cells known as astrocytes help to recycle neurotransmitters after they are released by neurons, which effectively limits the amount of time the neurotransmitters can stimulate a neighboring cell. In the young brain, since astrocytes are not recycling neurotransmitters as efficiently because of their immaturity, the neurons they are supporting may get over-excited, leading to seizure-like activity (Engel, 2013). With time, as astrocytes continue to mature, the threshold for seizure activity gradually rises, decreasing the likelihood of seizures.

Another cell, the inhibitory interneuron, is also important for seizure propensity. Even though inhibitory neurons are some of the first cells to be produced in the embryonic brain, their synapses are some of the last to mature after birth (Engel, 2013). This invariably leads to lopsided excitation–inhibition between the excitatory pyramidal neurons and the inhibitory interneurons, with the former overpowering the latter. As we see with the immature astrocytes, immature inhibitory synapses decrease the threshold for seizure activity in the infant/toddler brain making excessive excitation all the more likely. However, as we described earlier, serious seizures are less likely to occur because the connections between neurons are also relatively immature, placing a developmental stopgap on the spread of seizure activity.

The excitatory–inhibitory imbalance in the young brain may be the main reason febrile (fever-induced) seizures are typically relegated to this age group. Scientists believe that certain immune factors known as "cytokines" not only trigger the induction of a fever but also increase excitation within the brain, leading to isolated seizure events in approximately 5 percent of children (Serdaroğlu et al., 2009; Stafstrom, 2002). As the child ages, risk for febrile seizures decreases as glial cells and inhibitory interneurons continue to mature.

How does seizure threshold relate to autism?

Similar to epilepsy, there is an excitatory–inhibitory imbalance in autism (Casanova et al., 2003; Rubenstein & Merzenich, 2003). Interestingly, the severity of autism symptoms tends to reach its zenith during the late infancy/toddler period—the same time in which the brain is especially hyper-excitable and seizure threshold is reduced. It is also during this period that autistic regression occurs, in some instances following an illness or other immune challenge. A notable example includes children with autism who also have a mitochondrial illness, in which the majority experience regression following a fever-associated illness or inoculation (Shoffner et al., 2010). The majority of individuals with Dravet syndrome, mentioned earlier, also experiences seizure onset and regression in skills following an immunological challenge, suggesting that the immune system and peculiarities of developmental timing as discussed above may play deciding roles in autistic regression and seizure onset (McIntosh et al., 2010).

EPILEPSY IN FEMALES ON THE AUTISM SPECTRUM
Hormones

The sex ratio in autism is roughly four males for every one female. Although there are twice as many autistic males as females who have epilepsy, this is because the absolute number of autistic boys far exceeds the number of girls. Instead, epilepsy rates are higher in girls by about 15% (for examples see Amiet et al., 2008; Blackmon et al., 2016; Bolton et al., 2011). Although epilepsy shares strong ties with intellectual disability and girls have a disproportionate rate of diagnosis, it is unlikely that the level of cognitive functioning is the sole reason for the discrepancy. It is well recognized, for instance, that idiopathic epilepsy is more common in women in general (McHugh & Delanty, 2008). And though the mechanisms of this vulnerability are not agreed upon by doctors and scientists, hormones—especially estrogen and progesterone—greatly affect seizure threshold.

Estrogen and progesterone are major hormones of the female body that help to drive the reproductive cycle. While estrogen often has an excitatory effect on the brain, progesterone in contrast behaves in an inhibitory manner. Therefore, the balance between progesterone and estrogen is vital in determining seizure threshold in women. During menstruation, for instance, a portion of women with epilepsy experience worsening of their seizures, which seems to be directly related to progesterone withdrawal (the inhibitory hormone) (El-Khayat et al., 2008). Many of these women who experience a worsening of their symptoms during menses also have a higher estrogen-to-progesterone ratio throughout their cycle compared to other women with epilepsy whose symptoms do not fluctuate as much with their cycles.

Low progesterone levels seen in some epileptic women can be a sign of a hormonal disorder. For example, it is a major feature of polycystic ovary syndrome (PCOS) (mentioned in Chapter 4), which is the most common cause of infertility in women, affecting roughly 10–12 percent of the female population (Amato et al., 2011; March et al., 2009). Unfortunately, there is evidence that the use of Depakote in the treatment of epilepsy—one of the most potent anti-seizure medications—can trigger PCOS in some women (Betts et al., 2003). However, even though drugs like Depakote have been linked with higher PCOS rates in epileptic women, people with epilepsy have higher rates of hormone disorders over all, males included (Herzog, 2008).

As we discussed in Chapter 4, studies indicate that autistic women and their mothers have higher rates of PCOS than the general population, suggesting links between autism, epilepsy, and hormonal disorders (Ingudomnukul et al., 2007). Interestingly, however, we have also found that women with both autism and generalized joint hypermobility (GJH) have unusually high rates of PCOS compared to their non-GJH counterparts (25% vs. 8%). This suggests that this subpopulation of women could be driving some of the effects we are seeing in the larger female ASD population (Casanova et al., 2018).

Male autism stereotypes and how they may affect prevalence rates

It has become better recognized that the diagnostic criteria for autism are biased towards males because they were primarily modeled after male patients. Many girls and women, including those whose IQs fall below 70, must often exhibit exaggerated symptoms compared to their male counterparts in order to receive the same diagnosis (Dworzynski et al., 2012). This can lead to an apparent skewing of the spectrum, overrepresenting girls who are more severely affected and giving an inaccurate picture of the full range of autism in females.

Because epilepsy and IQ share a strong relationship with one another, this can also lead to the appearance that epilepsy is more common in autistic women than in men (Bolton et al., 2011). However, rates of epilepsy in women with IQ > 70 are similar to those seen in high-functioning autism in general (~6–7%) (Ingudomnukul et al., 2007; Tuchman et al., 2009).

Children with brain malformations, such as the focal cortical dysplasia we discussed earlier, are more likely to develop epilepsy that is less responsive to pharmacologic intervention. Interestingly, scientists have found that although autistic males outnumber autistic females by about four-to-one, the gender ratio in cases with treatment-resistant epilepsy is closer to two-to-one (Blackmon et al., 2016). In addition, girls with these features are more likely to have mild brain malformations than their male counterparts.

While some consider this evidence that autistic females are more severely affected than males, the gender-biased diagnostic rates and protective effects of estrogen instead suggest that females have a higher developmental threshold that must be met to reach autism cut-off. In essence, because we use "autism" as the main inclusion criteria for our studies, we are preferentially sampling females who are more severely affected.

But why do women have higher rates of epilepsy in general? Although further research is needed to fully explore this, one possibility is sex differences in brain connectivity. We discussed earlier that the infant/toddler brain is highly excitable and may occasionally give rise to isolated seizures, however, it is less prone towards epilepsy because its cells are immature and the brain is poorly connected overall. When it comes to sex differences in the brain, scientists have found that men tend to have poorer connectivity between the hemispheres of the brain, meanwhile they have enhanced short-range connectivity and modularity within the two hemispheres (a trend shared with autism). Women, on the other hand, usually have stronger connectivity between the hemispheres and the different modules of the brain (Ingalhalikar et al., 2014).

This long-range connectivity may be a major risk factor in the development of epilepsy. Significant seizures result not only from hyperexcitable neurons but also through the synchronous spread of activity to other regions of the brain. Male-specific connectivity patterns may effectively limit the spread and entrenchment of epilepsy—meanwhile, female-typical connectivity patterns provide more avenues for seizures to spread. In addition, cyclic changes to the female hormonal milieu, especially during times of low progesterone (an anticonvulsant hormone), may lower seizure threshold and increase the likelihood of seizure occurrence (Frye & Scalise, 2000).

CLINICAL CONSIDERATIONS

Because epilepsy occurs with such frequency within the autism spectrum and can confer considerable morbidity (and in rare instances even lead to death), there is much interest in its identification and treatment. Usually, treatment involves the use of typical anticonvulsants, however in the case of postpubertal females with epilepsy, hormone medications, such as birth control, may offer another useful avenue to complement anticonvulsant therapy.

In a minority of people whose epilepsy is poorly controlled with medications, they may be candidates for surgical resection (removal of an area of brain tissue). This can be done provided a single focal point for the seizures exists, doctors are able to identify that focal point with certainty, and it does not occur in an area vital for brain function, such as Wernicke's area that is necessary for the understanding of language. In certain types of extreme and uncontrolled generalized seizures, patients may also be helped by a corpus callosotomy, in which the white matter bridging the two cerebral hemispheres is cut to prevent excessive spread of seizures. These individuals will continue to have seizure activity, but the seizures are limited to a single hemisphere of the brain, preventing the occurrence of "drop attacks" in about 50–75 percent of postsurgical cases.

Many individuals who develop epilepsy may do so because of another disease process, such as a brain tumor or a neurodegenerative disease. As one would expect, mortality rates are high in these subpopulations—the cause generally being unrelated to the epilepsy. However, epilepsy itself can be deadly and approximately 1 in every 100 persons with the condition will die prematurely (Shackleton et al., 1999). In a significant minority of these cases, the cause is unknown and is labeled as *sudden unexpected death in epilepsy* (SUDEP). In these instances, it is not always obvious that the person has died due to convulsions. Some scientists believe that seizures may trigger an irregular heart rhythm leading to heart failure, meanwhile others suspect impairments in breathing or even suffocation from bedding may occur, as is sometimes seen in sudden infant death syndrome (SIDS).

While the causes of SUDEP are poorly understood, it is recommended that the best prevention is through seizure management. For these reasons, it is also important that children, teens, and adults on the autism spectrum are regularly screened for signs of epilepsy, especially in those individuals who may have impairments in communication and cannot describe behavioral manifestations of the condition. Although epilepsy can arise at any time, there are two developmental time periods of vulnerability in autism: preschool and adolescence (Rossi et al., 2000). Therefore, screening during and immediately after these periods is particularly important in the identification of epilepsy and abnormal EEG discharges in autism. In individuals with abnormal EEG but no outward signs of epilepsy, follow-up should be performed regularly should seizures eventually arise.

Chapter Seven

THE NEURODEVELOPMENTAL SPECTRUM

Mental Health for the 21st Century

CONDITIONS THAT OCCUR ALONGSIDE AUTISM

Our understanding of neurodevelopmental conditions has been slowly changing over time. With the advent of the Human Genome Project and the progressive identification of numerous risk genes, it is now apparent that few genetic variations produce the same phenotype across all affected individuals. While a young boy may display fullblown autism, his mother may have generalized anxiety, sensory issues, attention-deficit/hyperactivity disorder (ADHD), and specific learning disability. While in the past we assumed the mother's and son's conditions were different, we are now recognizing that these phenotypic relationships may be two different sides of the same die.

With this in mind, we will review many of the neurodevelopmental conditions that are comorbid with autism, as well as occur at increased frequencies in autism families. Finally, we will show how, at least with some conditions, we are realizing that the same biological propensity can be expressed differently across family members, varying by sex, genetic background, and environmental stressors.

Attention-deficit/hyperactivity disorder

People with ADHD experience challenges with inattention and/or hyperactivity-impulsivity that are often lifelong and begin in early childhood. Although previous editions of the *Diagnostic and Statistical Manual of Mental Disorders* (DSM) designated autism as an exclusionary criterion for ADHD, growing awareness of their overlap has resulted in the removal of that criterion from DSM-5 (American Psychiatric Association, 2013), and the two conditions can now be diagnosed comorbidly.

About 30–50 percent of individuals on the autism spectrum fulfill criteria for ADHD. Likewise, it is estimated that approximately two thirds of those with ADHD have at least some features of autism (Leitner, 2014). People with both autism and ADHD tend to have poorer adaptive functioning and quality of life than those with autism alone, and they are more likely to have additional comorbid psychiatric conditions (Mansour et al., 2017).

Although the two conditions' respective diagnostic criteria share little in common, the conditions nevertheless overlap one another neurobehaviorally. This overlap occurs in areas such as the use of pragmatic language, deficits in theory of mind, and alexithymia (the inability to identify and understand one's emotions) (reviewed in Leitner, 2014). Children with ADHD often experience significant social challenges, although social problems are not considered a core of the condition (Friedman et al., 2003). They may be subjected to peer rejection due to behaviors related to their ADHD, including bossiness, argumentativeness, and inattention. However, there is also a significant minority who experience challenges in social "savoir faire," more akin to the social deficits associated with autism (Cantwell, 1996).

Executive dysfunction, on the other hand, is not a core feature of autism yet is central to ADHD. However, many with autism have challenges in transitioning between tasks, impulse control, verbal and spatial working memory, flexibility, and planning—all of which are subsumed under executive functioning (Hughes, Russell, & Robbins, 1994; Lai et al., 2016). Impairments in cognitive flexibility (i.e. task switching) and planning tend to characterize individuals with both autism and ADHD. Meanwhile, features such as inattentiveness and working memory deficits are nonspecific and occur across any combination of these comorbid conditions (Craig et al., 2016).

Intellectual disability and specific learning disorder

We will be discussing autism and intellectual disability (ID) extensively in Chapter 9 and, therefore, won't preview the material except to say that a large minority of those on the autism spectrum test within the intellectually disabled range. However, people with autism may also have learning disabilities.

To the chagrin of those communicating between English-speaking countries, we use the term, "learning disability," to mean two different things. Those within the Americas (the United States and Canada) use the terms "specific learning disorder" and "learning disability/ disorder" interchangeably, referring to deficits in specific areas of learning in an individual who has otherwise average or above-average intelligence. People within the United Kingdom and Australia, however, use "learning disability" to refer to those with an IQ < 70. Instead, they use the terms, "learning difficulties," or "specific learning difficulties" to refer to challenges in academic learning in a person with normal intelligence. This accidental overlap in terminology can prove challenging to anyone studying the literature on learning disabilities. Here, however, we elect to use the Americanized interpretation of the term "learning disability" when referring to isolated learning deficits, so please keep that in mind.

The definition of "learning disability" may vary according to context. In everyday use it refers to learning difficulties in one or more of the following:

- auditory/visual perception

- sequencing, abstraction, and organization of information

- working, short-term, and long-term memory

- expressive language

- fine or gross motor coordination.

In medicalese, "learning disability" refers to deficits in reading, mathematics, or written expression. Within the legal realm, it includes "such conditions as perceptual disabilities, brain injury, minimal brain dysfunction, dyslexia, and developmental aphasia" but not "the result of visual, hearing, or motor disabilities, of mental retardation, of emotional disturbance, or of environmental, cultural, or economic disadvantage" (20 U.S. Code Section 1401 (30)). As you can see, the term describes a variety of deficits in various stages of information processing.

Here, we will focus on the term as it is defined by the DSM-5, due to the research literature available on the subject. (See Table 7.1 for a description of the recognized learning disabilities.)

Table 7.1: Recognized learning disabilities

Impairment in reading	Impairment in written	Impairment in mathematics
includes any of the following: • word reading accuracy • reading rate or fluency • reading comprehension	includes any of the following: • spelling accuracy • grammar and punctuation accuracy • clarity of organization or written expression	includes any of the following: • number sense • memorization of arithmetic facts • accurate or fluent calculation • accurate math reasoning

Reading

Most readers are likely familiar with the term "dyslexia," which refers to deficits in basic phonological decoding skills (i.e. the sound of words) that leads to problems in both reading and writing. Though the science is sparse, previous research suggests that dyslexia occurs in about one in seven individuals with high-functioning autism (Hofvander et al., 2009). (Intellectual disability is an exclusionary criterion for specific learning disorder, therefore learning disabilities are only diagnosed in individuals with an IQ > 70.)

In contrast, non-dyslexic deficits in reading comprehension have garnered more attention in autism research due to interest in the condition known as "hyperlexia." Hyperlexia is the precocious ability to read—a feature sometimes accompanied by poor reading comprehension. Therefore, while a child may be capable of decoding words phonologically above his or her age level, he or she may have little to no understanding of what is being read.

According to Darold Treffert (2011), a world expert on savantism, precocious readers with hyperlexia can be divided into three subtypes:

• those without autism or autistic-like traits

• those with an autism spectrum condition

• those with autistic-like traits but who fail to meet full autism criteria.

Like most complex conditions, the background on which hyperlexia rests forms a spectrum of severity ranging from those with fullblown autism to gifted children with relatively preserved sociocommunication skills.

Though not all children with hyperlexia experience deficits in reading comprehension, many do. They may exhibit exceptional skill in phonological decoding yet fail to use context to aid in that decoding (Aram, 1997). For instance, some hyperlexic children have difficulty pronouncing homonyms correctly, which are words that are spelled the same but sound different based on contextual meaning of the sentence itself. An example is "lead," which can be interpreted either as "to go in front of" or "a type of metal." Similar to hyperlexic children, children with autism may display dissociations between phonological decoding and comprehension, though most are not precocious readers (Jones et al., 2009; Nation et al., 2006).

Mathematics

Colloquially, deficits in mathematics are known as "dyscalculia." Although this condition has not been studied well in relation to autism, there is some evidence suggesting a small minority of autistic individuals have deficits in the ability to understand and perform mathematical calculations. According to one study, about 6 percent of those with autism have a mathematical deficiency in relation to their general levels of intelligence (Jones et al., 2009). Meanwhile, roughly 16 percent of individuals exhibit particular skill in numerical operations. Interestingly, both people with talents and deficits in numerical ability have similar IQs (~96), while those with average math skills score lower (~80). This suggests that autistic people with mathematical talents and deficits may share more in common than meets the eye.

Mood disorders

Major depression

It can be a challenge to identify mood disturbances in a person who has difficulty communicating. For this reason, it has traditionally been easier to gauge rates of depression in children and adults with autism who are able to clearly identify and communicate those feelings. However, according to parent report, children with poor language skills also experience depressive symptoms similar to their communicative counterparts (Mayes et al., 2011).

Major depression seems to occur in under 20 percent of children with an autism spectrum condition—however, parental reports typically shed light on a further 20–30 percent who have subclinical symptoms (Kim et al., 2000; Mayes et al., 2011). This suggests that sadness and depression are serious comorbid issues impairing quality of life for a large portion of those on the spectrum.

About half of verbal adults with autism report some symptoms of depression and anxiety, while approximately one third of the broader spectrum has a comorbid diagnosis of major depression (Eaves & Ho, 2008; Marriage, Wolverton, & Marriage, 2009). Interestingly, individuals diagnosed with autism after the age of 18, who are typically higher-functioning than their earlier-diagnosed counterparts (in terms of IQ), have almost double the rates of major depression. While this has sometimes been explained away by differences in capacity for self-awareness and self-reflection (How can you be sad if you don't know you're different?), it may also be biology.

Surprisingly, the occurrence of depression in autism seems to be linked with a familial propensity. Although it was a small pilot study, Ghaziuddin and Greden (1998) reported that families of autistic children with depression were themselves more likely to exhibit depression. The authors suggested that depression was therefore a condition distinct from autism. However, we would disagree given the high rates of depression, particularly in mothers of those on the spectrum (Mazefsky, Connor, & Oswald, 2010; Mazefsky, Folstein, & Lainhart, 2008). Were there no shared causal relationship, inheritance patterns would not likely differ so markedly from the general population. Clearly, autism and depression coincide in families more often than expected at random. And therefore autism with and without depression are probably two behaviorally overlapping yet unique biological entities. In addition, familial, and especially maternal, depression may be a risk factor for high-functioning autism.

Bipolar disorder

Bipolar disorder is characterized by alternating moods of mania and depression. In contrast to bipolar I disorder, bipolar II is typified not by manic episodes but by *hypomania*, which is elation or irritability that is less extreme and impairing than genuine mania. About 2.5 percent of the adult population has a diagnosis of a bipolar spectrum disorder, with roughly equal numbers falling under the I and II category headings (Merikangas et al., 2007). Mean age of onset is roughly 25 years.

Although it hasn't been well studied, it is estimated that about 7 percent of the adult autism spectrum population fulfills criteria for bipolar disorder (Stahlberg et al., 2004). And, as with major depression, bipolar is more common in those with high-functioning autism as well as their families, once again suggesting a link between autism severity and familial mood disorders (DeLong & Dwyer, 1988; DeLong, Ritch, & Burch, 2002; Munesue et al., 2008). The relationship vaguely reminds one of the quote by the Roman philosopher Seneca: "*Nullum magnum ingenium sine mixture dementiae fuit*" – "There is no great genius without a mixture of madness."

Anxiety disorders and obsessive-compulsive disorder

There are many types of anxiety disorders, though they each share a common core of excessive fear and anxiety. Under current DSM-5 classification, they include: separation anxiety disorder, selective mutism, specific phobia, social anxiety disorder, panic disorder, agoraphobia, and generalized anxiety disorder. Obsessive-compulsive disorder, though once subsumed under "anxiety disorders," now comprises its own category under anxiety and trauma-based disorders.

In contrast to many other psychiatric conditions, anxiety disorders have been studied comparatively well in autism. About 40 percent of children with autism have at least one anxiety disorder, the most prevalent being specific phobia (Van Steensel, Bögels, & Perrin, 2011). Fear of needles and/or shots is the most common phobia reported in children with autism (~30%), followed by a phobia of loud noises (~10%). In contrast, autistic children tend to have lower rates of phobias common to children in the general population, such as flying, stores, standing in line, bridges, and tunnels (Leyfer et al., 2006). Separation anxiety and social phobia are also common in autism, together comprising about 10 percent of the subpopulation (Leyfer et al., 2006).

Anxiety disorders are extremely common in adults with autism. One small pilot study estimated that more than three quarters of the participants and one third of their first-degree relatives had some form of anxiety disorder (Mazefsky et al., 2008). Within the high-functioning population, Hofvander et al. (2009) estimated that about half suffer from clinical anxiety. Meanwhile, those with autism and intellectual disability have significantly higher levels of panic disorder, agoraphobia, social anxiety, and generalized anxiety compared with individuals with ID alone (Gillot & Standen, 2007). Unfortunately, high levels of anxiety associate with poorer ability to cope with life stressors and represent a significant daily impairment in the lives of those on the spectrum.

Like anxiety disorders, OCD is a common co-occurring condition in autism. Using an assessment adapted for communicative impairment, Leyfer et al. (2006) estimated that about 37 percent of children in their study fulfilled criteria for OCD, while another 6 percent presented with subclinical symptoms. Likewise, they reported that children on the spectrum with ID were fourteen times more likely to have OCD than those with ID alone. Interestingly, however, research suggests autism-associated OCD is less severe than those with pure OCD (Cath et al., 2008).

Motor disorders

Motor delays and developmental coordination disorder

Mood and anxiety disorders typically fall under the purview of psychiatry. For this reason, developmental history does not play an integral part in their respective diagnoses. Some motor disorders, however, are defined in reference to deviations from age norms. For instance, if a three-year-old child exhibits the sociocommunicative and motor skills of a two-year-old, we would say he or she is "delayed." If on the other hand that same child is a toe-walker—a feature atypical for most children—we would refer to the toe walking as a "divergent" symptom because it doesn't normally occur during development. Finally, if we see a child who has age-appropriate skills in socialization and communication but is motorically delayed or divergent, we say that child has "dissociated" development (Pellegrino, 2013). Delay, divergence, and dissociation are helpful terms for the clinician to communicate a child's deficits to parents and other clinicians as well as to aid in the formulation of a therapeutic plan.

The official label used for people who have significant motor skills deficits, which are not otherwise due to intellectual disability, visual impairment, or some other neurological impairment, is *developmental coordination disorder* (DCD). Often, people with this condition may be clumsy, inaccurate, or slow when performing motor tasks. They may have difficulty playing sports; may drop or bump into objects frequently; and may have poor handwriting, a deficit that overlaps with specific learning disorders of written expression.

Not all individuals with motor delays will go on to receive the label of DCD. For instance, one study found that while 63 percent of young autistic children had motor deficits, similar deficits were present in only 38 percent of older children, suggesting some outgrow their motor delays or the deficits had become subclinical (Ming, Brimacombe, & Wagner, 2007). Although boys and girls can differ in the rate of acquisition of motor milestones, frequency of motor delay is not significantly different between girls and boys on the spectrum (Giarelli et al., 2010). Interestingly, this differs from DCD in general, in which boys are preferentially more affected than girls (Kirby & Sugden, 2007).

Tic disorders

Tics are sudden twitches, movements, or vocalizations. Though they are not "involuntary" like a reflex, they are considered "*un*voluntary" and can be temporarily suppressed. Suppression, however, usually causes the individual significant distress, leading to the re-emergence of the tic at a later time. As described by Dr. Samuel Zinner, an expert in the study of tic disorders, "Tics are a semi-voluntary or voluntary response to involuntary sensation" (Seattle Children's Hospital Research Foundation, 2013). He further explains that, "If you ask a person with a tic disorder, they can describe an unpleasant urge/sensation right before the tic occurs." Zinner relates this to a similarly unpleasant sensation we have all experienced: trying to resist the urge to blink. The longer we hold our eyes open, the more unpleasant the sensation becomes and the more difficult it is to resist the urge. Similar to the blinking scenario, the person with a tic disorder experiences a sensation of relief after performing the tic. Therefore, even though compulsions, habits, and stereotypies in autism may appear similar to tics to an outside observer, only tics are associated with internal sensations of initial urgency and then relief upon completion of the tic (Seattle Children's Hospital Research Foundation, 2013).

The DSM-5 recognizes several different tic disorders. The best known tic disorder is Tourette's syndrome, in which the individual presents with multiple motor and vocal tics. Tourette's occurs in approximately 1 percent of the general population according to Dr. Zinner. The other tic disorders are similar but have fewer tics and/or occur for a shorter duration of time.

Tic disorders, though not extremely common in autism, occur at elevated rates within the spectrum. Studies have typically reported a 6–8 percent occurrence rate, which is several times higher than rates seen in the general population (Baron-Cohen et al., 1999; Bitsko et al., 2014; Seattle Children's Hospital Research Foundation, 2013). In contrast, more than one fifth of people with Tourette's syndrome meet cutoff for autism, suggesting that while Tourette's may not be extremely common in autism, autism is very common in Tourette's syndrome (Darrow et al., 2017). In addition, similar to autism, boys are more likely to have tic disorders than girls for reasons not well understood (Centers for Disease Control and Prevention, 2017).

Psychotic disorders

We have already discussed bipolar disorder, which, though considered a mood disorder, can also present with symptoms of psychosis during episodes of mania. However, it is not considered a psychotic disorder as such. Instead, most psychotic disorders are collected in the DSM-5 under the umbrella label "Schizophrenia Spectrum and Other Psychotic Disorders." They comprise schizophrenia, schizophreniform disorder, schizoaffective disorder, catatonia, delusional disorder, and brief psychotic disorder.

Although all of these conditions vary from one another, they share many of the key features that define psychotic disorders. Classically, these are broken down into positive and negative symptoms. According to the DSM-5, positive symptoms include:

- hallucinations

- delusions

- disorganized thinking or speech

- disorganized or abnormal motor behavior, such as catatonia (reduced reactivity to the environment; see Figure 7.1).

Figure 7.1: Catatonic patients with various psychoses
pictured around the turn of the 20th century
(Image from Nervous and Mental Diseases by Church and Peterson, 1908)

In contrast, negative symptoms primarily include reduced emotional expression and avolition (lack of motivation). These symptoms account for most of the impairment in schizophrenia, even though the psychosis itself can be extremely distressing. For instance, individuals may sit for long periods of time, showing minimal interest in life and everyday activities. This can lead to career loss, damage to relationships with family and friends, and reinforce the isolation a person with schizophrenia is likely to be feeling. Elyn Saks, a well-known lawyer with schizophrenia who wrote her autobiography, *The Center Cannot Hold*, explains some of the thought patterns that produced her poverty of speech:

> I couldn't speak on the phone with my family or friends in America, either—I decided that it cost too much, that it was therefore 'forbidden.' By whom, I couldn't have said; there just seemed to be some kind of vague but absolute rule against it. Of course, my family would have gladly paid the phone bill, but my distorted judgment told me I did not deserve to spend money on myself, or to have others spend money on me. Besides, nothing I had to say was worth hearing or so said my mind. It's wrong to talk. Talking means you have something to say. I have nothing to say. I am nobody, a nothing.

> Talking takes up space and time. You don't deserve to talk. Keep quiet. Within weeks after my arrival at Oxford, almost everything I said came out in monosyllables. (Saks, 2007, p. 55)

Autism and schizophrenia share a modest overlap of traits, which will be discussed in further detail in upcoming sections. Despite this overlap, reported rates of psychotic disorders and schizophrenia in autism are conflicting. Most studies report higher frequencies of psychotic disorders in autism. However, rarely are they in the form of fullblown schizophrenia, especially in individuals diagnosed with either classic autism or Asperger's syndrome (Hofvander et al., 2009; Stahlberg et al., 2004). Interestingly, individuals with autism often score high for traits associated with schizotypal personality disorder, which is considered the lightest variant of the schizophrenia spectrum (Barnevald et al., 2011). In fact, Elyn Saks herself displayed traits consistent with Asperger's syndrome. In general, however, rates of psychotic disorders in autism are similar to that of bipolar disorder, averaging approximately 8 percent (Stahlberg et al., 2004).

CHANGING HOW WE VIEW NEURODEVELOPMENTAL CONDITIONS

In their 2010 article in the *British Journal of Psychiatry*, Nick Craddock and Michael Owen wrote:

> The history of medicine suggests that therapeutic and prognostic decision-making are usually facilitated, often greatly, as classifications move closer to the underlying biological mechanisms. For this reason, it is desirable to move towards a classification that maps the expression of illness onto the underlying biological systems.

Schizophrenia is an excellent example of how definitions and perceptions change over the centuries. It's a condition that is intimately linked with the roots of psychiatry and the concepts that began in those bleak asylums of the early 19th century, concepts that still influence us today. Therefore, in order to understand our modern conceptual limitations of conditions like autism, we must look to the assumptions of the past.

The Kraepelinian dichotomy

The late 19th century saw phenomenal changes in medicine. Except for the field of surgery, medical specialism didn't develop until the 20th century. However, there were doctors who devoted their practices to the treatment of those with psychiatric and neurological conditions. But it wasn't until the 1800s that physicians realized asylums could provide more than just confinement for the "insane" as they had done for hundreds of years—they could in fact be *therapeutic*. Out of this mindset, psychiatry was born (Shorter, 2008).

In 1863, the Prussian psychiatrist, Karl Kahlbaum, published *The Classification of Psychiatric Diseases*, which provided the first medical taxonomic framework for psychiatric illnesses, bringing a sense of order to an otherwise disordered field of study. Close on the heels of Kahlbaum's work, the German psychiatrist, Emil Kraepelin, published his book *Psychiatry: A Textbook for Students and Physicians*, in which he divided psychoses into two major divisions: the schizophrenias and the manic-depressives (the latter now known as "bipolar disorder") (Kraepelin, 1899). Since that time, psychiatry has continued to apply Kraepelin's dichotomy, despite growing evidence of diagnostic and etiological overlap between the two conditions. For instance, an entirely new condition, "schizoaffective disorder," was coined in order to more accurately label those individuals who had both symptoms of schizophrenia *and* bipolar disorder. But does this mean that schizophrenia and bipolar are as separate and unique as the early psychiatrists liked to think? Biology suggests otherwise.

Symptoms of autism in schizophrenia

Like bipolar disorder and schizophrenia, autism and schizophrenia also share an intertwined and convoluted past. Interestingly, Leo Kanner originally considered autism an infantile form of schizophrenia. However, the term "autism," was first coined by the psychiatrist, Eugene Bleuler, in his book *Dementia Praecox*, to describe symptoms of withdrawal in his schizophrenic patients:

> The most severe schizophrenics, who have no more contact with the outside world, live in a world of their own. They have encased themselves with their desires and wishes…they have cut themselves off as much as possible from any contact with the external world…

> This detachment from reality, together with the relative and absolute predominance of the inner life, we term *autism* [our emphasis]. (Bleuler, 1950, p. 63)

We now view autism and schizophrenia as separate conditions, particularly in light of the different ages of onset: one arises during the first few years of life, the other usually begins in adolescence or early adulthood. But are they as separate as we assume? For instance, both conditions may exhibit:

- blunted affect

- poverty of speech

- problems with apathy and blunted emotional experiences

- social disinterest

- loss of motivation.

People with autism or schizophrenia also share sensory disturbances, though in schizophrenics these disturbances are more apparent in the early stages of psychosis:

> During the last while back I have noticed that noises all seem to be louder to me than they were before. It's as if someone had turned up the volume. … I notice it most with background noises—you know what I mean, noises that are always around but you don't notice them. Now they seem to be just as loud and sometimes louder than the main noises that are going on. … It's a bit alarming at times because it makes it difficult to keep your mind on something when there's so much going on that you can't help listening to. (Description from a patient with schizophrenia, from Torrey, 2001, p. 34)

Auditory hypersensitivity (also known as hyperacusis) occurs in autism too, as the noted autistic psychologist and author Dr. Wenn Lawson describes:

> Yesterday I connected my noise canceling headphones to my laptop so I could watch and listen to one of the videos I had downloaded as part of a TV series. The problem was though the lowest volume setting on my headphones was still too "loud" for my ears. Therefore, because I was in a public place with others I had to read from my Kindle instead. Very frustrating when it's not what I had hoped to

be doing. This morning I visited the podiatrist for a "foot" check and she clipped my toenails. Each "clip-chunk" of her nail cutters upon my toenails sounded like someone had clapped loudly in my ears and it was hard not to jump! As a youngster I heard the school bus coming from a ways off, well before other children. Even the direction indicator lights sounded loud enough for me to recognise which bus it was. Living with auditory hypersensitivity is an overwhelming experience that I can't escape from, even with earplugs in my ears and headphones over the top! It's also very uncomfortable to appreciate other people (family, friends, the public) don't truly get how painful auditory hypersensitivity can be. I'm not trying to be difficult when I complain something hurts my ears, nor am I doing this for attention. I'm complaining because it's painful and a small thing, like turning the volume down or wearing noise cancelling headphones can mean the difference between being able to go shopping, or having to leave the shop, pub, party, classroom, outing and so on, and live with the gossip of being thought of as "difficult, not normal and/or a person with special needs"! (Dr. Wenn Lawson, personal communication)

Autistic people and schizophrenics share not just sensory overlap, but deficits in socialization (Couture et al., 2010). Theory of mind (ToM) is the ability to attribute mental states to oneself and to others. The concept originally arose within the field of philosophy and was later applied to psychology. In the 1980s, Uta Frith and her then-student, Simon Baron-Cohen, began to use the term to describe deficits in autistic children (Baron-Cohen, Leslie, & Frith, 1985). Later in the 1990s Uta Frith's husband, Christopher Frith, applied the term to similar deficits seen in schizophrenia (Corcoran, Mercer, & Frith, 1995; Frith, 2014).

People with various lesions to the frontal lobes of the brain often display a variety of social deficits (Sarazin et al., 1998). Consider Phineas Gage, the railroad worker who was involved in a construction accident during which a tamping spike was driven through the front of his brain following an explosion (Figure 7.2). It was miraculous he survived, which was largely thanks to the brilliance of the attending physician, Dr. J. M. Harlow. Following the incident, Gage's personality changed so vehemently that despite his survival and recovery he was not able to retain his former position. It took several years for him to recover some of his previous social skills and executive functioning. Unfortunately, he died 12 years after the accident due to repeated and prolonged seizures related to the head injury, finally succumbing to *status epilepticus.*

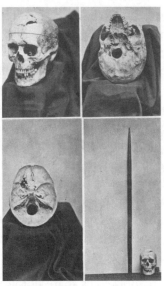

Figure 7.2: Multiple views of the exhumed skull of Phineas Gage, alongside the tamping iron that so severely injured him

(Reproduced from Wikimedia Commons)

Given the overlapping social deficits, it is unsurprising that studies have shown that autism and schizophrenia share functional similarities within the frontal and temporal lobes and some of the underlying limbic structures of the brain. Both conditions display reduced activation during specific social tasks within areas known as the *medial prefrontal cortex*, the *superior temporal sulcus*, and *amygdala* (Sugranyes et al., 2011). People with either autism or schizophrenia also tend to have lower gray-matter volume in various limbic circuitry, although they differ in regard to which specific nuclei are affected (Cheung et al., 2010).

It is challenging to untangle the reasons why autism and schizophrenia rarely occur together and yet overlap significantly in symptomology. Some research suggests that schizophrenics during childhood exhibit high rates of autistic-like symptoms, blurring the lines between the two conditions (Hallerbäck, Lugnergård, & Gillberg, 2012).

It is possible some types of autism and schizophrenia lie on a continuum where symptomology differs primarily according to the age at which it occurs. In modest support of this, a large population study performed in Sweden reported higher rates of schizophrenia in parents of autistic children, as well as higher rates of mood and personality disorders (Daniels et al., 2008).

Why are we talking about psychoses?

Although there is overlap between schizophrenia, mood disorders, and autism, why have we chosen to focus a large portion of this chapter on the history of psychiatry and psychotic disorders? We have chosen to do so because the study and treatment of modern mental health began in those 19th-century asylums. Much of our modern diagnostic taxonomy for neurodevelopmental conditions has grown out of those early traditions, which envisioned symptom clusters as unique and non-overlapping. And thus our concepts of autism have been hemmed in by the same assumptions that reflect obsolete notions of schizophrenia and bipolar disorder.

However, nowadays we know that a single genetic syndrome can sometimes express itself in a variety of ways in different family members. Reminiscent of the many-sided die metaphor we used at the beginning of the chapter, this concept is known as "pleiotropy." Pleiotropy is the production of two or more apparently unrelated phenotypes (expressions) from a single genotype.

Different conditions, same genes

Unfortunately, the genetics of conditions such as ADHD, Tourette's, OCD, and learning disabilities have been poorly studied compared to autism, schizophrenia, and bipolar disorder. For that reason, we will continue to focus on the latter three conditions as illustration, with the expectation that we may find similar trends across all these disorders in future.

One of the key findings that suggests boundaries between autism, schizophrenia, and bipolar disorder are more fluid than we thought is the complex developmental and psychiatric backgrounds of the families of affected individuals. For instance, when researchers studied more than two million Swedish families with first-degree relatives with either schizophrenia or bipolar disorder, they found that family members were at an increased risk for developing either condition (Lichtenstein et al., 2009). This is in contrast to the antiquated theory that such conditions tend to "breed true," an old medical wives' tale. Likewise, when you look at first-degree family members of those with autism, they also have an increased risk for developing schizophrenia and bipolar (Sullivan et al., 2012).

Another finding concerns the genetic overlap we see between these different conditions. For instance, certain types of rare mutations in schizophrenia overlap mutations found in autism, especially in genes involved in epigenetic patterning (McCarthy et al., 2014). Other researchers have also identified overlap of common gene variants between autism, schizophrenia, and bipolar disorder, particularly in calcium channel genes involved in regulating the flux of calcium into the cell (Cross-Disorder Group of the Psychiatric Genomics Consortium, 2013).

On the other hand, some scientists have suggested that although autism and schizophrenia share overlapping gene targets, when they do overlap the effects of these mutations are quite different. For example, there are four known instances in which large chromosomal rearrangements occur in the same genetic loci in both autism and schizophrenia. Scientists have found that deletions in these regions predispose towards autism, while duplications predispose towards schizophrenia, suggesting that even though the same genes are affected in both conditions, the mutations probably affect the functions of the genes very differently (Crespi et al., 2010).

Certain growth-signaling pathways also tend to be upregulated in autism as a result of major loss-of-function mutations. In contrast, schizophrenia tends to be associated with reduced activation in those same pathways (Crespi et al., 2010). Interestingly, however, there are genetic syndromes that are "polar opposites" yet both predispose towards autism. One notable pair is Rett syndrome and Lubs X-linked mental retardation. Rett syndrome is most typically the result of a functional loss of the *MECP2* gene, meanwhile, Lubs is due to duplication of genetic material containing *MECP2* (similar to the autism–schizophrenia examples above.) It is therefore possible that the autism–schizophrenia dichotomy, as has been proposed by some researchers, may not be as simple as it sounds.

In general, high-functioning autism has higher rates of comorbid psychotic and bipolar disorders (Hofvander et al., 2009). In addition, family members of those with high-functioning autism are also at significant risk for these conditions. In contrast, the families of autistic individuals with lower IQ are significantly less likely to experience psychiatric illness than their higher-IQ counterparts, suggesting that the underlying causes of these conditions vary according to cognitive functioning (Robinson et al., 2014). This may also indicate that schizophrenia and bipolar disorder share more in common with high-functioning autism.

CLINICAL CONSIDERATIONS

Clinicians have realized over time that autism spectrum conditions come with a cornucopia of comorbid conditions. Because autism is pervasive and affects the entirety of the brain, almost any neurodevelopmental condition can be a comorbid feature. For these reasons, it is important not just to assess an individual for autism but to run a full work-up on other associated conditions, as these other issues may lead to significant daily impairment.

For example, ADHD and other learning disabilities can significantly impede academic achievement. Individuals with impairments in executive function, regardless of ADHD diagnosis, experience considerable academic challenges, and are at risk for grade retention and overall poor academic achievement (Biederman et al., 2004). In particular, learning disabilities in ADHD children compound the problem and increase the likelihood of grade retention, the necessity of in-school tutoring, and placement in special education classes (Faraone et al., 2001).

Most alarming of all, approximately 14 percent of children on the autism spectrum have considered or attempted suicide (Mayes et al., 2011). Demographics that increase the likelihood of suicide attempts in children with autism are: age (10+ years), race (black or hispanic), lower familial economic status, and sex (males). Children with depression, behavior problems, and those who have been the victims of bullying are all at significantly increased risk. It is therefore vital to identify depressive symptoms and behavior problems, as well as stimuli (e.g. bullying) that are driving these issues, because of the extreme danger they pose should they go unrecognized.

Chapter Eight

THE BROADER AUTISM PHENOTYPE

WHAT IS THE BROADER AUTISM PHENOTYPE?

The term broader autism phenotype (BAP) is not a diagnosis. Instead, it is typically used to describe subclinical traits in relatives of those with autism. Symptoms can include minor impairments in socialization and communication; obsessive, rigid, and inflexible behaviors; and problems with depression and anxiety. These individuals, however, do not reach the cut-off for a full diagnosis of autism. BAP also carries no apparent risk for intellectual disability and little additional risk for epilepsy (Parr & Le Couteur, 2013).

Although most BAP research has focused on family members of affected individuals, there are a few investigators who have studied subclinical traits in the general population. In general, this research has shown that social and communicative deficits associated with autism are continuously distributed throughout the human population and are moderately to highly heritable. Similar to autism, females tend to be less susceptible and are usually less affected than males (Constantino & Todd, 2003; Hoekstra et al., 2007).

RESEARCH INTO THE BROADER AUTISM PHENOTYPE

Kanner, Asperger, and early days

The study of BAP is as old as the study of autism itself. Leo Kanner's original manuscript, "Autistic disturbances of affective contact" (1943), is littered with descriptions of families of the children who formed his first cases studies. Hans Asperger's manuscript, "Autistic psychopathy in childhood" (translated in Frith, 1991), also highlighted similar peculiarities in most of the parents in his first case studies, although his familial descriptions were more limited than Kanner's. These descriptions foreshadow the later recognition of BAP.

In reading Kanner's original manuscript, a number of common features stand out amongst the parents. For instance, BAP traits were most obvious in the fathers whom Kanner was studying, a probable reflection of the unbalanced sex ratio in autism favoring males over females. The parents were also typically well educated, although there have been concerns raised over ascertainment bias in Kanner's first cases, preferencing white, well-educated families who had the means to seek help from Kanner. In fact, four of the eleven fathers were psychiatrists themselves! We know today, however, that although highly educated families may be at greater risk for autism, poor education (e.g. lack of a high school degree) is also an associated risk factor. Therefore, increased familial risk can be seen on both ends of the economic spectrum (Rai et al., 2012; Van Meter et al., 2010).

Interestingly, eccentricities, high achievement, and even language delay were noted in the families of Kanner's original cases:

> The father is the second of five children. The oldest is a well known newspaper man and author of a best-seller. A married sister, "high-strung and quite precocious," is a singer. Next comes a brother who writes for adventure magazines. The youngest, a painter, writer, and radio commentator, "did not talk until he was about 6 years old," and the first words he is reported to have spoken were, "When a lion can't talk he can whistle." (p. 224)

Although Kanner recanted his support for the Refrigerator Mother Theory of autism—instead describing most parents in his original publication as well intentioned, intelligent, and educated—there was one family in particular, the parents of Virginia, case no. 6, who may have provided inspiration for the disastrous theory:

> Virginia, the younger of two siblings, was the daughter of a psychiatrist, who said of himself… "I have never liked children, probably a reaction on my part to the restraint from movement (travel), the minor interruptions and commotions."
>
> Of Virginia's mother, her husband said: "She is not by any means the mother type. Her attitude [toward a child] is more like toward a doll or pet than anything else."

Virginia's brother, Philip, five years her senior, when referred to us because of severe stuttering at 15 years of age, burst out in tears when asked how things were at home and he sobbed: "The only time my father has ever had anything to do with me was when he scolded me for doing something wrong."

His mother did not contribute even that much. *He felt that all his life he had lived in "a frosty atmosphere" with two inapproachable strangers* [our emphasis]. (p. 230)

It wasn't Kanner, however, who popularized the Refrigerator Mother Theory but Bruno Bettelheim in his book *The Empty Fortress* (1967). Although Bettelheim held a doctorate, it was in philosophy or art history (historians aren't exactly certain) but certainly not psychology for which he was later known. An Austrian-born Jew, Bettelheim was imprisoned by the Nazis in the Dachau and Buchenwald concentration camps for ten-and-a-half months. After he was released, he emigrated to America, arriving in New York in late 1939. By 1944, he had passed himself off as a trained psychologist and was hired by the University of Chicago as professor and director of the Orthogenic School, a place for the treatment of emotionally disturbed children. Ironically, Bettelheim had only ever taken three introductory courses in psychology. Yet despite the subterfuge and underqualification, Bettelheim died in 1990 with reputation relatively intact. Posthumously, however, his work on autism has been extensively discredited and his professional fraud revealed.

Besides Kanner, other researchers who were steeped in a stifling Freudian scientific culture slowly added to the Refrigerator Mother Theory that so emboldened Bettelheim. For instance, Eisenberg (1957) described the fathers of autistic children as portraying "cool detachment, obsessive perfectionism and the single minded pursuit of, often scientific, interests but without original achievements" (reported in Wolff, Narayan, & Moyes, 1988). Creak and Ini (1960) later described parents of autistic children as "reserved," the mothers as "cold," and the fathers as "detached." This trend of viewing the parent–child relationship through a Freudian lens continued until Bernard Rimland, whom we discussed in Chapters 1 and 3, wrote his groundbreaking book, *Infantile Autism*. Though the change was slow, Rimland's book marked the beginning of the parents' movement and was the first time anyone had popularized a biological cause for autism. Kanner, an opponent of Freudian psychology, avidly supported Rimland's work and even wrote the introduction to his tome.

The first generation of BAP research

In the early days of familial research, Joseph Piven perceptively wrote:

> Studies of families ascertained through a single autistic proband suggest that the genetic liability for autism may be expressed in nonautistic relatives in a phenotype that is milder but qualitatively similar to the defining features of autism. (Piven et al., 1997, p. 185)

These early hereditary studies on autism were also some of the first addressing the broader phenotype, although the term didn't come into use until the 1990s. In 1977, Folstein and Rutter reported on 21 twin pairs in which either one or both twins were diagnosed with autism. In 11 of the identical twin pairs, four shared an autism diagnosis; in another five, one twin had autism while the other had subclinical traits; and finally two pairs were completely discordant. Meanwhile, none of the fraternal twin pairs were concordant for autism, and only one sibling had subclinical symptoms. We now know that non-identical siblings share significant risk for autism if one sibling is diagnosed, however, risk usually hovers between 10 and 20 percent, whereas in identical twin pairs it ranges between 60 and 90 percent (Bailey et al., 1995). Nowadays, those figures are based on an interpretation of the autism spectrum label that is decidedly broader than was acknowledged in the 1970s.

This early research on inheritance patterns spurred further behavioral and cognitive studies. One early study, for instance, found that half of autism parents had what the researchers called "schizoid traits" (Wolff et al., 1988). Interestingly, many traits of schizoid personality disorder (SPD), such as introversion, a preference for solitary activities, limited close friendships, and blunted emotional expression, all share significant overlap with symptoms common to autism. In fact, according to a more recent study, more than one third of males with Asperger's syndrome also fulfill criteria for SPD, suggesting some cases of SPD may in fact be developmental—rather than personality—disorders (Lugnegård, Hallerbäck, & Gillberg, 2012).

In 1994, Patrick Bolton, then at the University of Cambridge, published the first study on what we now call the broader autism phenotype. His team found that family members of those with autism displayed many subclinical traits, including social communication deficits and certain stereotyped behaviors (Bolton et al., 1994). In addition, about 12–20 percent of siblings fulfilled criteria for "Pervasive Developmental Disorder–Not Otherwise Specified (PDD-NOS)," a now-obsolete variant of autism. Piven and colleagues went further in depth to describe the social deficits and repetitive behaviors seen in BAP parents (Piven et al., 1997). For example, they found that a large minority of autism fathers had a history of conflict with coworkers or supervisors, leading to their resignation or discharge. By contrast, almost no fathers of children with Down syndrome reported the same. In addition, 50 percent of autism fathers had few or no adult friendships, compared to 3 percent of fathers in the Down's group. Mothers of autistic children also had more deficits in social communication skills and had more repetitive behaviors than mothers of those with Down's. The differences between the two groups of mothers were, however, less extreme than those of the fathers, once again highlighting the female protective effect.

Scientists have also identified differences in intellect across autism family members. Eric Fombonne and his colleagues observed, for instance, that autism parents and unaffected siblings tend to score higher on tests of verbal IQ than controls. Meanwhile, siblings with BAP generally have lower IQ scores than non-BAP siblings. In addition, they also tend to fare more poorly in the areas of reading and spelling (Fombonne et al., 1997).

Many readers have probably read or heard of the *WIRED* magazine article "The geek syndrome," describing an epidemic of autism in Silicon Valley, one of the great tech capitals of the world (Silberman, 2001). This follows on the idea of assortative mating or "like attracts like." Although some have questioned the veracity of the article's claims as it was based primarily on anecdotal evidence, more recent research supports the idea that autism rates are indeed higher in tech cities and areas characterized by higher parental education (Roelfsema et al., 2012; Van Meter et al., 2010). Research by Simon Baron-Cohen in particular suggests that autism parents, especially fathers, are more likely to select careers in engineering, physics, and mathematics (Baron-Cohen, 1998; Baron-Cohen et al., 1997).

It's difficult, however, to be certain if these tech-savvy geographic autism clusters are due to genuine heritability or simply to the fact that educated families have more resources and are therefore more likely to successfully seek diagnosis. But given the heritability of intelligence and the high rates of superior IQ in autism itself, this suggests that at least some of the "Silicon Valley Effect" is the result of assortative mating amongst people with subclinical autism who are indeed drawn towards STEM careers (Kim et al., 2011).

BAP research in the 21st century

Early studies assumed that BAP was a discrete entity, which was either present or absent. These studies were mostly performed using observation and interview and depended on qualitative data. With the new millennium, however, new research brought new tools such as the Social Responsiveness Scale, the Broader Autism Phenotype Questionnaire, and the Autism-Spectrum Quotient, all of which have provided a more quantitative measure of the BAP spectrum. In addition, BAP research has expanded to study subclinical traits in the general population. Since that time, we've gained a better idea about the range of traits that define the broader phenotype.

Sociocommunication deficits in BAP

Pragmatics refers to nuances of social language that include tone of voice, body language, and the use of situational context in order to communicate. Studies typically agree that deficits in social pragmatics best characterize language impairments in BAP parents (see Sucksmith, Roth, & Hoekstra, 2011, for review). For instance, using the Communication Checklist, scientists have found that the majority of BAP parents either perform poorly in the areas of pragmatic language or social engagement (Whitehouse et al., 2010). Specifically, BAP fathers tend to be more socially aloof, while BAP mothers have deficits in the use of pragmatics. These peculiarities are reminiscent of the "aloof" vs. "active but odd" categories of autism proposed by the well-known researcher Lorna Wing (Wing, 1981).

Significant language deficits often occur in siblings of those with autism. Roughly one fifth of siblings experience language delay, as well as delays in comprehension and other aspects of language expression (Sucksmith et al., 2011). Some of these features are also associated with delays in motor development. Interestingly, motor milestones are typically used in developmental pediatrics as a gauge of early neurological development, since motor delays in young infants can often be harbingers of delays or deficits in other areas of development still to come.

Other social peculiarities are seen in BAP. A prime example is taken from Hans Asperger's own initial case study, describing the behaviors of the mother of the boy known as "Fritz":

> Very characteristic, for instance, was the situation when mother and son walked to the hospital school together, but each by themselves. The mother slouched along, hands held behind her back and apparently oblivious to the world. Beside her the boy was rushing to and fro, doing mischief. They gave the appearance of having absolutely nothing to do with each other. One could not help thinking that the mother found it difficult to cope not only with her child but with the practical matters of life. She was certainly not up to running the household. Even living, as she did, in the upper echelons of society, she always looked unkempt, unwashed almost, and was always badly dressed. …
>
> It was clear that this state of affairs was due not only to the boy's own internally caused problems, but also to the mother's own problems in relating to the outside world, showing as she did a limited intuitive social understanding. Take the following typical trait: whenever things became too much for her at home she would simply walk out on her family and travel to her beloved mountains. She would stay there fore a week or more at a time, leaving the rest of the family to struggle for themselves. (translated in Frith, 1991, p. 41)

Indeed, given this quote, one wonders not only whether Fritz's mother had features of BAP but also may have been autistic herself according to today's diagnostic criteria. However, one of the parents from Asperger's other case studies, "Harro," is more typical of the aloofness seen in BAP:

> The father, who himself comes from peasant stock, is a typical intellectual. He professed to be completely and painfully self taught. One could make out from what he said that he had nothing to do with anyone in the village where he lived and where he must have been considered highly eccentric. He said himself that he was nervous and

highly strung but that "he controlled himself to such an extent that he appeared to be indifferent." (translated in Frith, 1991, pp. 51–52)

When studying at-risk siblings of those with autism, infants and young children with BAP tend to engage in fewer joint attention tasks with caregivers compared to controls. Likewise, when BAP siblings are engaged in joint attention with parents or other caregivers, similar to autism, they're less inclined to look at the eyes and instead tend to look at the mouth. Some researchers have even suggested eye-gaze differences could be a useful biomarker for the identification of BAP or autism in at-risk siblings (Sucksmith et al., 2011).

People with BAP may also struggle with the recognition of emotional expression and, in particular, the identification of neutral expressions (Kadak et al., 2014). Parents from multiplex families (which have higher rates of BAP) score lower in tests that require the identification of basic emotions than parents of simplex families, although autism parents as a whole don't differ significantly from controls (Bölte & Poutska, 2003). When tested on specific, isolated portions of the face, BAP parents also fare poorly in reading emotional expression from the eyes (Adolphs et al., 2008). More surprisingly, however, they fare *better* at reading emotions from the region of the mouth—the portion of the face those with BAP or autism tend to look at the most. Since people with BAP are still clearly missing important facial cues necessary for navigating the social world, the eyes surely convey a great deal of information necessary for translating human emotions.

The recognition of emotion may also be further complicated by deficits in facial memory. For instance, some scientists have found that autism fathers tend to perform poorly on the Cambridge Face Memory Test (Figure 8.1), which requires participants to recognize faces to which they had earlier been exposed (Wilson et al., 2010). Interestingly, this same trend is seen in the general population: men who score higher on the Autism-Spectrum Quotient (AQ) (a positive measure of BAP) fare more poorly on facial memory tasks. And more surprisingly, women who score higher on the AQ tend to perform *better* on facial memory tasks (Rhodes et al., 2013). This suggests that social skills in BAP women may not be as complicated by impairments in facial recognition as they are in men. Similar to other savant skills in autism, facial recognition in BAP is characterized by extremes of the human spectrum of ability, with high proportions of both "super-recognizers" and "prosopagnosics" (people who are face blind).

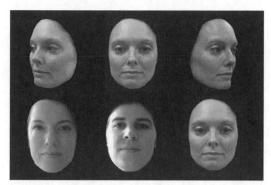

Figure 8.1: An example of one of the types of tasks
used in the Cambridge Face Memory Test

The test taker is first exposed to the top row, which contains a single person's
face from different perspectives. The test taker is then shown another set of
images (bottom row) and asked to identify the face previously seen.

Interestingly, people with BAP not only have greater problems recognizing faces and emotions of others, they're also more likely to struggle to identify their own emotions (Szatmari et al., 2008). This deficiency in emotional identification and understanding is known as *alexithymia*. People with alexithymia often have difficulty identifying and naming the emotional sensations they're experiencing; they may have a poor understanding of why they're feeling the way they're feeling, and they may have difficulty expressing those feelings to other people. Like most of the traits discussed in this chapter, alexithymia occurs on a spectrum of severity that bleeds into normality with the general population.

In terms of sex differences, BAP tends to be more strongly expressed in males for reasons still unknown but which are probably similar to those that underlie the sex-skewed ratio in autism. When, however, mothers are as severely affected as their BAP husbands, social impairment tends to be more severe in the autistic child, suggesting an additive or exponential hereditary effect (Constantino & Todd, 2005). The propensity for "like attracting like" is believed to account for approximately 30 percent of the variation in social impairment observed in children with autism. This suggests that BAP individuals, based on common personality characteristics, are more likely to pair with one another than expected at random, increasing risk for autism in the children.

Repetitive and restricted behaviors and interests

Unfortunately, most of the few studies to date investigating restricted and repetitive behaviors and interests (RRBI) in families of those with autism have been qualitative rather than quantitative. However, a number of studies suggest that RRBI in parents and siblings are less extreme but similar in nature to those seen in autism. For instance, young unaffected siblings of those with autism tend to show more repeated play behaviors than control children (reviewed in Sucksmith et al., 2011). In addition, BAP parents are sometimes described as rigid and perfectionistic, and may exhibit intense special interests, often of an intellectual nature (Sucksmith et al., 2011). Leo Kanner (1943) describes the obsessiveness of one of the mothers of his patients:

> His mother brought with her copious notes that indicated obsessive preoccupation with details and a tendency to read all sorts of peculiar interpretations into the child's performances. She watched (and recorded) every gesture and every "look," trying to find their specific significance and finally deciding on a particular, sometimes very farfetched explanation. She thus accumulated an account that, though very elaborate and richly illustrated, on the whole revealed more of her own version of what had happened in each instance than it told of what had actually occurred. (p. 225)

Cognition in BAP

Many studies report deficits in executive functioning in first-degree relatives of those with autism. Executive functions are a set of cognitive skills important for regulating one's behaviors that includes features such as the control of attention, working memory, self-control and planning, and cognitive flexibility. Although it's clear family members of those with autism sometimes have notable impairments in executive functioning, results have differed markedly across studies and are likely a reflection of different methodologies. Many studies, for instance, have failed to use typical controls and have instead utilized other affected groups such as parents of those with obsessive-compulsive disorder or schizophrenia. And so although autism parents may not perform differently from parents of children with other neurodevelopmental conditions, it doesn't address whether autism parents' abilities differ from the general population and are comparatively impaired. Therefore, results in this area of research are still somewhat sketchy. However, reported differences to date include deficits in: planning ability; spatial and verbal working memory; task-shifting; and ideational fluency, which is the ability to rapidly produce multiple ideas related to a particular object or condition (Gokcen et al., 2009; Hughes, Plumet, & Leboyer, 1999; Koczat et al., 2002; Nydén et al., 2011; Wong et al., 2006).

Other studies have found that parents with the broader phenotype are also prone to weak central coherence,[1] especially when examined using visuospatial tests like the Embedded Figures Task, in which the individual must find a hidden figure within a drawing as quickly as possible. Conversely, autism parents tend to have lower performance IQ than typical controls, especially in the area of matrix reasoning, which is a test that requires pattern recognition (Figure 8.2) (Bölte & Poutska, 2006; Schmidt et al., 2008).

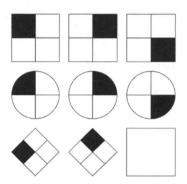

Figure 8.2: An example of matrix reasoning similar to that seen in the Raven's Progressive Matrices

(Reproduced with permission of Life of Riley from Wikimedia Commons)

Psychiatric symptoms

Autism parents are at increased risk for the development of various psychiatric disorders compared to parents of typically developing children and children with conditions like Down syndrome (Yirmiya & Shaked, 2005). Surprisingly, however, they have less psychiatric

---

1   A cognitive style in which the perception of detail is enhanced yet the capacity to generalize that detail into a contextual gestalt is comparatively limited. For this reason, individuals with Weak Central Coherence tend to perform better on the Embedded Figures Task, which requires the ability to ignore the visual gestalt and identify hidden targets.

risk than parents of children who have learning disabilities or children who later go on to develop schizophrenia.

Additional studies have found that parents of children with autism are more likely to have a history of hospitalization for a mental disorder and to have been diagnosed with schizophrenia. Autism mothers are also more likely to have been diagnosed with depression or a personality disorder (Daniels et al., 2008). And, interestingly, related research has revealed that while a mother's depression is in part related to the stress of caring for an autistic child relative to the severity of the child's behavior, risk for depression increases in association with maternal autism traits (Ingersoll, Meyer, & Becker, 2011).

Scientists have also found that in the general population, people with higher BAP scores report more loneliness and social isolation than their non-BAP counterparts (Jobe & White, 2007).

BAP in multiplex vs. simplex families

We've already alluded to the fact that multiplex and simplex families exhibit different risk patterns for BAP. These patterns suggest that risk inheritance is different in the two groups, although the roots of that variability have not been well defined. Some studies suggest, for instance, that children from multiplex families are more likely to inherit an increased load of common genetic risk variants, likely driven by assortative mating in the parents (Klei et al., 2012; Klusek, Losh, & Martin, 2014).

In support of this hypothesis, simplex parents have lower rates of BAP than those of multiplex families, suggesting that BAP personalities tend to attract each other (Davison et al., 2014). In addition, simplex cases of autism are on average more severely affected, a feature that's linked with higher rates of *de novo* (new) mutations in contrast to heritable forms passed from parent to child (Gerdts et al., 2013; Taylor et al., 2015). Unaffected siblings in multiplex families, like their parents, also share more BAP traits than siblings from simplex families (Constantino et al., 2006; Gerdts et al., 2013).

The BAP brain

Most BAP brain studies to date have focused on high-risk siblings, born out of some of the "baby sibs" projects that have become popular in the new millennium, such as the Baby Siblings Research Consortium. Studies thus far have found that the brains of high-risk infants process information differently than typically developing infants, even in those cases that don't go on to develop autism.

For instance, nine-month-old high-risk siblings look at the mouth and eyes in a similar pattern to that of low-risk infants, but process this information using different brain regions. In addition, these results seem to correlate with the child's communication abilities: the more abnormal the processing pattern, the more social communication deficits are evident at this young age (Key & Stone, 2013).

By 12 months of age, BAP infants have noticeably diverged from typically developing children, exhibiting more extensive delays and other abnormalities in cognition, motor development, language development, and social skills (Ozonoff et al., 2015). By mid-childhood, gaze fixation also diverges from controls, becoming more similar to that of their autistic siblings. As we've noted earlier, they spend more time looking at the mouth rather than the eyes, a trait commonly reported in autism. In addition, during these tasks high-risk siblings exhibit reduced activation of the fusiform gyrus, an area integral to facial processing, suggesting they're depending more heavily on other areas of the brain during facial-processing tasks, which may leave them at a decided social disadvantage (Dalton et al., 2007).

Internal noise and gamma oscillations

Internal noise is a property of the brain that affects the transduction of neural signals. In essence, it's the culmination of many factors, ranging from microscopic to large modular systems such as the regulation of attention and arousal. In concert, these variables provide the background on which neurons communicate with one another. Greater background noise impairs the processing of key neuronal signals, making it more difficult for the brain to assess, plan, and execute specific behaviors (Vilidaite, Yu, & Baker, 2017). Imagine the difficulty we may experience attending to a conversation while in an extremely noisy room. In this example, the noisy room is the "internal noise" in the brain, and the conversation we're trying to hear and be a part of is the target signal. A noisy background means that the brain is more likely to miss key segments of that all-important neural conversation.

As you may have guessed by now, autistic people have higher and more variable internal noise. And so it's harder for their brains to weed out all that background information and home in on predictable external and internal stimuli. Hypersensitivity that often accompanies sensory processing disorder is a prime example of when the brain isn't able to dampen background signals that most people (at least most of the time) are able to ignore with relative ease. Instead, some sensory perceptions in autism can be so strong as to be painful and may cause a person to withdraw simply to avoid the noxious stimulus—a stimulus that others without autism may not even notice.

Perhaps even more interesting is the fact that the severity of the brain's internal noise varies in the general population according to whether a person falls within the broader phenotype: people who score higher on BAP scales have more internal noise as measured across a variety of tasks (Vilidaite et al., 2017). Abnormalities in sensory sensitivity also seem to be somewhat heritable in autism families, with autism parents (some of whom are presumably BAP) reporting hypersensitivities and more avoidance behaviors than parents of typically developing children. In particular, autism mothers report high sensitivity to the perceptions of taste and smell (Glod et al., 2017).

The neurons of the brain communicate in waveforms, with waves of neural activity often acting rhythmically. These waves oscillate at varying frequencies. It is believed that *gamma oscillations* in particular are the means by which different areas of the brain synchronize, binding different types of sensory information into a larger usable gestalt (Tallon-Baudry & Bertrand, 1999). An example would be the way in which we watch and enjoy television. Our brains must bind together the sound of different syllables into a single word; single words into a sentence; sentences into dialogue; colors, shapes, and movement into form; and finally bind our visual and auditory percepts together so that all the stimuli we're deriving are perceived as a single television show or movie. The way the brain knows that these stimuli relate to one another is that they eventually synchronize, forming gamma oscillations. Without this synchronicity, the brain doesn't easily grasp that the stimuli are related.

High levels of internal noise can make it difficult for the brain to dissociate signal from background. In this way, the autistic brain remains poorly synchronized, making it more difficult for autistic people to relate incoming sensory experiences to one another (Casanova, Baruth, et al., 2013). For this reason, some people with autism report challenges both in looking at and listening to a person at the same time, sometimes preferring to look away in order to better understand what the other person is saying. Some also report difficulty watching television, preferring to have subtitles on to supplement conversation they may have otherwise missed. Similar to autism, people with BAP also exhibit high internal noise and reduced gamma oscillations, suggesting that they struggle similarly in relating different sensory perceptions to one another, although likely to a milder degree (Elsabbagh et al., 2009; Rojas et al., 2011; Vilidaite et al., 2017).

CLINICAL CONSIDERATIONS

According to inheritance patterns, there are no clear demarcations indicating the point at which autism ends and BAP begins, suggesting BAP is indeed a continuation of the autism spectrum, which is itself highly heterogeneous. However, parent and sibling studies of simplex and multiplex families suggest that BAP shares stronger ties with "higher-functioning" multiplex inheritance patterns, which themselves have ties with other psychiatric and neurodevelopmental conditions, such as mood and psychotic disorders. In summary, evidence suggests that although there is overlap, the autism spectrum is composed of two major entities represented by: (1) simplex cases with greater autism severity whose families exhibit fewer BAP traits and lower rates of major depression, bipolar disorder, and schizophrenia; and (2) multiplex cases with comparatively lighter autism variants whose families have higher rates of BAP, mood, and psychotic disorders. While this is a simplification of reported trends with cases undoubtedly available to the contrary, it's a useful generalization that allows us to make important predictions about the different heritable factors that likely underlie these two groups.

Chapter Nine

AUTISM, INTELLECTUAL DISABILITY, AND GENIUS

AUTISM VS. INTELLECTUAL DISABILITY

Although the association between autism and high intelligence has been culturally popularized, autism also shares much in common with intellectual disability (ID). It's estimated that about 30 percent of those on the spectrum test at or below an intelligence quotient (IQ) of 70, which places them in the intellectually disabled range. An additional ~20 percent test within the borderline range (IQ = 71–85), while the other half of the spectrum tests in the normal or above-average intelligence ranges (Centers for Disease Control and Prevention, 2014). However, there are many concerns about the reliability of those numbers and whether traditional IQ tests, such as the Wechsler and Stanford–Binet, adequately address underlying intelligence in someone who may have deficits in language or attention, both of which facilitate traditional testing methods (Nader et al., 2016).

While it's difficult to test around severe deficits in attention, there are, however, other ways to gauge development independent of language in young children, such as the Bayley Scales of Infant Development, Griffith's Mental Development Scales, and Mullen Scales of Early Learning. These tests address a young child's cognitive, language, and motor skills, giving a better estimate of how he or she processes a variety of types of novel information and adapts to it. Unfortunately, even during tasks that are not social- or language-based, a significant portion of young children with autism show measurable developmental delays (Akshoomoff, 2006).

Nevertheless, data suggest that when cognitive abilities are measured in autistic children prior to the age of three, more than half of those children who score within the ID range have by age nine lost that diagnosis, indicating that cognitive abilities in many cases improve with time and can genuinely be considered "delays" (Turner et al., 2006). Language scores also exhibit similar gains by middle childhood. In addition, in those cases in which ID is still present by later childhood, the majority score within the mildly affected range (Charman et al., 2011).

Some scientists, clinicians, and stakeholders have been critical of the means by which we attempt to measure general intelligence in autism (i.e. Stanford–Binet, Wechsler). As an alternative approach, some scientists have applied the Raven's Progressive Matrices as a measure of fluid intelligence, which doesn't rely on language as a communicative medium. Testing both children and adults, they have found that autistic people score significantly higher on the Raven compared to the Wechsler (Dawson et al., 2007; Soulières et al., 2011). In fact, autistic children that were studied scored on average 30 percentile points higher than they did on the Wechsler. These data together suggest that traditional IQ tests are not as capable of gauging intellectual potential as once believed.

AUTISM, INTELLECTUAL DISABILITY, AND OBSESSIVE-COMPULSIVE DISORDER

As discussed, a large minority of those with autism have an additional diagnosis of ID, however, there are many forms of ID that don't co-occur with autism. Therefore, one may wonder what the difference between the two conditions is despite their similarities and comorbidity.

Scientists have attempted to address this question from a behavioral standpoint. One group of researchers studied numerous cases of ID with and without autism, investigating which DSM autism criteria were most specific to the autism spectrum (Pedersen et al., 2016). They found that many individuals with ID and autism share speech and language impairments, indicating language is commonly impaired across all forms of ID regardless of autism diagnosis.

In contrast, they discovered that restricted and repetitive interests are most characteristic of autism. In particular, *stereotyped patterns of interest* and *inflexible adherence to routine* are the criteria with highest sensitivity and specificity for the condition. Meanwhile, *delays in or lack of development in spoken language* and *impairment in the ability to initiate and sustain conversations* are the criteria with least specificity for autism.

These data suggest that restricted and repetitive interests are particularly unique to the autism spectrum, regardless of comorbidity.

However, many of the restricted and repetitive symptoms overlap those of obsessive-compulsive disorder (OCD)—which, like ID, often co-occurs with autism. Therefore, if restricted and repetitive interests are specific to autism yet also overlap symptoms of OCD, how then do these two conditions differ?

Although research is early, the fundamental difference between OCD and autism seems to be the quality of the obsessions and compulsions (Paula-Pérez, 2013). In OCD, thoughts and impulses are intrusive and unwanted, and provide the individual with measurable anxiety. In contrast, when an autistic person engages in restricted and repetitive behaviors, these behaviors don't cause the individual anxiety—unless of course the person with autism is prevented from performing them. As many a family member and individual with autism knows, a meltdown can ensue if the autistic person is prevented from engaging in his or her routine or interests.

SAVANTISM
"Idiots savants"

Beate Hermelin, a pioneering psychologist in the field of autism research, once said that autistic savants were incapable of true human creativity but were limited to feats of rote mimicry (Snyder, 2004). Sadly, her ideas of autism were limited by the era in which she worked, one which didn't recognize Asperger's. Her early investigations were also biased by the preferential study of autistic savants living in psychiatric institutions.

More recent studies suggest that roughly 20 percent of people diagnosed with the older nosological term "autistic disorder," display at least modest savant skills. A further ~10 percent show outstanding skill on one or more of the Wechsler IQ subtests, suggesting approximately 30 percent of this population has some form of advanced skill relative to typically developing individuals. What's more, savantism is rarely associated with moderate-to-profound ID, arguing against the obsolete stereotype of the "idiot savant" (Howlin et al., 2009). Beate Hermelin herself recognized the misnomer:

> We knew of course that accounts of 'idiots savants' had been given for over 100 years. The Frenchman Alfred Binet, who invented the first intelligence test, had introduced the term to describe those people who had great learning difficulties and could not cope with life on

their own, but yet showed an outstanding ability in a specific area. In fact, as only those with the very lowest intelligence levels [(IQ < 20)] fell into the category of 'idiots', the term 'idiot savant' was probably never quite appropriate. (Hermelin, 2001, p. 16)

Bernard Rimland, a major proponent of the biological theory of autism and leader of the early parents' movement, whom we covered in Chapter 1, called attention to misuse of the term in an article for *Psychology Today* (1978)—instead suggesting that the term be replaced by "autistic savant." As he explains a few years later:

When prodigious abilities occur in individuals who have not developed normally (the developmentally disabled), we employ a rather derogatory misnomer: the idiot savant. Most of the otherwise mentally handicapped individuals who have developed special skills are not so disabled that the term idiot would be applicable, even in its once legitimate usage to mean the more profoundly retarded. In our own usage we shall omit the term idiot, and simply use savant, which is not appropriate either, but serves as a compromise with tradition. (Rimland & Hill, 1984, p. 155)

Rimland later provided professional expertise to the cast and crew of the movie *Rain Man*, suggesting that Dustin Hoffman's now-famous character, Raymond, be rewritten as an *autistic* rather than an "idiot" savant. He also arranged for Hoffman to meet a number of savants to study, and upon which to base his portrayal (Rimland, 1990). One of these young men, who was known back then only anonymously as "Peter," was in all likelihood the now-famous savant Kim Peek (Figure 9.1).

Figure 9.1: The megasavant Kim Peek
(Reproduced with permission of Dmadeo from Wikimedia Commons)

Laurence Kim Peek (aka Kim Peek) was born in 1951 after what seemed a normal pregnancy. However, from the very beginning his parents knew Kim was different. He didn't respond to stimuli normally, he didn't play, he couldn't walk until well after age four, and his eyes moved independently of one another. Doctors diagnosed Kim with ID and recommended his parents institutionalize him. Thankfully for Kim, his parents refused, keeping him at home with the family. Instead, to pass the time, they constantly read to him, as he slowly followed the words with his fingers. According to his father, one day Kim asked him what the term, "confidential," meant. His father, Fran, told the story years later:

> ...without thinking, I jokingly told him to look it up in the family dictionary. He did. About 30 seconds after putting his head down, crawling like a snowplow to the dictionary, he found the word and read out the definition. Thereafter he never stopped reading and memorizing everything he could get his hands on including phone directories, atlases, biographies, and histories (Opitz, Smith, & Santoro, 2008, p. 143).

Kim Peek was what is colloquially known as a *megasavant*. By the end of his life at age 58, he had read and memorized over 12,000 books, whose text he was able to retrieve with almost perfect recall. He also had considerable talents in music, both in terms of perfect pitch and musical memory.

In addition to ID, Kim was originally diagnosed with autism, although by the end of his life that diagnosis was changed to FG syndrome (FGS). FGS is composed of several different subtypes, each underlayed by different mutations. However, all affected individuals present with poor muscle tone at birth, speech delays, relative macrocephaly, facial malformations, and severe constipation and/or malformations of the anus (OMIM, 2014). Kim also had a missing corpus callosum, the fibrous axons that connect the two hemispheres of the brain—a feature that is not uncommon in FGS.

Although most people with FGS don't fulfill all autism criteria, many display abnormal social skills and withdrawal, echolalia, stereotypies, and substantial repetitive behaviors, suggesting autistic-like features are common in this syndrome (Battaglia, Chines, & Carey, 2006; Ozonoff et al., 2000). This overlap is probably the reason Kim received the earlier "autism" diagnosis.

Savantism with normal intelligence

Because of the "idiot savant" stereotype, much attention has been paid to savants who have some form of cognitive impairment—perhaps because the extreme dichotomy is so fascinating to us. But do autistic savants with normal or superior IQ exist? And if so, how common are they?

When calculating the general and special education populations combined, roughly 63 percent of children on the autism spectrum score within the average to very superior ranges of IQ (Kim et al., 2011). Approximately 6 percent score at or above the superior range of intelligence (IQ ≥ 120), which is roughly three-fold more common than in the general population. Unfortunately, there are no current prevalence rates that tell us how common savantism is in this subpopulation. However, Darold Treffert, a world expert on savantism, suggests that it is:

> very common [in Asperger's], and generally include[s] prodigious memory. When [savant skills] do occur, in my experience, those special abilities in Asperger's tend to involve numbers, mathematics, mechanical and spatial skills. Many are drawn to science, inventions, complex machines and particularly, now, computers. (Treffert, 2004)

Additional research has also shown that people with high-functioning autism are more sensitive to minute changes in auditory pitch, a potential precursor to musical savantism (Bonnel et al., 2003). Interestingly, musicians who display perfect pitch exhibit more autistic traits than musicians without this ability, suggesting even subclinical personality traits share links with enhanced perceptual processing (Dohn et al., 2012).

There are many famous savants. However, most tend to have some mild cognitive impairment or developed savantism following brain injury. Daniel Tammet (Figure 9.2), however, is a notable exception:

> I was born on January 31, 1979—a Wednesday. I know it was a Wednesday, because the date is blue in my mind and Wednesdays are always blue, like the number 9 or the sound of loud voices arguing. I like my birth date, because of the way I'm able to visualize most of the numbers in it as smooth and round shapes, similar to pebbles on a beach. That's because they are prime numbers: 31, 19, 197, 97, 79,

and 1979 are all divisible only by themselves and 1. I can recognize every prime up to 9,973 by their "pebble-like" quality. It's just the way my brain works. (Tammet, 2006, p. 1)

Daniel was a shy child, enraptured by a world of numbers. The eldest of nine children, he suffered from epilepsy, which was eventually controlled by medications. It wasn't until adulthood, however, after his initial rise to fame that he was diagnosed with Asperger's syndrome by the Autism Research Centre at Cambridge University.

Lending to his prodigious memory feats, Daniel also has a mixed form of synesthesia. Synesthesia is a perceptual phenomenon in which stimulation of one sense triggers activation of another typically unrelated sense. In the case of Daniel, he experiences numbers associated with color, physical features like size and spatial arrangement, and even emotion. In this way, he's able to "walk through a landscape" in his mind, each number up to 10,000 having a unique identity or "personality."

Figure 9.2: The autistic savant Daniel Tammet
(Reproduced with permission of MelodyNelson18 from Wikimedia Commons)

Although he became famous for incredible feats of memory, notably memorizing and reciting pi (π) to 22,514 digits, Daniel is an equally accomplished polyglot and author, and besides penning three autobiographies he has written a book on language as well as his first novel, *Mishenka*, published in French. In the television documentary *The Boy with the Incredible Brain*, Daniel accepted and won the challenge to learn conversational Icelandic within a single week, supposedly one of the most difficult languages to master.

When savantism crosses into pure genius

Jacob (Jake) Barnett (Figure 9.3) is a mathematician currently working on his doctorate degree at the world-renowned Perimeter Institute for Theoretical Physics in Waterloo, Canada. According to those around him, he is on the short-track to a Nobel Prize. He is also the youngest student to be accepted to the institute at the age of 15.

Figure 9.3: The autistic savant Jacob Barnett
(Reproduced with permission of Álvaro from Wikimedia Commons)

Jake was diagnosed with autism at two years of age following an episode of regression so severe that doctors and teachers told his parents he would probably never talk. His parents enrolled him in the usual slew of behavioral therapies, hopeful he could recover the skills he'd lost, yet within a short time his mother, Kristine, could tell his therapies were only causing him to withdraw further into himself:

> Most of the time, it didn't even feel as though he was in the room. He had stopped speaking entirely. He no longer made eye contact with anyone, nor did he respond when he was spoken to. If you hugged him, he'd push away. (Jack M., 2016)

Enough was enough. Kristine took him out of therapy and began to homeschool him, letting him focus on and indulge in the things he loved. Even as a toddler, Jake adored math, drawing, and solving puzzles, and within a short time he began to blossom under his mother's tutelage. He did so well that Kristine opened an evening program called Little Light for local families with autism, aimed at using the children's strengths to improve their weaknesses, an approach strongly advocated by Temple Grandin. The program was a smashing success, helping children who had been written off by the school systems achieve greater levels of integration in school than were ever thought possible. And more importantly, the young people were measurably happier, eagerly allowed to take part in the things that interested them most.

Thanks to Kristine's gut instincts and motherly support, by age three Jake could speak four languages, was teaching himself Braille, and was able to recreate street maps using only Q-tips. By age five, he was able to enter kindergarten full-time without the need for special education. By age eight, he was auditing classes on astronomy at Indiana University, impressing the professors so much that the university eventually invited him to enroll. By age ten he began college, at age 11 he was giving TED talks, and by 13 he was a published physicist.

After Jake's initial brush with the media following an article in *The Indiana Star*, he was invited to participate in a research study on autism and savantism run by Dr. Joanne Ruthsatz at Ohio State University. As part of the study, she tested Jake using the Stanford–Binet, an IQ test ideal for testing people with either low or high IQ due to the low floor and high ceiling the test offers respectively. Shockingly, Jake reached the Stanford–Binet's ceiling, managing to test out on all the subtests. Nobody had ever done that before! Even the Stanford–Binet couldn't measure Jake's IQ, which was well over 170. Now at age 19 Jake is working to complete his PhD in physics and astronomy at the Perimeter Institute and is undoubtedly slated for great things in his future career (Andrews, 2017).

Dr. Beate Hermelin did not believe that splinter skills in autism reflected genuine intelligence, a case that has been argued by many. However, there have been both modern and historical cases in which prodigious ability in autism lends itself to true creativity and, at times, pure genius. Daniel Tammet and Jacob Barnett are excellent modern examples and historical figures abound, such as Wolfgang Amadeus Mozart, Ludwig van Beethoven, Albert Einstein, Henry Cavendish, Nikola Tesla, and Isaac Newton to name just a few (Fitzgerald, 2005, 2007). Although such profound prodigies are exceptionally rare—perhaps one in a million—the application of prodigious ability is limited only by an individual's creative capacity. What's more, our definitions of "creativity" are both variable and subjective, suggesting our concepts of creative ability may be biased by our perceptions of autism.

For example, although Stephen Wiltshire (Figure 9.4), the autistic savant artist, draws his incredible cityscapes true to form based on a prodigious memory, his drawings and paintings are still exceptional forms of artistic expression. No artist in the world would doubt his creative capacity. And his incredible memory aids that natural talent, but is not the source of his gift—anymore than Da Vinci's model was the origin of his masterpiece, the *Mona Lisa*. It's true that not every savant is gifted with remarkable creativity to match his or her prodigious ability. But neither is savantism an impassionate endeavor, defined by the exercising of eidetic memory. As anyone who is autistic, or has loved, lived, or worked with someone with autism knows, they can be remarkably original and creative people, regardless of their cognitive abilities.

Figure 9.4: The autistic savant artist Stephen Wiltshire
(Reproduced from Wikimedia Commons)

HUMAN INTELLIGENCE

As we discussed in the first chapter of this book, Leo Kanner, the Father of Autism, was the first to notice autistic traits in the parents and family members of his original case studies. He also noted that most of the parents of the children he studied had attained high educational status, including the mothers—an occurrence especially unusual for that era. As may be of little surprise to the reader, we now know that high intelligence, socioeconomic status, and educational achievement share a strong interrelationship (Deary & Johnson, 2010; Deary et al., 2007). As we discussed in the chapter on genetics (Chapter 3), the tendency for like attracting like is referred to as *assortative mating* (Hugh-Jones et al., 2016; Plomin & Deary, 2015). In short, people with similar backgrounds tend to intermarry more often than expected at random.

We know that mate patterns affect intelligence and development of the human brain in modern times. But what drove brain evolution throughout prehistory? Is the human brain uniquely different from those of our primate cousins? To address these questions, we're going to have to travel back several million years in time.

The evolution of human intelligence

The humanoid line contains all of our known ancient relatives from the ape-like protohuman, *Ardipithecus ramidus*, who lived over 4.4 million years ago (Figure 9.5), to us, *Homo sapiens*. As animals go, the size of our brains isn't unique. In fact, several lines of placental mammals have also experienced dramatic increases in brain size relative to body size, including certain cetaceans (e.g. dolphins) and elephants (Herculano-Houzel et al., 2014; Marino, 1998). We do however top the list, having the biggest brains for our body size with an encephalization quotient (EQ) of roughly 6 (Boddy et al., 2012). (Any EQ greater than 1 indicates a brain that is larger than expected with respect to its body size.)

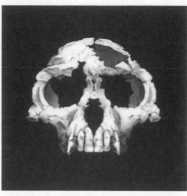

Figure 9.5: A reconstruction of the skull of *Ardipithecus ramidus*, one of our oldest known humanoid relatives who lived approximately 4.4 million years ago

(Accessed on 17 July 2018 at www.hindawi.com/journals/ert/2014/582039/)

Other primates, such as the baboon lineage, don't appear to have experienced significant increases in brain volume during recent evolution (Elton, Bishop, & Wood, 2001). This, however, is not the case for the human lineage. While genera like the robust Australopithecus, an early form of human-like ancestor similar to "Lucy," experienced some mild increases in size, our genus, Homo, is the only one to exhibit substantial increases in overall brain volume (De Sousa & Wood, 2007). In fact, brain size in our ancestral lineage has increased nearly five-fold, a figure that diverges significantly from what we would expect given increases in body size over that same time period (Boddy et al., 2012).

But dolphins have an EQ of 4–4.5, and although we know they're very smart, why aren't they making tools, building skyscrapers, and developing complex social societies? Surely our humanness isn't rooted solely in our capacity to manipulate objects with our hands but is buried deep in our cerebrum.

The answer may lie in connectivity. Although the surface of a dolphin's brain is inordinately more complex than our own, having twice the gyrification index as that of the human brain, their interhemispheric connections are comparatively sparse. In part, this is due to the fact that because a dolphin is a mammal and must breathe air, it must continue to swim and surface at all times. In order to achieve this feat, similar to nesting birds, only half of the dolphin's brain sleeps at any given time. Therefore, each hemisphere serves almost entirely as a brain unto itself, necessitating few connections to its mirror partner (Tarpley & Ridgway, 1994). In contrast, the human brain, though anatomically and functionally asymmetric, nevertheless functions as a whole and displays considerable interconnectivity alongside its substantial gray matter. We'll discuss more about connectivity in relation to human intelligence and autism in later sections.

Brain evolution at the DNA level

We share roughly 70 percent of our protein-coding genes with zebrafish, yet our two species shared their last common ancestor over 450 million years ago. We have a lot in common at the genetic level (Howe et al., 2013), but, in spite of that commonality, few would deny that humans and zebrafish look radically different. These differences are due in large part to the evolution that's taken place *around* protein-coding segments of DNA in regions that regulate the expression of those genes. These are known as *regulatory sequences*. They tell a gene *when*, *where*, and *how* it should be expressed. Because mutations within coding sequences of a gene are more likely to harm the organism, evolution preferentially tinkers with the more dispensable regulatory sequences. Rather than change the structure and function of the proteins themselves, variation within regulatory DNA has allowed evolution to create different patterns of gene expression and promote biological diversity.

Now think of chimpanzees and humans. We share about 98 percent of our protein-coding sequences with chimps. And though our two species look more alike than either of us do compared to a zebrafish, we are still radically different species with roughly 6–13 million years of divergent evolution between us. What's more, our encephalization quotient is almost three-fold greater than a chimp's (Roth & Dicke, 2005). So how can we be so similar and yet our brains so different?

Scientists have found that both the human and chimp ancestral lineages experienced accelerated evolution within the regulatory DNA in and around genes associated with the central nervous system. However, even though both species share this accelerated evolution, there's almost no overlap in the specific sequences affected in our two species (Prabhakar et al., 2006). In other words, neural genes in humans and chimps have dramatically evolved since the time both species split but in different ways, which has led to significant differences in brain size and function between us.

Many regulatory sequences are derived from *mobile elements* (Feschotte, 2008). These "jumping genes" are segments of DNA that use cut/copy and paste methods to move around the genome.

Mobile elements are extremely old and can be found in vertebrates like ourselves, in invertebrates such as fruit flies, plants, and even in bacteria. This means that mobile elements probably arose more than two to three billion years ago!

Because these jumping genes often contain repetitive DNA content, once they've managed to insert into the genome they're inherently unstable, leading to mispairings during DNA replication. These mispairings can result in the gain or loss of DNA material (discussed in Chapter 3). Sometimes that material contains regulatory DNA, which can change how a nearby gene functions.

Interestingly, deletion of significant regulatory content has occurred in the human lineage. Scientists have identified over 500 conserved regulatory sequences that humans have lost since the time of our last common ancestor with chimpanzees, but which the chimpanzee still retains (McLean et al., 2011). What's more, these sequences tend to be near neural genes.

Although it may seem strange to the reader, the loss of a regulatory element doesn't equate to an evolutionary regression or devolution. Instead, the loss of regulatory DNA may simply change *when*, *where*, or *how* that gene is expressed. Some regulatory sequences, for instance, aid in methylating genes, whereby a methyl group is attached to a target in the DNA, determining whether the gene can be expressed. Most typically, methylation will suppress gene expression.

However, if a methylation target is deleted, gene expression may also change. Interestingly, scientists have found that humans have hundreds of promoter regions that are undermethylated compared to the chimpanzee, leading to higher gene expression levels in those genes. What's more, these genes are especially enriched within the central nervous system (Zeng et al., 2012). So neural genes have been under strong selection in both humans and chimps for millions of years, yet evolution has worked in different ways, likely leading to the remarkable differences in brain size and function across our two species.

Is it all about brain size?

Humans have the largest brain-to-body-mass ratio of any organism studied to date. And though bigger brains may provide an animal with the ability to process more information, *how* the brain processes data is just as important. When we compare human, chimpanzee, and the macaque monkey, there are clear differences in brain size, with humans topping the list. However, geneticists have identified important differences in a part of the human brain known as the frontal cortex that differentiate us from our primate cousins.

As the term suggests, the frontal cortex lies at the front of the brain, directly behind the forehead and the frontal portion of the scalp. Although it is multifunctional, this area of the brain is best known for its involvement in "executive functions." Executive functions include such skills as the regulation of attention, working memory, multitasking, self-inhibition, and planning. These are the skills with which people with ADHD tend to have their greatest challenges.

Interestingly, geneticists have found that gene expression patterns in the human frontal cortex (specifically within the most anterior region known as the "frontal pole") are more complex than we see in our primate cousins such as chimps and macaques (Konopka et al., 2012). Of the gene profiles we have studied so far, about 30 percent are differentially expressed in humans compared to apes and monkeys. These genes span a variety of cellular functions, affecting different stages of neuron development and communication, as well as immune system function.

The frontal pole is also decidedly larger in humans compared to other primates and has an exceptional microanatomy contained within its layers, leading to enhanced connectivity throughout the brain (Semendeferi et al., 2001). This finding suggests that, aside from having more processing power, the human brain is better able to integrate incoming information compared to other animals. Think back to our earlier example of the dolphin and its "two brains." Interestingly, this ability to "integrate" disparate forms of information is one of the main impairments in autism, which we'll talk about in the next section.

Although the entirety of the human brain has radically evolved over millions of years, the frontal cortex is uniquely affected. This lobe is partly responsible for the intricacies of our social networks; our ability to plan, build, and adapt useful tools; our capacity for complex language that allows us to verbally inherit ideas over generations, tinkering as we go; and our ability to work together to achieve common goals. This is the biological counterpart of the cultural "ratchet effect," in which human traits are inherited behaviorally rather than genetically (Tomasello, 2009). Our genetics provides the means for these abilities and our culture ensures their inheritance.

INTELLIGENCE IN AUTISM
Connectivity

Cerebral connectivity can be broken down into two major forms: long-range and short-range. Most of the connections within the cortex are short-range, linking neurons that fall within several hundred micrometers of one another. They are primarily responsible for generating information. Long-range connections on the other hand are necessary for linking disparate areas of the brain with one another so that information can be integrated into a usable gestalt (Sporns & Zwi, 2004). For instance, people with face blindness (prosopagnosia) have difficulty recognizing familiar people because they are unable to integrate the varied information of the human face into an identifiable whole. Therefore, when they are able to recognize people, it's often because of select features such as hairstyle, a person's nose, or unusual glasses. They have challenges integrating these different types of facial information due, in part, to reduced connectivity or damage between brain regions integral in consolidation (Thomas et al., 2009).

Connections within the brains of infants who develop autism tend to develop at a faster pace than their typical counterparts. Connectivity initially skyrockets, particularly within the frontal cortex, but over time that growth plateaus compared to other children (Bashat et al., 2007; Wolff et al., 2012). This premature development is what evolutionary biologists call *peramorphosis*, meaning that particular stages of development in a specific organ or tissue have occurred earlier than they did in the same organs or tissues of their ancestors. The opposite of peramorphosis is *pedomorphosis*, in which select developmental stages have occurred later. Pedomorphosis is apparent in many aspects of human development. For instance, our extended childhood and adolescent periods are pedomorphic compared to other primates who reach sexual maturity at younger ages than ourselves (Marson et al., 1991; McNamara, 2012).

In spite of our extended childhoods, the brains of human infants are in some ways peramorphic (developmentally advanced) compared to chimpanzees. Scientists have found that, despite the larger size of our brains, connectivity develops earlier and faster than in our closest relative, the chimp—especially within the frontal cortex (Sakai et al., 2011). Ultimately, this leads to an enlarged white matter volume in the frontal cortex of humans compared to other primates (Schoenemann, Sheehan, & Glotzer, 2005).

Connectivity in autism, on average, develops even earlier than in typical infants, indicating that they may lie on the extreme end of a human continuum that preferences early development of brain connectivity compared to our primate ancestors. This suggests that hereditary influences responsible for this human trend have been under strong evolutionary pressures and may underlie aspects of autism risk. How premature development leads to the long-range underconnectivity and short-range overconnectivity patterns we see in autism is uncertain. However, a few possibilities spring to mind.

One explanation involves pruning. During early development, subsets of neurons in the cerebral cortex form numerous connections within the brain, connecting to regions not only within the same hemisphere but with the contralateral (opposite) hemisphere, forming the naïve corpus callosum. Through infancy and early childhood, however, as experience and learning drive patterns of activity, unused connections will be pruned. In the case of autism, peculiarities of neural activity may preference the activity of short-range connections over long ones, leading to more extensive pruning within white-matter structures like the corpus callosum. This in turn would lead to a decrease in the volume of this important structure.

Metabolic injury could lead to a loss of connectivity within the brain, a scenario that may be relevant in cases of autistic regression. Since long-range fibers are less plastic than smaller ones and can't reconnect to their original targets due to the sheer distance they must traverse, this connectivity is permanently lost following injury. Meanwhile, short-range fibers are able to recapitulate their earlier connections more easily.

Finally, the last scenario involves developmental mistiming. Because nerve fibers don't connect to targets randomly but are guided by important molecular signals (often provided by glial cells), premature development in autism may precede the presence of those all-important guiding signals. In order to aid in development of the corpus callosum, glial cells sit in the middle of the developing cerebrum, forming a pathway between which newborn nerve fibers are guided and eventually synapse onto neurons on the other side of the brain. If those fibers reach the midline of the brain before the glia are ready for them, this leads to a backlog of fiber tracts that are either pruned away or seek out alternate targets within the same hemisphere.

Interestingly, postmortem studies in autism suggest this does occur in a subset of cases (Wegiel et al., 2017).

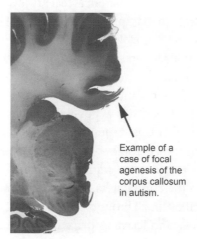

Example of a case of focal agenesis of the corpus callosum in autism.

Figure 9.6: Focal agenesis of the corpus callosum in autism

This is evidence of disturbances to developmental connectivity, particularly to long fiber tracts of the brainThese impairments can lead to deficits in communication between distant regions of the brain involved in complex cognitive processes such as socialization and language.

(Courtesy of Dr. Jerzy Wegiel)

Connectivity and cognition in autism

A preference for short-range connections over long ones emphasizes information generation. When this is at the expense of long-range connectivity, the brain isn't capable of integrating all the information it generates. This may partly explain why autistic individuals are often attuned to details yet struggle with skills that require the coordinated efforts of multiple disparate brain regions, such as socialization, language, and motor movements.

However, provided cognition isn't overly impaired, an emphasis on information generation may be beneficial, leading to detailed perception and potentially higher intelligence. This may explain some of the savantism, creativity, and intelligence we see in portions of the spectrum. It may also explain why people with high intelligence sometimes have autistic-like features. And in this way we can begin to understand how the evolution of human intelligence may share some of its story with conditions like autism.

However, as with many things in life, cognition teeters in a delicate balancing act: too much one way and we don't perceive enough detail; too much the other way and we can't construct a coherent whole. It is in this way that the autism spectrum can range from peaks of incredible genius to the most intellectually impaired of individuals, all determined by the ways in which the brain communicates within itself.

CLINICAL CONSIDERATIONS

Intellectual delays and impairment are significant issues in the diagnosis and treatment of people with autism. Although the majority of individuals by middle childhood are not intellectually disabled, a substantial minority retain the diagnosis of mild cognitive impairment. There are also some cases, often syndromic in nature, who have severe cognitive challenges and require significant supports for the entirety of their lives.

On the other hand, there are individuals on the spectrum who are eventually capable of independence, going on to hold jobs, and have careers and families of their own. Many a parent reading this book, for instance, may have realized his or her own autistic challenges during the process of his or her child's assessment and diagnosis.

Many cultural factions have argued over what autism is and isn't, attempting to draw a dividing line through ever-shifting sand. And while definitional dividing lines may be possible when addressing rare conditions, when we are dealing with a complex condition, by definition the causes will be numerous and the severity variable. That is the nature of complex conditions such as autism, schizophrenia, ADHD, heart disease, and Alzheimer's.

Autism isn't a single condition, but a large collection of different but overlapping syndromes that all share common behavioral features. And we call those features *autism*. Therefore, while one person's "autism" may be the result of a fragile X mutation leading to significant cognitive impairment, another person's "autism" may be linked with maternal immune activation during pregnancy and other hereditary and environmental factors, leading to a milder presentation of symptoms. The same concept can be extended to individuals with subclinical traits.

Autism, like the term *intellectual disability*, is a descriptive diagnosis, not a single condition with a single underlying cause—even though clinicians, scientists, and laymen have usually treated it as such. And although there is probably a common biological underpinning that causes this syndrome (e.g. widespread effects to specific systems within the brain), the factors that lead to its phenotype are numerous. Therefore, we must begin to rethink how we use the term *autism* and the implications that go with it. People across the spectrum may have the same syndrome, but they don't all share the same condition.

Chapter Ten

TOWARD A DEFINITION
OF AUTISM

Although Leo Kanner and Hans Asperger had published their manuscripts in the early 1940s, "autism" was not its own official diagnostic entity until 1980, a single year before Kanner passed away. In the first and second editions of the *Diagnostic and Statistical Manual of Mental Disorders* (DSM), published in 1952 and 1968 respectively, autism was subsumed under the broader diagnosis of *childhood schizophrenia*, used simply as an adjective to describe children who manifested atypical withdrawal behaviors. Given the rarity of childhood schizophrenia today, it's likely that many of these children were autistic by modern diagnostic standards.

By the time of the DSM-III's (1980) publication, *infantile autism* had been inducted as an official diagnosis, although its criteria were simplistic compared to later iterations. "Childhood Onset Pervasive Developmental Disorders" were also included in this version of the DSM, covering other variants of autism that supposedly had symptom onset after 30 months of age.

During this same period, renowned psychiatrist Dr. Lorna Wing (Figure 10.1) was working and publishing on a diagnostic entity she referred to as Asperger's syndrome (Wing, 1981). Wing's daughter was diagnosed with Kanner's autism in the 1950s. From that point onwards, Wing relinquished a blossoming line of research in electrophysiological studies of various mental health conditions and focused her professional career on autism. In 1964, she established the Camberwell Case Register and, alongside then-graduate student Judith Gould, assessed children with special needs coming through the Maudsley Hospital in southeast London (Watts, 2014).

Figure 10.1: The renowned autism researcher Dr. Lorna Wing
(Courtesy of Dr. Judith Gould and The Lorna Wing Centre for Autism)

As they collected data on these young patients for the register, they realized that while some children had classic autism, other children had features of autism but also characteristics that didn't precisely match Kanner's original profile. Instead, Wing came to recognize that autism existed as a *spectrum*, appreciating that the autistic phenotype was more variable than Kanner had envisioned.

Later, her husband, Dr. John Wing, happened across Hans Asperger's manuscript, which described children with social impairments, poor nonverbal communication, and physical clumsiness. Lorna Wing realized that Asperger's patients had features in common with Kanner's original cases but they were also different in other ways.

Although Asperger himself did not feel his patients lay on the same spectrum as that of Kanner's, Wing nevertheless helped to popularize the concept of an autism spectrum (including Asperger's syndrome) in her 1981 article "Asperger's syndrome: A clinical account." Interestingly, Wing precociously recognized in those early years of research that the etiological roots of autism spectrum conditions were quite variable:

> [Individuals] with the triad of symptoms all require the same kind of structured, organised educational approach, although the aims and achievements of education will vary from minimal self-care up to a university degree, depending on the skills available to the person concerned.

This hypothesis does not suggest that there is a common gross aetiology. This is certainly not the case, since many different genetic or pre-, peri- or post-natal causes can lead to the same overt clinical picture (Wing & Gould, 1979). It is more likely that all the conditions in which the triad occurs have in common impairment of certain aspects of brain function that are presumably necessary for adequate social interaction, verbal and non-verbal communication and imaginative development. (Wing, 1981)

By 1992, Asperger's syndrome was inducted into the World Health Organization's *International Classification of Diseases* (ICD) and in 1994 was subsumed in the DSM-IV-TR under the larger umbrella "Pervasive Developmental Disorders," alongside autistic disorder and other conditions such as Rett syndrome.

Although Asperger's syndrome is still an ICD diagnosis and is in use outside the United States, the term is currently obsolete within the U.S., and people with the condition now fall under the umbrella diagnosis *autism spectrum disorder* in the new DSM-5. Unfortunately, it now appears more difficult for individuals who once fulfilled Asperger criteria to garner an autism spectrum disorder diagnosis due to an increase in the number of criteria a person is required to meet within the sociocommunication domain. This has undoubtedly left a number of children and adults in the lurch, with no appropriate diagnosis to help them get the treatment and accommodations they may need. It's uncertain whether nosology (classification) will change again in future—however, fluctuating criteria are a reflection of the ongoing debate concerning the boundaries where autism ends and "normality" (for want of a better word) begins. Since biology rarely provides such clean delineation when it comes to complex conditions, it's likely these sorts of dividing lines are relatively arbitrary and may be more heavily driven by clinician opinion than hard data.

By now it should be clear to the reader that the etiology of autism is complex and varies across individuals. As we concluded in the previous chapter, "People across the spectrum may have the same syndrome, but they don't all share the same condition." Like the term, "intellectual disability," we are coming to understand "autism" as a behavioral label rather than a single entity—although there are undoubtedly subgroups of people who share similar etiologies. As science continues to plod onwards, we hope to identify these subgroups, which may afford individuals more tailored treatment options and accommodations should they wish.

LOOKING AT LESION STUDIES TO UNDERSTAND AUTISM

According to Lorna Wing's friend and collaborator Judith Gould, Wing was "rather like a detective. She could look at the bits of a puzzle and put it together" (Watts, 2014, p. 658). Despite working during the infancy of autism research, Wing already grasped that the autism spectrum was not only behaviorally but etiologically heterogeneous. Although in the early days she may not have realized the sheer breadth of that heterogeneity, she understood that disturbances to specific regions of the brain might lead to a common syndrome:

> It is more likely that all the conditions in which the triad occurs have in common impairment of certain aspects of brain function that are presumably necessary for adequate social interaction, verbal and non-verbal communication and imaginative development. (Wing, 1981, p. 124)

Here, we will review specific lesion studies to illustrate how regional effects in the brain can produce the primary symptoms associated with autism. Sometimes these cases are the result of brain injury, such as blunt trauma or stroke; other times, they are congenital. In reviewing this material, we can better understand which systems in the brain may be responsible for the criteria we consider the "core" of this complicated syndrome, even though different genetic and environmental factors drive symptomology across groups of people.

Sociocommunication

As we briefly discussed in Chapter 8, *pragmatics* is the social use of language. This includes what we say, how we say it, to whom we say it, our body language, and other aspects of context important for understanding the mood of the speaker and his or her likely response in such a situation. As you might imagine, in order to use social language well we must attend to and process many stimuli at once in order to alter our behaviors appropriately. Without that ability, we may be apt to tell rude jokes at the wrong time, be honest when our conversation partner is wanting reassurance rather than honesty, or give away private information to a stranger. Considering the social world's complexity, it may be unsurprising to know that pragmatic language continues to develop throughout childhood and well into adolescence and early adulthood (Nippold, 1993). Deficits in pragmatic language are also a fundamental feature of the sociocommunicative traits we see in autism (APA, 2013).

The frontal cortex, temporal cortex, and portions of the corpus callosum bridging these regions are areas integral to the production and comprehension of social language. Children who have experienced traumatic brain injury (TBI) to any of these regions often have deficits in social communication, particularly during the acute phase after injury (Ryan et al., 2015). With enough time and therapy, they may regain some of the skills they had lost, although some deficits may be permanent.

Individuals who are born with a congenitally missing corpus callosum (Figure 10.2) have a condition known as *agenesis of the corpus callosum* (ACC). Sometimes the agenesis is partial, affecting one or more of the subregions of the structure. Other times, the agenesis is complete and the entirety of the corpus callosum is missing. Interestingly, a body of evidence suggests that people with ACC have particular difficulties with social language, even when overall IQ is accounted for.

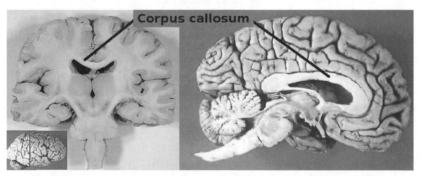

Figure 10.2: Coronal (left) and sagittal (right) sections of the corpus callosum, the white matter tract that connects the two hemispheres of the brain

(Reproduced with permission of user: Looie496 and John A. Beal, PhD, from Wikimedia Commons)

Parents often report that their children with ACC have difficulties with the nuances of social interaction, frequently misconstruing jokes and stories. Based on this anecdotal evidence, scientists have studied

ACC children's abilities to grasp humor, finding that while their comprehension of humor through the use of cartoons is relatively unimpaired, children with ACC do indeed have a poorer grasp of language-based jokes, the use of figurative language, and proverbs (Brown et al., 2005). Other studies have also found they have deficits in the perception of affective prosody, which refers to variations in vocal tone, rhythm, pitch, and volume that communicate emotion to the listener (Paul et al., 2003).

Further research has revealed that ACC children also struggle with social insight, social logic, and self-perception, indicating that the corpus callosum is necessary in coordinating numerous aspects of socialization in humans. However, these same children experience challenges in general reasoning, problem solving, and the ability to abstract and generalize non-social information as well, suggesting that social deficits are secondary to those occurring in more foundational cognitive processes (Brown & Paul, 2000).

When we compare children with ACC versus those with autism, those with ACC tend to be less impaired socially and have fewer problems with attention, anxiety, and depression than autistic children. However, although they experience social deficits to a lesser degree, the quality of impairments is similar across the two conditions. Meanwhile, children with ACC don't usually display the repetitive and restricted behaviors that are so characteristic of the autism spectrum (Badaruddin et al., 2007).

As we reviewed in Chapter 2, the corpus callosum is significantly smaller in autism (Casanova et al., 2011). Although we don't yet know the precise cause(s), this can be due to any of a number of factors: (1) fewer neuronal axons traverse the hemispheres of the brain; (2) a similar number of axons traverse the hemispheres but the diameters of these axons are thinner; or (3) a similar number of axons traverse the hemispheres but they have less white matter insulating them. The prevailing theory, however, purports that there are fewer axons forming the corpus callosum in autism, resulting in smaller overall volume of this all-important structure.

Because the corpus callosum is affected in autism and ACC and both conditions share similar social impairments that are separated by degree rather than by kind, this suggests that the structure and the regions of cortex it integrates are responsible for many of the sociocommunicative and higher-order cognitive deficits we see in the two conditions.

Restricted and repetitive behaviors and interests

While impairment in the frontotemporal regions and/or a loss of connectivity within major white-matter structures like the corpus callosum may be largely responsible for the sociocommunicative deficits in autism, we must turn to other brain structures to understand what could drive the restricted and repetitive behaviors and interests (RRBI) that, as some studies suggest, are most unique to the autism spectrum (Pedersen et al., 2016).

Although we discussed some of the differences between autism and obsessive-compulsive disorder (OCD) in the previous chapter, there are nevertheless obsessive-compulsive qualities that are characteristic of autism. In addition, lesion studies on acquired OCD are plentiful within the literature. For these reasons, we'll draw from this area of research to better understand aspects of RRBI in autism.

Many neurological syndromes and TBI can result in what is known as "acquired OCD." In these instances, there is usually no hereditary pattern within the extended family and OCD symptoms begin as a result of injury or disease progression. Examples of conditions that may result in acquired OCD include Huntington's disease, progressive supranuclear palsy, frontotemporal dementia, stroke, and even streptococcal infection. In the case of acquired OCD following a strep infection in childhood, this syndrome is known as "Pediatric Autoimmune Neuropsychiatric Disorders Associated with Streptococcal Infections" (PANDAS). Conditions like Tourette's syndrome may also occur with PANDAS.

In general, people with OCD, regardless of whether it's acquired or idiopathic (of unknown cause), tend to share certain cognitive deficits in addition to the obsessional and compulsive qualities that characterize the condition. Most typically, they experience challenges in attention, executive function, memory, and learning (Berthier et al., 1996). All of these processes are rooted within the frontal and temporal lobes of the brain.

Interestingly, when scientists perform neuroimaging on people with acquired OCD, they often find lesions within the frontotemporal regions, especially in cases of severe OCD (Berthier et al., 1996, 2001). Lesions sometimes also are found within the cingulate gyrus, a portion of cerebral cortex that lies directly above the corpus callosum, and within a subcortical region known as the basal ganglia, which is a limbic structure highly interconnected with the frontal lobes that helps to fine-tune their activities (Berthier et al., 1996; Laplane et al., 1989). Together, the frontal cortex, the cingulate, the basal ganglia, and the thalamus (a way station for neural information) all form a loop that regulates numerous aspects of human behavior and cognition (Figure 10.3). When damage occurs to any one of these structures, that loop is interrupted and can lead to a number of syndromes, including OCD. In the case of autism and idiopathic OCD, structures within this loop, as well as the fibers that are meant to connect them, probably didn't form properly or were lost.

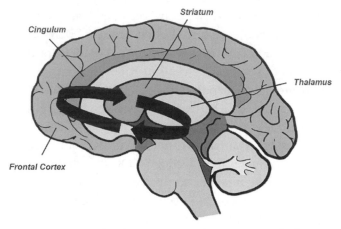

Figure 10.3: The obsessive-compulsive circuit in the brain

Stereotyped motor behavior, otherwise known as stereotypies or "stimming," is repetitive rhythmic movement that is used primarily for the purposes of self-stimulation or self-calming. Examples include thumb sucking, nail/lip biting, hand flapping, body rocking, head nodding, and head banging. When a stereotypy occurs in a child without any apparent developmental condition such as autism, it is referred to as a *primary motor stereotypy*. Otherwise, stereotypies are typically secondary symptoms to childhood neurodevelopmental conditions.

The basal ganglia, which we discussed above in relation to obsessive-compulsive behaviors, contain two opposing but complementary pathways. Through the *direct* or *striatonigral pathway*, the basal ganglia amplify motor and other behavioral patterns. Meanwhile, via the *indirect* or *striatopallidal pathway* they inhibit undesirable actions.

Both of these pathways connect the frontal cortex with deeper structures like the thalamus and the midbrain (Figure 10.4). Stereotyped behaviors arise whenever either of these two pathways is unbalanced, since they regulate one another. If the direct pathway is suppressed or if the indirect pathway is overactivated, this will result in repetitive mannerisms, not unlike those seen in conditions such as autism, OCD, and Tourette's (Langen et al., 2011).

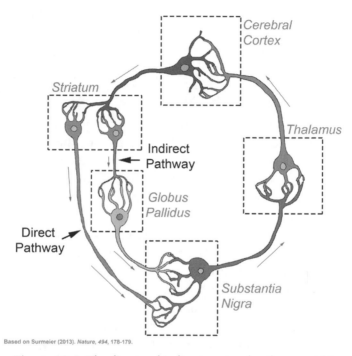

Based on Surmeier (2013). *Nature, 494*, 178-179.

Figure 10.4: The direct and indirect neuronal pathways within the part of the limbic system known as the basal ganglia

Dysfunction within these pathways is thought to be responsible for the symptoms of OCD and may also play important roles in the restricted and repetitive behaviors characteristic of autism.

Because RRBI are a core feature of autism, there have been many neuroimaging studies investigating the structure of the basal ganglia in the condition. Some of these studies report contradictory findings, which are likely due to differences in methodology. However, in general, the basal ganglia appear to be modestly larger in autism, even after accounting for overall brain size (Langen et al., 2009).

Unfortunately, there have been few postmortem studies to look at the microstructure of the basal ganglia in autism to determine what may be the cause of this volumetric increase. However, Jerzy Wegiel, a neuropathologist at the New York Institute for Basic Research in Developmental Disabilities, suggests that it may be due to increased neuron production with the subependymal layer in the basal ganglia, noting that a similar process occurs in the brains of people with Huntington's disease, a neurodegenerative condition that can develop obsessive-compulsive symptoms as the disease progresses (Wegiel et al., 2010). This increase in overall neuron number leads to larger basal ganglia volume.

Locating autism in the brain

Autism is a pervasive condition that has the propensity to affect almost all areas of the brain in some way. This is especially the case when we examine all the possible secondary symptoms that occur alongside those symptoms considered the "core" of the syndrome. However, since the medical community uses the core symptoms to define autism, it's important to identify the neural systems that underlie these cognitive functions in the hopes of moving closer towards a biological definition of these heterogeneous conditions, even if the precise impairments in those systems vary across people.

Although we have only viewed the question "Where is autism located in the brain?" in a simplified manner, we can come to a few tentative conclusions (Figure 10.5). First of all, the sociocommunicative deficits that are considered part of the core of the syndrome are likely the result of functional impairments in the frontotemporal lobes and/or the structures (i.e. corpus callosum) that connect them. Poor communication between these structures limits the individual's capacity to integrate different types of information, preventing him or her from forming a useful gestalt of social situations and reacting accordingly. In essence, the autistic person is only picking up parts of the social situation and is therefore acting on a more limited range of information.

Secondly, based on lesion studies investigating OCD, Tourette's, and stereotyped behaviors, we can conclude that many of the RRBI associated with autism are likely the result of disturbances to the communicative loops that connect the frontal cortex, cingulate, basal ganglia, thalamus, and midbrain, which regulate a variety of important behaviors. When these loops are dysregulated, this leads to different types of repetitive behaviors. Disturbances to this system can be either congenital or acquired.

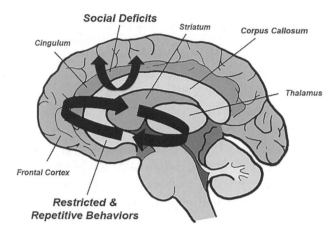

Figure 10.5: The circuits of the brain that are most likely responsible for the core features of autism

"Social deficits" are represented by the double-headed arrow traversing the corpus callosum, linking the two hemispheres. Meanwhile, "restricted and repetitive behaviors" are represented by the circuit running through the frontal cortex, the limbic system, and the thalamus.

When we look at the overlap between lesions that impair social communication and those that produce repetitive behaviors, we can see that the frontotemporal lobes and the fibers that provide interhemispheric, subcortical, and midbrain connections between them are all suspect. Therefore, in theory, any condition that targets these structures increases the likelihood of autism.

ONE SYNDROME—MANY AUTISMS

In this section we'll review a couple of the different conditions that claim autism as an associated feature. In this way you may begin to see (if you don't already) that although the term *autism* refers to a single syndrome, it occurs as a primary or secondary feature of many different conditions. And as Lorna Wing so aptly suggested, the feature that likely draws them under a single diagnostic umbrella is an overlapping impairment in key neural systems. In the above sections, we hypothesized that those core systems involve the frontotemporal regions and their interhemispheric and subcortical connections.

Rett syndrome

At one point in time, Rett syndrome was considered part of the Pervasive Developmental Disorders. However, with the acceleration of genetics research, the mutated gene responsible for most cases of Rett syndrome was identified (*MECP2*) and Rett's was removed from the DSM. It is now considered a "syndromic" or "genetic" form of autism, although hopefully in reading this book you have by now realized that the distinction of these labels is exceedingly gray and fuzzy.

The course of Rett syndrome includes a period of apparently normal development (although subtle features can be detected), followed by a regression in skills and the appearance of distinctive behaviors. Often, language and motor abilities regress, the latter frequently leading to the characteristic hand-wringing movements that typify the condition. The children also develop *dyspraxia* or *apraxia*, which significantly impairs their fine and/or gross motor abilities. Finally, intellectual disability, autism or autistic-like features, and epilepsy are very common in Rett's.

Similar to autism, the corpus callosum in Rett syndrome is demonstrably smaller than expected for overall cerebral volume, suggesting impairments in its ability to coordinate social and other complex forms of information. This is especially the case within segments known as the *genu* and *splenium*, which connect the most anterior and posterior portions of the brain respectively (Mahmood et al., 2010). Interestingly, Rett's patients whose speech is impaired also have smaller volume in a structure known as the *superior longitudinal fasciculus*, which is a long tract of white matter that connects all lobes with one another within the same hemisphere. A similar finding occurs in people with autism who have significant speech impairment, suggesting this structure is vital in the production of language and is probably an integral part of the "cortical language circuit" (Friederici, 2012; Nagae et al., 2012).

The entirety of the brain in Rett's is hypoplastic (underdeveloped) (Murakami et al., 1992). It is a progressive condition whose severity depends on the specific mutation involved and usually results in brain atrophy over time (Horská et al., 2009). As we find with autism, the frontal lobes are indeed targeted in Rett's and the hypoplasia in these regions is also relative to the severity of the condition (Carter et al., 2008). The frontal lobes exhibit reduced blood flow, suggesting low oxygen intake and reduced neural activity in these areas (reviewed in Villemagne et al., 2002).

Like the frontal lobes, the basal ganglia in Rett's are reduced in overall size (Murakami et al., 1992). Interestingly, postmortem analysis of the Rett's brain has shown that subunits of the basal ganglia known as the putamen and caudate nucleus express unusually low levels of excitatory receptors (AMPA, NMDA, kainate), meanwhile the caudate nucleus has high levels of inhibitory receptors, suggesting that the excitatory–inhibitory balance within the basal ganglia in Rett's is seriously disturbed and is likely responsible for the repetitive behaviors characteristic of the condition (Blue, Naidu, & Johnston, 1999).

Obviously not all cases of autism have Rett syndrome. Meanwhile, not all cases of Rett's fulfill autism criteria. However, the extensive overlap we see in the two conditions may be due, as we've discussed, to impairments in specific systems within the brain. Rett's shows evidence of structural and functional impairment within the frontal cortex, the basal ganglia, and large white-matter structures that support interhemispheric and subcortical connectivity, all of which may produce the core features of autism. Likewise, similar impairments are seen in "idiopathic" autism, suggesting that the reason for their symptom overlap is not a common etiology in the molecular sense but dysfunction within common systems.

22q11.2 deletion syndrome

22q11.2 deletion syndrome is caused (as the name implies) by a deletion of genetic material near the middle of the 22nd chromosome. People with the condition often have heart abnormalities, cleft palate, and other distinctive facial features. Many other features can occur but vary considerably between cases. This symptom variability meant that different groupings of clinical features were once described under different names, including DiGeorge syndrome, velocardiofacial syndrome, and conotruncal anomaly syndrome. More recently, however, they have all been subsumed under the single diagnostic label 22q11.2 deletion syndrome, based on the specific gene mutation that underlies this broad syndrome.

Children with 22q11.2 deletion typically experience developmental delays and are at significantly increased risk for developing ADHD and autism. Autism and autism-like symptoms occur in approximately 20–25 percent of children and adolescents with the condition (Fine et al., 2005; Schneider et al., 2014). In addition, adults with 22q11.2 deletion are at significantly elevated risk for developing schizophrenia (23–43%), as well as anxiety (40–76%) and mood disorders (9–35%) (reviewed in Schneider et al., 2014). Overall, this deletion syndrome predisposes towards a variety of neurodevelopmental and psychiatric conditions.

Similar to what we see with the other clinical features, brain abnormalities across this group of people differ considerably. And while there is typically an overall reduction in brain volume, effects to the frontal lobes, for instance, are quite variable (Zinkstok & Amelsvoort, 2005). In people with features reminiscent of the now-obsolete velocardiofacial syndrome, frontal lobe volume is typically increased in size, particularly within regions known as the *right middle* and *superior frontal gyri* (Simon et al., 2005). However, children with 22q11.2 deletion in general have a reduction in overall white matter volume (connectivity) within the frontal lobes, suggesting significant potential impairment in these regions that may affect social communication skills (Campbell et al., 2006).

People with 22q11.2 deletion also have midline defects within the brain, affecting structures like the corpus callosum as well as the cingulum bundle, which is the bilateral tract of fibers that connects the cingulate with the hippocampus (Kates et al., 2015; Tan et al., 2009). In addition, they are likely to retain a fluid-filled embryologic structure known as the *cavum septum pellucidum*, which is a midline anatomical variation occurring in a minority of the typical population and is colloquially known as the "sixth ventricle" (Shashi et al., 2004; Tan et al., 2009). The basal ganglia are also affected in 22q11.2 deletion. Not only are the caudate heads increased in volume similar to what we see in idiopathic autism, there is sometimes abnormal asymmetry within the structures, with the left side greater in volume than the right (Eliez et al., 2002).

Although these brain anomalies are more variable than we noted with Rett syndrome, which has an extremely high incidence of comorbid autism, some of the structures that are affected in 22q11.2 deletion syndrome (frontal lobes, cingulate, corpus callosum, basal ganglia, etc.) are the same structures likely responsible for the core symptoms of autism and may give rise to the high comorbidity rates seen in this genetic syndrome.

AUTISM OR AUTISMS?

Although the core symptoms of autism may be due to dysfunction within specific structures and systems of the brain, it's clear that autism has many different causes, as discussed by Lynn Waterhouse:

> In 1975 when I began studying autism I believed it was a distinct behavioral syndrome, and believed a unitary brain basis for it would soon be discovered. But by the middle of the 1990s many brain deficits had already been found in association with autism. Evidence suggested that subsets of individuals diagnosed with autism had deficits in one or more brain regions and brain neurochemicals, including the amygdala, the hippocampus, temporal and parietal regions of the cortex, and the neurohormone oxytocin (Waterhouse, Fein, & Modahl, 1996). Our research group did find evidence for abnormal oxytocin in autism (Green et al., 2001; Modahl et al., 1998). However, despite substantial financial support from the National Institutes of Mental Health, National Institute of Child Health and Human Development, and support from several private funding agencies, and despite the intellectual effort of all on our research teams, we failed to find meaningful brain-based behavioral subgroups of autism (Stevens et al., 2000; Waterhouse et al., 1996). Our problems reflected the field's problems. (Waterhouse, 2013, p. 2)

Research suggests that this heterogeneity or variability can result in many different anomalies within the brain and is often structurally and functionally pervasive. Therefore, although impairments in the frontotemporal lobes, the cingulate, the basal ganglia, and their respective white-matter connections may underlie the core features of autism, these findings may be lost amidst a sea of other abnormalities that mask their relevance. In addition, the specific structural and functional abnormalities within these core systems vary across individuals but still inevitably lead to similar impairments. For instance, we may envision macrocephaly (unusually large head size) and microcephaly (unusually small head size) as polar opposites yet both occur frequently in association with autism (Fombonne et al., 1999).

For these reasons, it is understandable as Lynn Waterhouse laments in the preceding quote that it has been challenging for us scientists to organize autistic people into subgroups based on specific neuroanatomical correlates. It is also easy to become distracted by the superfluous findings that occur in the brain outside the systems that are likely responsible for the core of autism. This, in the end, has led to much confusion and continues to delay our understanding of these conditions at the biological level.

Yet, ironically, the behavioral syndrome is robust, as even cognitive studies suggest that despite etiological heterogeneity autistic people actually have a lot in common with one another (Cantio et al., 2016). This indicates that the function of the brain and its resultant behaviors are the core of our definitions for autism, not genes, proteins, or compartmentalized structures of cells. While there are undoubtedly molecular and microscopic subgroups in autism, our definitions of these subgroups will likely only be realized at a broader systems level, not in terms of specific gene function or synaptic structure.

CONCLUSIONS

It is now 75 years since Leo Kanner published his original manuscript describing eleven children with the condition we call "autism." It was almost 40 years later that the diagnostic entity was finally acknowledged by mainstream psychiatry. Autism, therefore, is a relatively young concept when compared to other neurodevelopmental conditions, such as schizophrenia or bipolar disorder. While there may well be hereditary and environmental variables that affect autism prevalence, "infantile autism" as a diagnosis is not much older than "Asperger's syndrome," the former predating the latter by 12 to 14 years. Undoubtedly, much of the boom in autism prevalence is not just the recognition of a broader spectrum but the recognition of autism, period.

With that in mind, we have nevertheless discussed environmental exigencies in Chapter 4 that have the potential to affect autism incidence, although to what extent is challenging to discern since we're attempting to measure effects of complex and fluctuating features. We also cannot say how heredity, especially assortative mating, continues to subtly alter the gene pool over time and thus autism risk. This question may be especially poignant considering the ease with which we now move and intermingle, which a couple hundred years ago was unheard of. Most people lived, married, and died in their local villages.

Besides autism prevalence, we have discussed important associated features such as epilepsy, intellectual disability, and regression, the latter having been painfully ignored by medical and research communities despite its clinical significance. We also reviewed what we know of the biology of these comorbid features, which, especially in the case of epilepsy and regression, may share some overlap.

Finally, we discussed the broader autism phenotype (BAP), which shares similar though muted impairments to those we see in autism and appears to be a significant hereditary risk factor for having a child on the spectrum. We learned that BAP can be subtle and, especially in women, may even be diagnosed as anxiety or depression, illustrating an etiologically related yet phenotypically broad neurodevelopmental spectrum.

In summary, this book is a work in progress. We have tried our best to present the current state of knowledge of autism research, but this work is a reflection of our (the authors') professional biases. In addition, in ten or twenty years' time scientists' perceptions of some of the information presented here may radically change based on new data and paradigm shifts within the field. That is the nature of science: a noble endeavor but inevitably colored by the humanness of the people pursuing it. The information reviewed here is no different. We only hope that our perspectives may inspire others to look at data in new imaginative ways, so that this field of work continues to evolve in a healthy and fruitful manner and leads to measurable positive differences in the lives of people on the autism spectrum and their families.

References

Ackerman, S., Schoenbrun, S., Hudac, C., & Bernier, R. (2017). Interactive effects of prenatal antidepressant exposure and likely gene disrupting mutations on the severity of autism spectrum disorder. *Journal of Autism and Developmental Disorders, 47*(11), 3489–3496.

Adamo, M. P., Zapata, M., & Frey, T. K. (2008). Analysis of gene expression in fetal and adult cells infected with rubella virus. *Virology, 370*(1), 1–11.

Adolphs, R., Spezio, M. L., Parlier, M., & Piven, J. (2008). Distinct face-processing strategies in parents of autistic children. *Current Biology, 18*, 1090–1093.

Ahmad, S. F., Zoheir, K. M., Ansari, M. A., Nadeem, A., et al. (2017). Th1, Th2, Th17, and T regulatory cell-related transcription factor signaling in children with autism. *Molecular Neurobiology, 54*, 4390–4400.

Akshoomoff, N. (2006). Use of the Mullen Scales of Early Learning for the assessment of young children with autism spectrum disorders. *Child Neuropsychology, 12*, 269–277.

Al Kaissi, A., Grill, F., Safi, H., Ben Ghachem, M., Ben Chehida, F., & Klaushofer, K. (2007). Craniocervical junction malformation in a child with oromandibular-limb hypogenesis-Möbius syndrome. *Orphanet Journal of Rare Diseases, 2*, 2.

Alarcón, M., Abrahams, B. S., Stone, J. L., Duvall, J. A., et al. (2008). Linkage, association, and gene-expression analyses identify CNTNAP2 as an autism-susceptibility gene. *American Journal of Human Genetics, 82*(1), 150–159.

Aldridge, K., George, I. D., Cole, K. K., Austin, J. R., et al. (2011). Facial phenotypes in subgroups of prepubertal boys with autism spectrum disorders are correlated with clinical phenotypes. *Molecular Autism, 2*, 15.

Allen, L. H. (1997). Pregnancy and iron deficiency: Unresolved issues. *Nutritional Reviews, 55*, 91–101.

Amato, M. C., Verghi, M., Galluzzo, A., & Giordano, C. (2011). The oligomenorrhoic phenotypes of polycystic ovary syndrome are characterized by a high visceral adiposity index: A likely condition of cardiometabolic risk. *Human Reproduction, 26*, 1486–1494.

APA (American Psychiatric Association). (2013). *Diagnostic and Statistical Manual of Mental Disorders* (5th edn). Washington, DC: American Psychiatric Publishing.

Amiet, C., Gourfinkel-An, I., Bouzamondo, A., Tordjman, S., et al. (2008). Epilepsy in autism is associated with intellectual disability and gender: Evidence from a meta-analysis. *Biological Psychiatry, 64*, 577–582.

Anderson, G. M., Gutknecht, L., Cohen, C. J., Brailly-Tabard, S., et al. (2002). Serotonin transporter promoter variants in autism: Functional effects and relationship to platelet hyperserotonemia. *Molecular Psychiatry, 7*(8), 831–836.

Andrews, A. (2017). Jacob Barnett's curious and computation mind. *Pacific Standard,* May 19.

Andrews, D. S., Avino, T. A., Gudbrandsen, M., Daly, E., et al. (2017). In vivo evidence of reduced integrity of the gray-white matter boundary in autism spectrum disorder. *Cerebral Cortex, 27,* 877–887.

Apostolou, P., & Fostira, F. (2013). Hereditary breast cancer: The era of new susceptibility genes. *BioMed Research International,* 747318.

Aram, D. M. (1997). Hyperlexia: Reading without meaning in young children. *Topics in Language Disorders, 17,* 1–13.

Arking, D. E., Cutler, D. J., Brune, C. W., Teslovich, T. M., et al. (2008). A common genetic variant in the neurexin superfamily member CNTNAP2 increases familiar risk of autism. *American Journal of Human Genetics, 82*(1), 160–164.

Arnold, S. E., Louneva, N., Cao, K., Wang, L. S., et al. (2013). Cellular, synaptic, and biochemical features of resilient cognition in Alzheimer's disease. *Neurobiology of Aging, 34,* 157–168.

Aronson, M., Hagberg, B., & Gillberg, C. (1997). Attention deficits and autistic spectrum problems in children exposed to alcohol during gestation: A follow-up study. *Developmental Medicine & Child Neurology, 39,* 583–587.

Ashwood, P., Schauer, J., Pessah, I. N., & Van de Water, J. (2009). Preliminary evidence of the in vitro effects of BDE-47 on innate immune response in children with autism spectrum disorders. *Journal of Neuroimmunology, 208,* 130–135.

Astiz, M., de Alaniz, M. J., & Marra, C. A. (2012). The oxidative damage and inflammation caused by pesticides are reverted by lipoic acid in rat brain. *Neurochemistry International, 61,* 1231–1241.

Autier, P., Boniol, M., Pizot, C., & Mullie, P. (2014). Vitamin D status and ill health: A systematic review. *Lancet Diabetes and Endocrinology, 2*(1), 76–89.

Avino, T. A., & Hutsler, J. J. (2010). Abnormal cell patterning at the cortical gray-white matter boundary in autism spectrum disorders. *Brain Research, 1360,* 138–146.

Badaruddin, D. H., Andrews, G. L., Bölte, S., Schilmoeller, K. J., et al. (2007). Social and behavioral problems of children with agenesis of the corpus callosum. *Child Psychiatry and Human Development, 38,* 287–302.

Baeza-Velasco, C., Pailhez, G., Bulbena, A., & Baghdadli, A. (2015). Joint hypermobility and the heritable disorders of connective tissue: Clinical and empirical evidence of links with psychiatry. *General Hospital Psychiatry, 37,* 24–30.

Bailey, A., Le Couteur, A., Gottesman, I., Bolton, P., et al. (1995). Autism as a strongly genetic disorder: Evidence from a British twin study. *Psychological Medicine, 25,* 63–77.

Baird, G., Charman, T., Pickles, A., Chandler, S., et al. (2008). Regression, developmental trajectory and associated problems in disorders in the autism spectrum: The SNAP study. *Journal of Autism and Developmental Disorders, 38*(10), 1827–1836.

Baird, G., Robinson, R. O., Boyd, S., & Charman, T. (2006). Sleep electrocencephalograms in young children with autism with and without regression. *Developmental Medicine and Child Neurology, 48,* 604–608.

Baker, J. P. (2013). Autism at 70—Redrawing the boundaries. *New England Journal of Medicine, 369,* 1089–1091.

Bandim, J. M., Ventura, L. O., Miller, M. T., Almeida, H. C., & Costa, A. E. (2003). Autism and Möbius sequence: An exploratory study of children in northeastern Brazil. *Arquivos de Neuro-psiquitria, 61*(2A), 181–185.

Barger, B. D., & Campbell, J. M. (2014). Developmental regression in autism spectrum disorders: Implications for clinical outcomes. In V. B. Patel, V. R. Preedy, & C. R. Martin (Eds.), *Comprehensive Guide to Autism* (pp. 1473–1493). New York, NY: Springer.

Barger, B. D., Campbell, J. M., & McDonough, J. D. (2013). Prevalence and onset of regression within autism spectrum disorders: A meta-analytic review. *Journal of Autism and Developmental Disorders, 43,* 817–828.

Barkovich, A. J., Dobyns, W. B., & Guerrini, R. (2015). Malformations of cortical development and epilepsy. *Cold Spring Harbor Perspectives in Medicine, 5,* a022392.

Barneveld, P. S., Pierterse, J., de Sonneville, L., van Rijn, S., et al. (2011). Overlap of autistic and schizotypal traits in adolescents with autism spectrum disorders. *Schizophrenia Research, 126,* 231–236.

Baron-Cohen, S. (1998). Does autism occur more often in families of physicists, engineers, and mathematicians? *Autism, 2,* 296–301.

Baron-Cohen, S. (2002). The extreme male brain theory of autism. *Trends in Cognitive Sciences, 6,* 248–254.

Baron-Cohen, S., Leslie, A. M., & Frith, U. (1985). Does the autistic child have a "theory of mind"? *Cognition, 21,* 37–46.

Baron-Cohen, S., Scahill, V. L., Izaguirre, J., Hornsey, H., & Robertson, M. M. (1999). The prevalence of Gilles de la Tourette syndrome in children and adolescents with autism: A large scale study. *Psychological Medicine, 29,* 1151–1159.

Baron-Cohen, S., Wheelwright, S., Stott, C., Bolton, P., & Goodyer, I. (1997). Is there a link between engineering and autism? *Autism, 1,* 101–109.

Bashat, D. B., Kronfeld-Duenias, V., Zachor, D. A., Ekstein, P. M., et al. (2007). Accelerated maturation of white matter in young children with autism: A high b value DWI study. *NeuroImage, 37,* 40–47.

Battaglia, A., Chines, C., & Carey, J. C. (2006). The FG syndrome: A report of a large Italian series. *American Journal of Medical Genetics Part A, 140,* 2075–2079.

Bauman, M. D., Iosif, A.-M., Ashwood, P., Braunschweig, D., et al. (2013). Maternal antibodies from mothers of children with autism alter brain growth and social behavior development in the rhesus monkey. *Translational Psychiatry, 3,* e278.

Behnke, M., Eyler, F. D, Garvan, C. W., & Wobie, K. (2001). The search for congenital malformations in newborns with fetal cocaine exposure. *Pediatrics, 107*(5), E74.

Ben-Ari, Y. (2002). Excitatory actions of GABA during development: The nature of the nurture. *Nature Reviews Neuroscience, 3*(9), 728–739.

Bercum, F. M., Rodgers, K. M., Benison, A. M., Smith, Z. Z., et al. (2015). Maternal stress combined with terbutaline leads to comorbid autistic-like behavior and epilepsy in a rat model. *Journal of Neuroscience, 35*(48), 15894–15902.

Berg, J. M., & Geschwind, D. H. (2012). Autism genetics: Searching for specificity and convergence. *Genome Biology, 13,* 247.

Berthier, M. L., Kulisevsky, J., Gironell, A., & Heras, J. A. (1996). Obsessive-compulsive disorder associated with brain lesions: Clinical phenomenology, cognitive function, and anatomic correlates. *Neurology, 47*, 353–361.

Berthier, M. L., Kulisevsky, J., Gironell, A., & López, O. L. (2001). Obsessive-compulsive disorder and traumatic brain injury: Behavioral, cognitive, and neuroimaging findings. *Cognitive and Behavioral Neurology, 14*, 23–31.

Betts, T., Yarrow, H., Dutton, N., Greenhill, L., & Rolfe, T. (2003). A study of anticonvulsant medication on ovarian function in a group of women with epilepsy who have only ever taken one anticonvulsant compared with a group of women without epilepsy. *Seizure, 12*, 323–329.

Beversdorf, D. Q., Manning, S. E., Hillier, A., Anderson, L., et al. (2005). Timing of prenatal stressors and autism. *Journal of Autism and Developmental Disorders, 35*, 471–478.

Biederman, J., Monuteaux, M. C., Doyle, A. E., Seidman, L. J., et al. (2004). Impact of executive function deficits and attention-deficit/hyperactivity disorder (ADHD) on academic outcomes in children. *Journal of Consulting and Clinical Psychology, 72*, 757.

Billes, S. K., Sinnayah, P., & Cowley, M. A. (2014). Naltrexone/bupropion for obesity: An investigational combination pharmacotherapy for weight loss. *Pharmacological Research, 84*, 1–11.

Biswas, S. K. (2016). Does the interdependence between oxidative stress and inflammation explain the antioxidant paradox? *Oxidative Medicine and Cellular Longevity*, 5698931.

Bitsko R. H., Holbrook, J. R., Visser, S. N., Mink, J. W., et al. (2014). A national profile of Tourette syndrome, 2011–2012. *Journal of Developmental and Behavioral Pediatrics, 35*, 317.

Blackmon, K., Bluvstein, J., MacAllister, W. S., Avallone, J., et al. (2016). Treatment resistant epilepsy in autism spectrum disorder: Increased risk for females. *Autism Research, 9*, 311–320.

Blaxill, M. F. (2004). What's going on? The question of time trends in autism. *Public Health Reports, 119*(6), 536–551.

Bleuler, E. (1950). *Dementia Praecox*. New York, NY: International University Press.

Blue, M. E., Naidu, S., & Johnston, M. V. (1999). Altered development of glutamate and GABA receptors in the basal ganglia of girls with Rett syndrome. *Experimental Neurology, 156*, 345–352.

Boddy, A. M., McGowen, M. R., Sherwood, C. C., Grossman, L. I., Goodman, M., & Wildman, D. E. (2012). Comparative analysis of encephalization in mammals reveals relaxed constraints on anthropoid primate and cetacean brain scaling. *Journal of Evolutionary Biology, 25*, 981–994.

Bölte, S., & Poutska, F. (2003). The recognition of facial affect in autistic and schizophrenic subjects and their first-degree relatives. *Psychological Medicine, 33*, 907–915.

Bölte, S., & Poutska, F. (2006). The broader cognitive phenotype of autism in parents: How specific is the tendency for local processing and executive dysfunction? *Journal of Child Psychology and Psychiatry, 47*, 639–645.

Bolton, P. F., Carcani-Rathwell, I., Hutton, J., Goode, S., Howlin, P., & Rutter, M. (2011). Epilepsy in autism: Features and correlates. *British Journal of Psychiatry, 198*, 289–294.

Bolton, P., MacDonald, H., Pickles, A., Rios, P., et al. (1994). A case-control family history study of autism. *Journal of Child Psychology and Psychiatry, 35*, 877–900.

Bonnel, A., Mottron, L., Peretz, I., Trudel, M., Gallun, E., & Bonnel, A. M. (2003). Enhanced pitch sensitivity in individuals with autism: A signal detection analysis. *Journal of Cognitive Neuroscience, 15*, 226–235.

Borrás, C., Sastre, J., García-Sala, D., Lloret, A., Pallardó, F. V., & Viña, J. (2003). Mitochondria from females exhibit higher antioxidant gene expression and lower oxidative damage than males. *Free Radical Biology & Medicine, 34*, 546–552.

Borsini, A., Zunszain, P. A., Thuret, S., & Pariante, C. M. (2015). The role of inflammatory cytokines as key modulators of neurogenesis. *Trends in Neurosciences, 38*, 145–157.

Boukhris, T., Sheehy, O., Mottron, L., & Bérard, A. (2016). Antidepressant use during pregnancy and the risk of autism spectrum disorder in children. *JAMA Pediatrics, 170*(2), 117–124.

Bren, L. (2001). Frances Oldham Kelsey: FDA medical reviewer leaves her mark on history. *FDA Consumer Magazine*, March–April.

Brodmann, K. (2006). *Brodmann's "Localization in the Cerebral Cortex"*. New York, NY: Springer. (Original work published 1909)

Brown, H. K., Ray, J. G., Wilton, A. S., Lunsky, Y., Gomes, T., & Vigod, S. N. (2017). Association between serotonergic antidepressant use during pregnancy and autism spectrum disorder in children. *JAMA, 317*, 1544–1552.

Brown, J., Bianco, J. I., McGrath, J. J., & Eyles, D. W. (2003). 1,25-dihydroxyvitamin D3 induces nerve growth factor, promotes neurite outgrowth and inhibits mitosis in the embryonic rat hippocampal neurons. *Neuroscience Letters, 343*, 139–143.

Brown, W. S., & Paul, L. K. (2000). Cognitive and psychosocial deficits in agenesis of the corpus callosum with normal intelligence. *Cognitive Neuropsychiatry, 5*, 135–157.

Brown, W. S., Paul, L. K., Symington, M., & Dietrich, R. (2005). Comprehension of humor in primary agenesis of the corpus callosum. *Neuropsychologia, 43*, 906–916.

Buchmann, K. (2014). Evolution of innate immunity: Clues from invertebrates via fish to mammals. *Frontiers in Immunology, 5*, 459.

Burton, H. (2003). Visual cortex activity in early and late blind people. *Journal of Neuroscience, 23*, 4005–4011.

Buxhoeveden, D. P., Switala, A. E., Roy, E., Litaker, M., & Casanova, M. F. (2001). Morphological differences between minicolumns in human and nonhuman primate cortex. *American Journal of Physical Anthropology, 115*, 361–371.

Byrnes, G. B., Southey, M. C., & Hopper, J. L. (2008). Are the so-called low penetrance breast cancer genes, *ATM, BRIP1, PALB2*, and *CHEK2*, high risk for women with strong family histories? *Breast Cancer Research, 10*, 208.

Callaway, E. (2012). Fathers bequeath more mutations as they age. *Nature, 488*(7412), 439.

Campbell, L. E., Daly, E., Toal, F., Stevens, A., et al. (2006). Brain and behaviour in children with 22q11.2 deletion syndrome: A volumetric and voxel-based morphometry MRI study. *Brain, 129*, 1218–1228.

Canitano, R., Luchetti, A., & Zapella, M. (2005). Epilepsy, electroencephalographic abnormalities, and regression in children with autism. *Journal of Child Neurology, 20*, 27–31.

Cantio, C., Jepsen, J. R. M., Madsen, G. F., Bilenberg, N., & White, S. J. (2016). Exploring 'the autisms' at a cognitive level. *Autism Research, 9*, 1328–1339.

Cantwell, D. P. (1996). Attention deficit disorder: A review of the past 10 years. *Journal of the American Academy of Child and Adolescent Psychiatry, 35*, 978–987.

Capone, G. T., Grados, M. A., Kaufman, W. E., Bernad-Ripoli, S., & Jewell, A. (2005). Down syndrome and comorbid autism-spectrum disorder: Characterization using the aberrant behavior checklist. *American Journal of Medical Genetics Part A, 134*, 373–380.

Cárdenas, A. M., Ardiles, A. O., Barraza, N., Baéz-Matus, X., & Caviedes, P. (2012). Role of tau protein in neuronal damage in Alzheimer's disease and Down syndrome. *Archives of Medical Research, 43*, 645–654.

Carlsen, M. H., Halvorsen, B. L., Holte, K., Bøhn, S. K., et al. (2010). The total antioxidant content of more than 3100 foods, beverages, spices, herbs and supplements used worldwide. *Nutrition Journal, 9*, 3.

Carter, C. J., & Blizard, R. A. (2016). Autism genes are selectively targeted by environmental pollutants including pesticides, heavy metals, bisphenol A, phthalates and many others in food, cosmetics or household products. *Neurochemistry International, 101*, 83–109.

Carter, J. C., Landham, D. C., Pham, D., Bibat, G., Naidu, S., & Kaufmann, W. E. (2008). Selective cerebral volume reduction in Rett syndrome: A multiple-approach MR imaging study. *American Journal of Neuroradiology, 29*, 436–441.

Carvill, G. L., Heavin, S. B., Yendle, S. C., McMahon, J. M., et al. (2013). Targeted resequencing in epileptic encephalopathies identifies de novo mutations in CHD2 and SYNGAP1. *Nature Genetics, 45*(7), 825–830.

Casanova, E. L., Gerstner, Z., Sharp, J. L., Casanova, M. F., & Feltus, F. A. (2017a). Widespread genotype-phenotype correlations in intellectual disability. *bioRxiv*, 220608.

Casanova, E. L., Sharp, J. L., Chakraborty, H., Sumi, N. S., & Casanova, M. F. (2016). Genes with high penetrance for syndromic and nonsyndromic autism typically function within the nucleus and regulate gene expression. *Molecular Autism, 7*, 18.

Casanova, E. L., Sharp, J. L., Edelson, S. M., Kelly, D. P., & Casanova, M. F. (2018). A cohort study comparing women with autism spectrum disorder with and without generalized joint hypermobility. *Behavioral Sciences, 8*, 35

Casanova, E. L., Switala, A. E., Dandamudi, S., & Casanova, M. F. (2017b). The feature landscape of autism risk genes suggests recent directional selection. Unpublished data.

Casanova, M F., El-Baz, A., Elnakib, A., Switala, A. E., et al. (2011). Quantitative analysis of the shape of the corpus callosum in patients with autism and comparison individuals. *Autism, 15*, 223–238.

Casanova, M. F. (1995) Elmer Ernest Southard (1876–1920). *Biological Psychiatry,* *38,* 71–73.

Casanova, M. F. (2007). The neuropathology of autism. *Brain Pathology, 17,* 422–433.

Casanova, M. F. (2014a). Autism as a sequence: From heterochronic germinal cell divisions to abnormalities of cell migration and cortical dysplasias. *Medical Hypotheses, 83,* 32–38.

Casanova, M. F. (2014b). The neuropathology of autism. In F. Volkmar, K. Pelphrey, R. Paul, & S. Rogers (Eds.), *Handbook of Autism and Pervasive Developmental Disorders: Volume I* (4th edn, pp. 497–531). New York, NY: Wiley.

Casanova, M. F., Baruth, J. M., El-Baz, A., Tasman, A., Sears, L., & Sokhadze, E. (2012). Repetitive transcranial magnetic stimulation (rTMS) modulates event-related potential (ERP) indices of attention in autism. *Translational Neuroscience, 3,* 170–180.

Casanova, M. F., Baruth, J., El-Baz, A. S., Sokhadze, G. E., Hensley, M., & Sokhadze, E. M. (2013). Evoked and induced gamma-frequency oscillations in autism. In M. F. Casanova, A. S. El-Baz, & J. S. Suri (Eds.), *Imaging the Brain in Autism* (pp. 87–106). New York, NY: Springer.

Casanova, M. F., Buxhoeveden, D. P., Switala, A. E., & Roy, R. (2002a). Minicolumnar pathology in autism. *Neurology, 58,* 428–432.

Casanova, M. F., Buxhoeveden, D. P., Switala, A. E., & Roy, R. (2002b). Asperger's syndrome and cortical neuropathology. *Journal of Child Neurology, 17,* 142–145.

Casanova, M. F., Buxhoeveden, D., & Gomez, J. (2003). Disruption in the inhibitory architecture of the cell minicolumn: Implications for autism. *The Neuroscientist, 9,* 496–507.

Casanova, M. F., Casanova, E. L., & Sokhadze, E. M. (2016). Leo Kanner, the anti-psychiatry movement and neurodiversity. *Siberian Journal of Special Education, 1–2,* 6–9.

Casanova, M. F., El-Baz, A. S., Kamat, S. S., Dombroski, B. A., et al. (2013). Focal cortical dysplasias in autism spectrum disorders. *Acta Neuropathologica Communications, 1,* 67.

Casanova, M. F., El-Baz, A., Mott, M., Mannheim, G., et al. (2009). Reduced gyral window and corpus callosum size in autism: Possible macroscopic correlates of a minicolumnopathy. *Journal of Autism and Developmental Disorders, 39,* 751–764.

Casanova, M. F., Sokhadze, E., Opris, I., Wang, Y., & Li, X. (2015). Autism spectrum disorders: Linking neuropathological findings to treatment with transcranial magnetic stimulation. *Acta Paediatrica, 104,* 346–355.

Casanova, M. F., Switala, A. E., Trippe, J., & Fitzgerald, M. (2007). Comparative minicolumnar morphometry of three distinguished scientists. *Autism, 11,* 557–569.

Casanova, M. F., Trippe, J., Tillquist, C., & Switala, A. E. (2009). Morphometric variability of minicolumns in the striate cortex of *Homo sapiens, Macaca mulatta,* and *Pan troglodytes. Journal of Anatomy, 214,* 226–234.

Casida, J. E. (2009). Pest toxicology: The primary mechanisms of pesticide action. *Chemical Research in Toxicology, 22,* 609–619.

Castillo, H., Patterson, B., Hickey, F., Kinsman, A., et al. (2008). Difference in age at regression in children with autism with and without Down syndrome. *Journal of Developmental and Behavioral Pediatrics, 29,* 89–93.

Castro, V. M., Kong, S. W., Clements, C. C., Brady, R., et al. (2016). Absence of evidence for increase in risk for autism or attention-deficit hyperactivity disorder following antidepressant exposure during pregnancy: A replication study. *Translational Psychiatry, 6*, e708.

Cath, D. C., Ran, N., Smit, J. H., van Balkom, A. J., & Comijs, H. C. (2008). Symptom overlap between autism spectrum disorder, generalized social anxiety disorder and obsessive-compulsive disorder in adults: A preliminary case-controlled study. *Psychopathology, 41*, 101–110.

Cederlöf, M., Larsson, H., Lichtenstein, P., Almqvist, C., Serlachius, E., & Ludvigsson, J. F. (2016). Nationwide population-based cohort study of psychiatric disorders in individuals with Ehlers-Danlos syndrome or hypermobility syndrome and their siblings. *BMC Psychiatry, 16*, 207.

Centers for Disease Control and Prevention. (2010). *Cytomegalovirus (CMV) and Congenital CMV Infection.* Accessed on 21 May 2018 at www.cdc.gov/cmv/congenital-infection.html

Centers for Disease Control and Prevention. (2014). Prevalence of autism spectrum disorder among children aged 8 years – Autism and developmental disabilities monitoring network, 11 sites, United States, 2010. *Morbidity and Mortality Weekly Report. Surveillance Summaries, 63*, 1–21.

Centers for Disease Control and Prevention. (2015). *Fetal Alcohol Spectrum Disorders.* Accessed on 21 May 2018 at www.cdc.gov/ncbddd/fasd/facts.html

Centers for Disease Control and Prevention. (2016a). *Epilepsy Fast Facts.* Accessed on 21 May 2018 at www.cdc.gov/epilepsy/basics/fast-facts.htm

Centers for Disease Control and Prevention. (2016b). *Autism Spectrum Disorder (ASD): Data & Statistics.* Accessed on 21 May 2018 at www.cdc.gov/ncbddd/autism/data.html

Centers for Disease Control and Prevention. (2017). *Tourette Syndrome (TS): Data & Statistics.* Accessed on 21 May 2108 at www.cdc.gov/ncbddd/tourette/data.html

Charman, T., Pickles, A., Simonoff, E., Chandler, S., Loucas, T., & Baird, G. (2011). IQ in children with autism spectrum disorders: Data from the Special Needs and Autism Project (SNAP). *Psychological Medicine, 41*, 619–627.

Cheeran, M. C., Lokensard, J. R., & Schleiss, M. R. (2009). Neuropathogenesis of congenital cytomegalovirus infection: Disease mechanisms and prospects for intervention. *Clinical Microbiology Reviews, 22*(1), 99–126.

Cheng, F., Vivacqua, G., & Yu, S. (2011). The role of α-synuclein in neurotransmission and synaptic plasticity. *Journal of Chemical Neuroanatomy, 42*, 242–248.

Chess, S. (1971). Autism in children with congenital rubella. *Journal of Autism and Childhood Schizophrenia, 1*(1), 33–47.

Cheung, C., Yu, K., Fung, G., Leung, M., et al. (2010). Autistic disorders and schizophrenia: Related or remote? An anatomical likelihood estimation. *PLoS One, 5*, e12233.

Cheung, I., & Vadas, P. (2015). A new disease cluster: Mast cell activation syndrome, postural orthostatic tachycardia syndrome, and Ehlers-Danlos syndrome. *Journal of Allergy and Clinical Immunology, 135*, AB65.

Choe, S.-Y., Kim, S.-J., Kim, H.-G., Lee, J. H., et al. (2003). Evaluation of estrogenicity of major heavy metals. *Science of the Total Environment, 312*, 15–21.

Comoletti, D., De Jaco, A., Jennings, L. L., Flynn, R. E., et al. (2004). The Arg451Cys-neuroligin-3 mutation associated with autism reveals a defect in protein processing. *Journal of Neuroscience, 24,* 4889–4893.

Connor, K., Ramamoorthy, K., Moore, M., Mustain, M., et al. (1997). Hydroxylated polychlorinated biphenyls (PCBs) as estrogens and antiestrogens: Structure-activity relationships. *Toxicology and Applied Pharmacology, 145,* 111–123.

Connors, S. L., Crowell, D. E., Eberhart, C. G., Copeland, J., et al. (2005). Beta2-adrenergic receptor activation and genetic polymorphisms in autism: Data from dizygotic twins. *Journal of Child Neurology, 20*(11), 876–884.

Constantino, J. N., & Todd, R. D. (2003). Autistic traits in the general population. *Archives of General Psychiatry, 60,* 524–530.

Constantino, J. N., & Todd, R. D. (2005). Intergenerational transmission of subthreshold autistic traits in the general population. *Biological Psychiatry, 57,* 655–660.

Constantino, J. N., Lajonchere, C., Lutz, M., Gray, T., et al. (2006). Autistic social impairment in the siblings of children with pervasive developmental disorders. *American Journal of Psychiatry, 163,* 294–296.

Cooper, G. S., & Stroehla, B. C. (2003). The epidemiology of autoimmune disease. *Autoimmunity Reviews, 2,* 119–125.

Corcoran, R., Mercer, G., & Frith, C. D. (1995). Schizophrenia, symptomatology and social inference: Investigating "theory of mind" in people with schizophrenia. *Schizophrenia Research, 17,* 5–13.

Couture, S. M., Penn, D. L., Losh, M., Adolphs, R., Hurley, R., & Piven, J. (2010). Comparison of social cognitive functioning in schizophrenia and high functioning autism: More convergence than divergence. *Psychological Medicine, 40,* 569–579.

Craddock, N., & Owen, M. J. (2010). The Kraepelinian dichotomy—going, going… but still not gone. *British Journal of Psychiatry, 196,* 92–95.

Craig, F., Margari, F., Legrottaglie, A. R., Palumbi, R., de Giambattista, C., & Margari, L. (2016). A review of executive function deficits in autism spectrum disorder and attention-deficit/hyperactivity disorder. *Neuropsychiatric Disease and Treatment, 12,* 1191–1202.

Creak, M., & Ini, S. (1960). Families of psychotic children. *Journal of Child Psychology and Psychiatry, 1,* 156–175.

Crespi, B., Stead, P., & Elliot, M. (2010). Evolution in health and medicine Sackler colloquium: Comparative genomics of autism and schizophrenia. *Proceedings of the National Academy of Sciences USA, 107,* 1736–1741.

Croen, L. A., Connors, S. L., Matevia, M., Qian, Y., Newschaffer, C., & Zimmerman, A. W. (2011). Prenatal exposure to β2-adrenergic receptor agonists and risk of autism spectrum disorders. *Journal of Neurodevelopmental Disorders, 3*(4), 307–315.

Croen, L. A., Grether, J. K., Yoshida, C. K., Odouli, R., & Hendrick, V. (2011). Antidepressant use during pregnancy and childhood autism spectrum disorders. *Archives of General Psychiatry, 68*(11), 1104–1112.

Croen, L. A., Najjar, D. V., Fireman, B., & Grether, J. K. (2007). Maternal and paternal age and risk of autism spectrum disorders. *Archives of Pediatrics & Adolescent Medicine, 161,* 334–340.

Cross-Disorder Group of the Psychiatric Genomics Consortium. (2013). Identification of risk loci with shared effects on five major psychiatric disorders: A genome-wide analysis. *The Lancet, 381*, 1371–1379.

Cunningham, C. (2013). Microglia and neurodegeneration: The role of systemic inflammation. *Glia, 61*, 71–90.

Dalton, K. M., Nacewicz, B. M., Alexander, A. L., & Davidson, R. J. (2007). Gaze-fixation, brain activation, and amygdala volume in unaffected siblings of individuals with autism. *Biological Psychiatry, 61*, 512–520.

Daniels, J. L., Forssen, U., Hultman, C. M., Cnattingius, S., et al. (2008). Parental psychiatric disorders associated with autism spectrum disorders in the offspring. *Pediatrics, 121*, e1357-e1362.

Darrow, S. M., Grados, M., Sandor, P., Hirschtritt, M. E., et al. (2017). Autism spectrum symptoms in a Tourette's disorder sample. *Journal of the American Academy of Child and Adolescent Psychiatry, 56*, 610–617.

Davis, E., Fennoy, I., Laraque, D., Kanem, N., Brown, G., & Mitchell, J. (1992). Autism and developmental abnormalities in children with perinatal cocaine exposure. *Journal of the National Medical Association, 84*(4), 315–319.

Davison, J., Goin-Kochel, R. P., Green-Snyder, L. A., Hundley, R. J., Warren, Z., & Peters, S. U. (2014). Expression of the broad autism phenotype in simplex autism families from the Simons Simplex Collection. *Journal of Autism and Developmental Disorders, 44*, 2392–2399.

Dawson, M., Soulières, I., Gernsbacher, M. A., & Mottron, L. (2007). The level and nature of autistic intelligence. *Psychological Science, 18*, 657–662.

De Rubeis, S., He, X., Goldberg, A. P., Poultney, C. S., Samocha, K., Cicek, A. E., et al. (2014). Synaptic, transcriptional and chromatin genes disrupted in autism. *Nature, 515*(7526), 209–215.

De Sousa, A., & Wood, B. (2007). The hominin fossil record and the emergence of the modern human central nervous system. In J. H. Kaas (Ed.), *Evolution of Nervous Systems: A Comprehensive Reference* (pp. 291–336). Amsterdam: Elsevier.

Deacon, T. W. (2000). Heterochrony in brain evolution: Cellular versus morphological analyses. In S. T. Parker, J. Langer, & M. L. McKinney (Eds.), *Biology, Brains, and Behavior: The Evolution of Human Development* (pp. 41–88). Santa Fe, NM/Oxford: School of American Research Press/James Currey.

Dean, J. C., Hailey, H., Moore, S. J., Lloyd, D. J., Turnpenny P. D., & Little, J. (2002). Long term health and neurodevelopment in children exposed to antiepileptic drugs before birth. *Journal of Medical Genetics, 39*(4), 251–259.

Deary, I. J., & Johnson, T. (2010). Intelligence and education: Causal perceptions drive analytic processes and therefore conclusions. *International Journal of Epidemiology, 39*, 1362–1369.

Deary, I. J., Strand, S., Smith, P., & Fernandes, C. (2007). Intelligence and educational achievement. *Intelligence, 35*, 13–21.

DeLong, G. R., Bean, S. C., & Brown, F. R. 3rd. (1981). Acquired reversible autistic syndrome in acute encephalopathic illness in children. *Archives of Neurology, 38*(3), 191–194.

DeLong, G. R., & Dwyer, J. T. (1988). Correlation of family history with specific autistic subgroups: Asperger's syndrome and bipolar affective disease. *Journal of Autism and Developmental Disorders, 18*, 593–600.

DeLong, G. R., Ritch, C. R., & Burch, S. (2002). Fluoxetine response in children with autistic spectrum disorders: Correlation with familial major affective disorder and intellectual achievement. *Developmental Medicine and Child Neurology, 44,* 652–659.

Dickerson, A. S., Rahbar, M. H., Bakian, A. V., Bilder, D. A., et al. (2016). Autism spectrum disorder prevalence and associations with air concentrations of lead, mercury, and arsenic. *Environmental Monitoring and Assessment, 188,* 407.

Dickerson, A. S., Rahbar, M. H., Han, I., Bakian, A. V., Bilder, D. A., Harrington, R. A., et al. (2015). Autism spectrum disorder prevalence and proximity to industrial facilities releasing arsenic, lead or mercury. *Science of the Total Environment, 536,* 245–251.

DiMario, Jr., F. J. (2004). Brain abnormalities in tuberous sclerosis complex. *Journal of Child Neurology, 19,* 650–657.

Dohn, A., Garza-Villarreal, E. A., Heaton, P., & Vuust, P. (2012). Do musicians with perfect pitch have more autism traits than musicians without perfect pitch? An empirical study. *PLoS One, 7,* e37961.

Donvan, J., & Zuker, C. (2016). *In a Different Key: The Story of Autism.* New York, NY: Crown Publishing Group.

Dooley, J. M., Stewart, W. A., Hayden, J. D., & Therrien, A. (2004). Brainstem calcification in Möbius syndrome. *Pediatric Neurology, 30*(1), 39–41.

Dubey, D., Hays, R., Alqallaf, A., Freeman, M., et al. (2016). Evaluating the prevalence of neurological autoantibodies among patients with epilepsy of unknown etiology: Ongoing prospective study (S52. 004). *Neurology, 86,* S52-004.

Duncan, A. J., & Heales, S. J. (2005). Nitric oxide and neurological disorders. *Molecular Aspects of Medicine, 26,* 67–96.

Duncan, R., Muller, J., Lee, N., Esmaili, A., & Nakhasi, H. L. (1999). Rubella virus-induced apoptosis varies among cell lines and is modulated by Bcl-XL and caspase inhibitors. *Virology, 255*(1), 117–128.

Durand, C. M., Betancur, C., Boeckers, T. M., Bockmann, J., et al. (2006). Mutations in the gene encoding the synaptic scaffolding protein SHANK3 are associated with autism spectrum disorders. *Nature Genetics, 39,* 25–27.

Dworzynski, K., Ronald, A., Bolton, P., & Happé, F. (2012). How different are girls and boys above and below the diagnostic threshold for autism spectrum disorders? *Journal of the American Academy of Child & Adolescent Psychiatry, 51,* 788–797.

Eaves, L. C., & Ho, H. H. (2008). Young adult outcome of autism spectrum disorders. *Journal of Autism and Developmental Disorders, 38,* 739–747.

Ebert, D. H., & Greenberg, M. E. (2013). Activity-dependent neuronal signaling and autism spectrum disorder. *Nature, 493*(7432), 327–337.

Eccles, J. A., Iodice, V., Dowell, N. G., Owens, A., et al. (2014). Joint hypermobility and autonomic hyperactivity: Relevance to neurodevelopmental disorders. *Journal of Neurology, Neurosurgery and Psychiatry, 85,* e3.

Eddleston, M., Buckley, N. A., Eye, P., & Dawson, A. H. (2008). Management of acute organophosphorus pesticide poisoning. *Lancet, 371,* 597–607.

Eiben, B., Bartels, I., Bähr-Porsch, S., Borgmann, S., et al. (1990). Cytogenetic analysis of 750 spontaneous abortions with the direct-preparation method of chorionic villi and its implications for studying genetic causes of pregnancy wastage. *American Journal of Human Genetics, 47*(4), 656–663.

Eisenberg, L. (1957). The fathers of autistic children. *American Journal of Psychiatry, 127*, 715–724.

El-Khayat, H. A, Soliman, N. A., Tomoum, H. Y., Omran, M. A., El-Wakad, A. S., & Shatla, R. H. (2008). Reproductive hormonal changes and catamenial pattern in adolescent females with epilepsy. *Epilepsia, 49*, 1619–1626.

Eliez, S., Barnea-Goraly, N., Schmitt, J. E., Liu, Y., & Reiss, A. L. (2002). Increased basal ganglia volumes in velo-cardio-facial syndrome (deletion 22q11.2). *Biological Psychiatry, 52*, 68–70.

Elsabbagh, M., Volein, A., Csibra, G., Holmboe, K., et al. (2009). Neural correlates of eye gaze processing in the infant broader autism phenotype. *Biological Psychiatry, 65*, 31–38.

Elton, S., Bishop, L. C., & Wood, B. (2001). Comparative context of Plio-Pleistocene hominin brain evolution. *Journal of Human Evolution, 41*, 1–27.

Engel, J., Jr. (2013). *Seizures and Epilepsy*. Oxford: Oxford University Press.

Englund, J., Walter, E. B., Fairchok, M. P., Monto, A. S., & Neuzil, K. M. (2005). A comparison of 2 influenza vaccine schedules in 6- to 23-month-old children. *Pediatrics, 115*, 1039–1047.

Ensembl. (2016). *rs1801133 SNP*. Accessed on 11 February 2016 at http://useast. ensembl.org/Homo_sapiens/Variation/Phenotype?db=core;r=1:11795821- 11796821;v=rs1801133;vdb=variation;vf=102375326

Epilepsy Foundation. (2016). *Epilepsy Statistics*. Accessed on 26 May 2016 at www. epilepsy.com/learn/epilepsy-statistics

Esser, N., Legrand-Poels, S., Piette, J., Scheen, A. J., & Paquot, N. (2014). Inflammation as a link between obesity, metabolic syndrome and type 2 diabetes. *Diabetes Research and Clinical Practice, 105*, 141–150.

Eyles, D., Burne, T., & McGrath, J. (2011). Vitamin D in fetal brain development. *Seminars in Cell & Developmental Biology, 22*, 629–636.

Falivelli, G., De Jaco, A., Favaloro, F. L., Kim, H., et al. (2012). Inherited genetic variants in autism-related CNTNAP2 show perturbed trafficking and ATF6 activation. *Human Molecular Genetics, 21*(21), 4761–4773.

Falter, C. M., Braeutigam, S., Nathan, R., Carrington, S., & Bailey, A. (2013). Enhanced access to early visual processing of perceptual simultaneity in autism spectrum disorders. *Journal of Autism and Developmental Disorders, 43*, 1857–1866.

Faraone, S. V., Biederman, J., Monuteaux, M., Doyle, A. E., & Seidman, L. J. (2001). A psychometric measure of learning disability predicts educational failure four years later in boys with attention-deficit/hyperactivity disorder. *Journal of Attention Disorders, 4*, 220–230.

Faretra, G. (1979). Lauretta Bender on autism: A review. *Child Psychiatry & Human Development, 10*, 118–129.

Fehlow, P., Bernstein, K., Tennstedt, A., & Walther, F. (1993). [Early infantile autism and excessive aerophagy with symptomatic megacolon and ileus in a case of Ehlers-Danlos syndrome]. *Padiatrie und Grenzgebiete, 31*, 259–267.

Fernell, E., Bejerot, S., Westerlund, J., Miniscalco, C., et al. (2015). Autism spectrum disorder and low vitamin D at birth: A sibling control study. *Molecular Autism, 6,* 3.

Ferrer, I. S., Alcantara, S., Zujar, M. J., & Cinos, C. (1993). Structure and pathogenesis of cortical nodules induced by prenatal X-irradiation in the rat. *Acta Neuropathologica, 85,* 205–212.

Feschotte, C. (2008). Transposable elements and the evolution of regulatory networks. *Nature Reviews Genetics, 9,* 397–405.

Fine, S. E., Weissman, A., Gerdes, M., Pinto-Martin, J., et al. (2005). Autism spectrum disorders and symptoms in children with molecularly confirmed 22q11.2 deletion syndrome. *Journal of Autism and Developmental Disorders, 35,* 461–470.

Fitzgerald, M. (2005). *The Genesis of Artistic Creativity: Asperger's Syndrome and the Arts.* London: Jessica Kingsley Publishers.

Fitzgerald, M., & O'Brien, B. (2007). *Genius Genes: How Asperger Talents Changed the World.* Shawnee Mission, KS: Autism Asperger Publishing Company.

Folstein, S., & Rutter, M. (1977). Infantile autism: A genetic study of 21 twin pairs. *Journal of Child Psychology and Psychiatry, 18*(4), 297–321.

Fombonne, E., Bolton, P., Prior, J., Jordan, H., & Rutter, M. (1997). A family study of autism: Cognitive patterns and levels in parents and siblings. *Journal of Child Psychology and Psychiatry, 38,* 667–683.

Fombonne, E., Rogé, B., Claverie, J., Courty, S., & Fremolle, J. (1999). Microcephaly and macrocephaly in autism. *Journal of Autism and Developmental Disorders, 29,* 113–119.

Foundation for a Drug-free World. (2016). *International Statistic: The Truth about Cocaine.* Accessed on 7 March 2016 at www.drugfreeworld.org/drugfacts/cocaine/international-statistics.html

Frantseva, M. V., Velazquez, J. P., Tsoraklidis, G., Mendonca, A. J., et al. (2000). Oxidative stress is involved in seizure-induced neurodegeneration in the kindling model of epilepsy. *Neuroscience, 97,* 431–435.

Friederici, A. D. (2012). The cortical language circuit: From auditory perception to sentence comprehension. *Trends in Cognitive Sciences, 16,* 262–268.

Friedman, S. R., Rapport, L. J., Lumley, M., Tzelepis, A., et al. (2003). Aspects of emotional competence in adult attention-deficit/hyperactivity disorder. *Neuropsychology, 17,* 50–58.

Frischmeyer-Guerrerio, P. A., Guerrerior, A. L., Oswald, G., Chichester, K., et al. (2013). TGF-beta receptor mutations impose a strong predisposition for human allergic disease. *Science Translational Medicine, 5,* 195ra94.

Frith, C. D. (2014). *The Cognitive Neuropsychology of Schizophrenia.* Hove: Psychology Press.

Frith, U. (1991). *Autism and Asperger Syndrome.* Cambridge: Cambridge University Press.

Frye, C. A., & Scalise, T. J. (2000). Anti-seizure effects of progesterone and 3α, 5α-THP in kainic acid and perforant pathway models of epilepsy. *Psychoneuroendocrinology, 25,* 407–420.

Frye, R. E., & Rossignol, D. A. (2011). Mitochondrial dysfunction can connect the diverse medical symptoms associated with autism spectrum disorders. *Pediatric Research, 69,* 41R–47R.

Fujita, E., Dai, H., Tanabe, Y., Zhiling, Y., et al. (2010). Autism spectrum disorder is related to endoplasmic reticulum stress induced by mutations in the synaptic cell adhesion molecule, CADM1. *Cell Death & Disease, 1,* e47.

Fullerton, P. M., & Kremer, M. (1961). Neuropathy after intake of thalidomide (Distaval). *British Medical Journal, 2*(5256), 855–858.

Gabel, H. W., Kinde, B., Stroud, H., Gilbert, C. S., et al. (2015). Disruption of DNA-methylation-dependent long gene repression in Rett syndrome. *Nature, 522*(7554), 89–93.

Gerdts, J. A., Bernier, R., Dawson, G., & Estes, A. (2013). The broader autism phenotype in simplex and multiplex families. *Journal of Autism and Developmental Disorders, 43,* 1597–1605.

Geschwind, D. H., & State, M. W. (2015). Gene hunting in autism spectrum disorder: On the path to precision medicine. *Lancet Neurology, 14*(11), 1109–1120.

Ghaziuddin, M., Al-Khouri, I., & Ghaziuddin, N. (2002). Autistic symptoms following herpes encephalitis. *European Child & Adolescent Psychiatry, 11*(3), 142–146.

Ghaziuddin, M., & Greden, J. (1998). Depression in children with autism/pervasive developmental disorders: A case-control family history study. *Journal of Autism and Developmental Disorders, 28,* 111–115.

Ghaziuddin, M., Tsai, L. Y., Eilers, L., & Ghaziuddin, N. (1992). Brief report: Autism and herpes simplex encephalitis. *Journal of Autism and Development Disorders, 22*(1), 107–113.

Giannotti, F., Cortesi, F., Cerquiglini, A., Miraglia, D., et al. (2008). An investigation of sleep characteristics, EEG abnormalities and epilepsy in developmental regressed and non-regressed children with autism. *Journal of Autism and Developmental Disorders, 38,* 1888–1897.

Giarelli, E., Wiggins, L. D., Rice, C. E., Levy, S. E., et al. (2010). Sex differences in the evaluation and diagnosis of autism spectrum disorders among children. *Disability and Health Journal, 3,* 107–116.

Gillberg, C. (1986). Onset at age 14 of a typical autistic syndrome: A case report of a girl with herpes simplex encephalitis. *Journal of Autism and Developmental Disorders, 16*(3), 369–375.

Gillberg, C., & Wahlström, J. (1985). Chromosome abnormalities in infantile autism and other childhood psychoses: A population study of 66 cases. *Developmental Medicine and Child Neurology, 27*(3), 293–304.

Gillberg, I. C. (1991). Autistic syndrome with onset at age 31 years: Herpes encephalitis as a possible model for childhood autism. *Developmental Medicine and Child Neurology, 33*(10), 920–924.

Gillot, A., & Standen, P. J. (2007). Levels of anxiety and sources of stress in adults with autism. *Journal of Intellectual Disabilities, 11,* 359–370.

Girirajan, S., Rosenfeld, J. A., Coe, B. P., Parikh, S., et al. (2012). Phenotypic heterogeneity of genomic disorders and rare copy-number variants. *New England Journal of Medicine, 367,* 1321–1331.

Giulivi, C., Zhang, Y. F., Omanska-Klusek, A., Ross-Inta, C., et al. (2010). Mitochondrial dysfunction in autism. *Journal of the American Medical Association, 304,* 2389–2396.

Glessner, J. T., Wang, K., Cai, G., Korvatska, O., et al. (2009). Autism genome-wide copy number variation reveals ubiquitin and neuronal genes. *Nature, 459*(7246), 569–573.

Glod, M., Riby, D. M., Honey, E., & Rogers, J. (2017). Sensory atypicalities in dyads of children with autism spectrum disorder (ASD) and their parents. *Autism Research, 10,* 531–538

Gockley, J., Willsey, A. J., Dong, S., Dougherty, J. D., Constantino, J. N., & Sanders, S. J. (2015). The female protective effect in autism spectrum disorder is not mediated by a single genetic locus. *Molecular Autism, 6,* 25.

Goin-Kochel, R. P., Trinh, S., Barber, S., & Bernier, R. (2017). Gene disrupting mutations associated with regression in autism spectrum disorder. *Journal of Autism and Developmental Disorders, 47,* 3600–3607.

Gokcen, S., Bora, E., Erermis, S., Kesikci, H., & Aydin, C. (2009). Theory of mind and verbal working memory deficits in parents of autistic children. *Psychiatry Research, 166,* 46–53.

Gonzalez, C. H., Marques-Dias, M. J., Kim, C. A., Sugayama, S. M., et al. (1998). Congenital abnormalities in Brazilian children associated with misoprostol misuse in first trimester of pregnancy. *Lancet, 351*(9116), 1624–1627.

Grant, W. B., & Soles, C. M. (2009). Epidemiologic evidence supporting the role of maternal vitamin D deficiency as a risk factor for the development of infantile autism. *Dermatoendocrinology, 1,* 223–228.

Gratten, J., Wray, N. R., Peyrot, W. J., McGrath, J. J., Visccher, P. M., Goddard, M. E. (2016). Risk of psychiatric illness from advanced paternal age is not predominantly from de novo mutations. *Nature Genetics, 48,* 718.

Guillette, L. J., Jr. (2000). Organochlorine pesticides as endocrine disruptors in wildlife. *Central European Journal of Public Health, 8,* 34–35.

Guimarães, L. E., Baker, B., Perricone, C., & Shoenfeld, Y. (2015). Vaccines, adjuvants and autoimmunity. *Pharmacological Research, 100,* 190–209.

Hagerman, P. J., & Hagerman, R. J. (2004). The fragile-X permutation: A maturing perspective. *American Journal of Human Genetics, 74*(5), 805–816.

Hallerbäck, M. U., Lugnegård, T., & Gillberg, C. (2012). Is autism spectrum disorder common in schizophrenia? *Psychiatry Research, 198,* 12–17.

Halliwell, B. (2001). Role of free radicals in the neurodegenerative diseases: Therapeutic implications for antioxidant treatment. *Drugs and Aging, 18,* 685–716.

Halliwell, B. (2006). Oxidative stress and neurodegeneration: Where are we now? *Journal of Neurochemistry, 97,* 1634–1658.

Hamblin, J. (2013). Why we took cocaine out of soda. *The Atlantic,* 31 January.

Hansson, A. C., Nixon, K., Rimondini, R., Damadzic, R., et al. (2010). Long-term suppression of forebrain neurogenesis and loss of neuronal progenitor cells following prolonged alcohol dependence in rats. *International Journal of Neuropsychopharmacology, 13*(5), 583–593.

Harris, S. R., MacKay, L. L., & Osborn, J. A. (1995). Autistic behaviors in offspring of mothers abusing alcohol and other drugs: A series of case reports. *Alcoholism, Clinical and Experimental Research, 19*(3), 660–665.

Harvey, L., & Boksa, P. (2014). Additive effects of maternal iron deficiency and prenatal immune activation on adult behaviors in rat offspring. *Brain, Behavior, and Immunity, 40*, 27–37.

Hashemi, E., Ariza, J., Rogers, H., Noctor, S. C., & Martinez-Cerdeno, V. (2017). The number of parvalbumin-expressing interneurons is decreased in the medical prefrontal cortex in autism. *Cerebral Cortex, 27*, 1931–1943.

Haykin, L. (2012). *On the sacred disease: The historical significance of Hippocratic humanism, rationality and scientific procedure.* Paper presented at the Young Historians Conference, Portland, OR, 26 April.

Hazell, A. S. (2007). Excitotoxic mechanisms in stroke: An update of concepts and treatment strategies. *Neurochemistry International, 50*, 941–953.

He, B. (2006). Viruses, endoplasmic reticulum stress, and interferon responses. *Cell Death and Differentiation, 13*, 393–403.

Hebert, K. J., Miller, L. L., & Joinson, C. J. (2010). Association of autistic spectrum disorder with season of birth and conception in a UK cohort. *Autism Research, 3*, 185–190.

Herbert, M. R., Ziegler, D. A., Makris, N., Filipek, P. A., et al. (2004). Localization of white matter volume increase in autism and developmental language disorder. *Annals of Neurology, 55*, 530–540.

Herculano-Houzel, S., Avelino-de-Souza, K., Neves, K., Porfírio, J., et al. (2014). The elephant brain in numbers. *Frontiers in Neuroanatomy, 8*, 46.

Hermelin, B. (2001). *Bright Splinters of the Mind: A Personal Story of Research with Autistic Savants.* London: Jessica Kingsley Publishers.

Hernández, A. F., Parrón, & Alarcón, R. (2011). Pesticides and asthma. *Current Opinion in Allergy and Clinical Immunology, 11*, 90–96.

Herzog, A. G. (2008). Disorders of reproduction in patients with epilepsy: Primary neurological mechanisms. *Seizure, 17*, 101–110.

Hill, D. S., Cabrera, R., Schultz, D. W., Zhu, H., Lu, W., Finnell, R. H., & Wlodarczyk, B. J. (2015). Autism-like behavior and epigenetic changes associated with autism as consequences of *in utero* exposure to environmental pollutants in a mouse models. *Behavioural Neurology*, 426263.

Hoekstra, R. A., Bartels, M., Verweij, C. J., & Boomsma, D. I. (2007). Heritability of autistic traits in the general population. *Archives of Pediatrics & Adolescent Medicine, 161*, 372–377.

Hoffman, E. J., Turner, K. J., Fernandez, J. M., Cifuentes, D., et al. (2016). Estrogens suppress a behavioral phenotype in zebrafish mutants of the autism risk gene, *CNTNAP2. Neuron, 89*, 725–733.

Hofvander, B., Delorme, R., Chaste, P., Nydén, A., et al. (2009). Psychiatric and psychosocial problems in adults with normal-intelligence autism spectrum disorders. *BMC Psychiatry, 9*, 1.

Holland, A. J., Hon, J., Huppert, F. A., Stevens, F., & Watson, P. (1998). Population-based study of the prevalence and presentation of dementia in adults with Down's syndrome. *British Journal of Psychiatry, 172*, 493–498.

Holmes, L. B. (2002). The teratogenicity of anticonvulsant drugs: A progress report. *Journal of Medical Genetics, 39*(4), 245–247.

Horská, A., Farage, L., Bibat, G., Nagae, L. M., et al. (2009). Brain metabolism in Rett syndrome: Age, clinical, and genotype correlations. *Annals of Neurology, 65*, 90–97.

Howe, K., Clark, M. D., Torroja, C. F., Torrance, J., et al. (2013). The zebrafish reference genome sequence and its relationship to the human genome. *Nature, 496*, 498.

Howlin, P., Goode, S., Hutton, J., & Rutter, M. (2009). Savant skills in autism: Psychometric approaches and parental reports. *Philosophical Transactions of the Royal Society of London B: Biological Sciences, 364*, 1359–1367.

Hoyme, H. E., May, P. A., Kalberg, W. O., Kodituwakku, P., et al. (2005). A practical clinical approach to diagnosis of fetal alcohol spectrum disorders: Clarification of the 1996 Institute of Medicine criteria. *Pediatrics, 115*(1), 39–47.

Hudak, M. L., & Tan, R. C., Committee on Drugs, Committee on Fetus and Newborn, American Academy of Pediatrics. (2012). Neonatal drug withdrawal. *Pediatrics, 129*(2), e540–560.

Hugh-Jones, D., Verqeij, K. J. H., St. Pourcain, B., & Abdellaoui, A. (2016). Assortative mating on educational attainment leads to genetic spousal resemblance for polygenic scores. *Intelligence, 59*, 103–108.

Hughes, C., Plumet, M.-H., & Leboyer, M. (1999). Towards a cognitive phenotype for autism: Increased prevalence of executive dysfunction and superior spatial span amongst siblings of children with autism. *Journal of Child Psychology and Psychiatry and Allied Disciplines, 40*, 705–718.

Hughes, C., Russell, J., & Robbins, T. W. (1994). Evidence for executive dysfunction in autism. *Neuropsychologia, 32*, 477–492.

Hughes, J. R., & Melyn, M. (2005). EEG and seizures in autistic children and adolescents: Further findings with therapeutic implications. *Clinical EEG and Neuroscience, 36*, 15–20.

Hunt, S., Russell, A., Smithson, W. H., Parsons, L., et al. (2008). Topiramate in pregnancy: Preliminary experience from the UK Epilepsy and Pregnancy Register. *Neurology, 71*(4), 272–276.

Hutsler, J. J., & Avino, T. (2015). The relevance of subplate modifications to connectivity in the cerebral cortex of individuals with autism spectrum disorders. In M. F. Casanova & I. Opris (Eds.), *Recent Advances on the Modular Organization of the Cortex* (pp. 201–224). Dordrecht: Springer Netherlands.

Hviid, A., Melbye, M., & Pasternak, B. (2013). Use of selective serotonin reuptake inhibitors during pregnancy and risk of autism. *New England Journal of Medicine, 369*(25), 2406–2415.

Ikonomidou, C., Bittigau, P., Ishimaru, M. J., Wozniak, D. F., et al. (2000). Ethanol-induced apoptotic neurodegeneration and fetal alcohol syndrome. *Science, 287*(5455), 1056–1060.

Ingalhalikar, M., Smith, A., Parker, D., Satterthwaite, T. D., et al. (2014). Sex differences in the structural connectome of the human brain. *Proceedings of the National Academy of Sciences, 111*, 823–828.

Ingemarsson, I. (1975). Effect of terbutaline on premature labour. *Acta Obstetrica et Gynceologica Scandinavica, 54*(S47), 37.

Ingersoll, B., Meyer, K., & Becker, M. W. (2011). Increased rates of depressed mood in others of children with ASD associated with the presence of the broader autism phenotype. *Autism Research, 4*, 143–148.

Ingudomnukul, E., Baron-Cohen, S., Wheelwright, S., & Knickmeyer, R. (2007). Elevated rates of testosterone-related disorders in women with autism spectrum conditions. *Hormones and Behavior, 51*, 597–604.

Iossifov, I., O'Roak, B. J., Sanders, S. J., Ronemus, M., et al. (2014). The contribution of de novo coding mutations to autism spectrum disorder. *Nature, 515*(7526), 216–221.

Jack M. (2016). Jacob is 17 years old, autistic, and on his way to getting a PhD in theoretical physics. *Plaid Zebra,* 18 January.

Jacquemont, S., Coe, B. P., Hersch, M., Duyzend, M. H., et al. (2014). A higher mutational burden in females supports a "female protective model" in neurodevelopmental disorders. *American Journal of Human Genetics, 94,* 415–425.

Jamain, S., Quach, H., Betancur, C., Råstam, M., et al. (2003). Mutations of the X-linked genes encoding neuroligins NLGN3 and NLGN4 are associated with autism. *Nature Genetics, 34*(1), 27–29.

Jambaque, I., Chiron, C., Dumas, C., Mumford, J., & Dulac, O. (2000). Mental and behavioural outcome of infantile epilepsy treated by vigabatrin in tuberous sclerosis patients. *Epilepsy Research, 38,* 151–160.

Janssens, S., Pulendran, B., & Lambrecht, B. N. (2014). Emerging functions of the unfolded protein response in immunity. *Nature Immunology, 15*(10), 910–919.

Jiang, Y. H., Yuen, R. K., Jin, X., Wang, M., et al. (2013). Detection of clinically relevant genetic variants in autism spectrum disorder by whole-genome sequencing. *American Journal of Human Genetics, 93*(2), 249–263.

Jobe, L. E., & White, S. W. (2007). Loneliness, social relationships, and a broader autism phenotype in college students. *Personality and Individual Differences, 42,* 1479–1489.

Johansson, M., Wentz, E., Fernell, E., Strömland, K., Miller, M. T., & Gillberg, C. (2001). Autistic spectrum disorders in Möbius sequence: A comprehensive study of 25 individuals. *Developmental Medicine and Child Neurology, 43,* 338–345.

Jones, C. R., Happé, F., Golden, H., Marsden, A. J., et al. (2009). Reading and arithmetic in adolescents with autism spectrum disorders: Peaks and dips in attainment. *Neuropsychology, 23,* 718.

Jones, K. L., Smith, D. W., Ulleland, C. N., & Streissguth, P. (1973). Pattern of malformation in offspring of chronic alcoholic mothers. *Lancet, 1*(7815), 1267–1271.

Judd, L. L., & Mandell, A. J. (1968). Chromosome studies in early infantile autism. *Archives of General Psychiatry, 18*(4), 450–457.

Kabat, J., & Król, P. (2012). Focal cortical dysplasia—Review. *Polish Journal of Radiology, 77,* 35.

Kadak, M. T., Demirel, O. F., Yavuz, M., & Demir, T. (2014). Recognition of emotional facial expressions and broad autism phenotype in parents of children diagnosed with autistic spectrum disorder. *Comprehensive Psychiatry, 55,* 1146–1151.

Kalueff, A. V., Minasyan, A., & Tuohimaa, P. (2005). Anticonvulsant effects of 1,25-dihydroxyvitamin D in chemically induced seizures in mice. *Brain Research Bulletin, 67,* 156–160.

Kanner, L. (1941). *In Defense of Mothers.* New York, NY: Dood, Mead & Company.

Kanner, L. (1943). Autistic disturbances of affective contact. *Nervous Child, 2,* 217–250.

Kanner, L. (1949). Problems of nosology and psychodynamics in early childhood autism. *American Journal of Orthopsychiatry, 19,* 416–426.

Kanner, L. (1965). Infantile autism and the schizophrenias. *Behavioral Science, 10,* 412–420.

Kanner, L. (1968). Infantile autism revisited. *Psychiatry Digest, 29,* 17–28.

Kanner, L. (1971a). Childhood psychosis: A historical view. *Journal of Autism and Childhood Schizophrenia, 1,* 14–19.

Kanner, L. (1971b). Retrospect and prospect [Editorial]. *Journal of Autism and Childhood Schizophrenia, 1,* 453–459.

Kanner, L. (1971c). The integrative aspects of ability. *Acta Paedopsychiatrica, 38,* 134–144.

Kanner, L. (1973). The birth of early infantile autism. *Journal of Autism and Childhood Schizophrenia, 3,* 93–95.

Kanner, L., Rodriguez, A., & Ashenden, B. (1972). How far can autistic children go in matters of social adaptation? *Journal of Autism and Childhood Schizophrenia, 2,* 9–33.

Kates, W. R., Olszewski, A. K., Gnirke, M. H., Kikinis, A., et al. (2015). White matter microstructural abnormalities of the cingulum bundle in youths with 22q11.2 deletion syndrome: Associations with medication, neuropsychological function, and prodromal symptoms of psychosis. *Schizophrenia Research, 161,* 76–84.

Kenneson, A., & Cannon, M. J. (2007). Review and meta-analysis of the epidemiology of congenital cytomegalovirus (CMV) infection. *Reviews in Medical Virology, 17*(4), 253–276.

Kern, J. K., Geier, D. A., Sykes, L. K., & Geier, M. R. (2013). Evidence of neurodegeneration in autism spectrum disorder. *Translational Neurodegeneration, 2*(1), 17.

Key, A. P. F., & Stone, W. L. (2013). Same but different: Nine-month-old infants at average and high risk for autism look at the same facial features but process them using different brain mechanisms. *Autism Research, 5,* 253–266.

Khemir, S., Halayem, S., & Azzouz, H. (2016). Autism in phenylketonuria patients: From clinical presentation to molecular defects. *Journal of Child Neurology, 31,* 843–849.

Kim, J. A., Szatmari, P., Bryson, S. E., Streiner, D. L., & Wilson, F. J. (2000). The prevalence of anxiety and mood problems among children with autism and Asperger syndrome. *Autism, 4,* 117–132.

Kim, Y. S., Leventhal, B. L., Koh, Y. J., Fombonne, E., et al. (2011). Prevalence of autism spectrum disorders in a total population sample. *American Journal of Psychiatry, 168,* 904–912.

King, B. H. (2017). Association between maternal use of SSRI medications and autism in their children. *Journal of the American Medical Association, 317,* 1568–1569.

Kirby, A., & Sugden, D. A. (2007). Children with developmental coordination disorders. *Journal of the Royal Society of Medicine, 100,* 182–186.

Klei, L., Sanders, S. J., Murtha, M. T., Hus, V., et al. (2012). Common genetic variants, acting additively, are a major source of risk for autism. *Molecular Autism, 3*(1), 9.

Klusek, J., Losh, M., & Martin, G. E. (2014). Sex differences and within-family associations in the broad autism phenotype. *Autism, 18,* 106–116.

Koczat, D. L., Rogers, S. J., Pennington, B. F., & Ross, R. G. (2002). Eye movement abnormality suggestive of spatial working memory deficit is present in parents of autistic probands. *Journal of Autism and Developmental Disorders, 32,* 513–518.

Kogan, M. D., Blumberg, S. J., Schieve, L. A., Boyle, C. A., et al. (2009). Prevalence of parent-reported diagnosis of autism spectrum disorder among children in the US, 2007. *Pediatrics, 124*(5), 1395–1403.

Kojima, H., Takeuchi, S., Itoh, T., Iida, M., Kobayashi, S., & Yoshida, T. (2013). In vitro endocrine disruption potential of organophosphate flame retardants via human nuclear receptors. *Toxicology, 314*, 76–83.

Kolevzon, A., Bush, L., Wang, A. T., Halpern, D., et al. (2014). A pilot controlled trial of insulin-like growth factor-1 in children with Phelan-McDermid syndrome. *Molecular Autism, 5*, 54.

Kollodge, T., & Hinkley, S. (2015). Retinoblastoma: A scientific and clinical review. *Vision Development & Rehabilitation, 1*, 39–45.

Konopka, G., Friedrich, T., Davis-Turak, J., Winden, K., Oldham, M. C., & Gao, F. (2012). Human-specific transcriptional networks in the brain. *Neuron, 75*, 601–617.

Kosidou, K., Dalman, C., Widman, L., Arver, S., Lee, B. K., Magnusson, C., & Gardner, R. M. (2016). Maternal polycystic ovary syndrome and the risk of autism spectrum disorders in the offspring: A population-based nationwide study in Sweden. *Molecular Psychiatry, 21*, 1441–1448.

Kotila, M., & Waltimo, O. (1992). Epilepsy after stroke. *Epilepsia, 33*, 495–498.

Kraepelin, E. (1899). *Psychiatrie: Ein Lehrbuch für Studirende und Arzte* [In 2 volumes]. Leipzig: Vertrag von Johann Ambresius. Barth.

Krakowiak, P., Goines, P. E., Tancredi, D. J., Ashwood, P., et al. (2015). Neonatal cytokine profiles associated with autism spectrum disorder. *Biological Psychiatry, 81*, 442–451.

Krüger, L., & Mandelkow, E. M. (2016). Tau neurotoxicity and rescue in animal models of human tauopathies. *Current Opinion in Neurobiology, 36*, 52–58.

Krumm, N., O'Roak, B. J., Shendure, J., & Eichler, E. E. (2014). A de novo convergence of autism genetics and molecular neuroscience. *Trends in Neurosciences, 37*(2), 95–105.

Kumar, S., Devendran, Y., & Devendran, R. (2017). Prevalence of autism spectrum disorders and its association with epileptiform activity among children with intellectual disability in a tertiary centre. *Journal of Indian Association for Child & Adolescent Mental Health, 13*, 26–47.

Kuniewicz, M. W., Wi, S., Qian, Y., Walsh, E. M., Armstrong, M. A., & Croen, L. A. (2014). Prevalence and neonatal factors associated with autism spectrum disorders in preterm infants. *Journal of Pediatrics, 164*, 20–25.

Kurita, H. (1985). Infantile autism with speech loss before the age of thirty months. *Journal of the American Academy of Child Psychiatry, 24*, 191–196.

Lai, C. L. E., Lau, Z., Lui, S. S., Lok, E., et al. (2016). Meta-analysis of neuropsychological measures of executive functioning in children and adolescents with high-functioning autism spectrum disorder. *Autism Research, 10*, 911–939.

Lainhart, J. E., Ozonoff, S., Coon, H., Krasny, L., et al. (2002). Autism, regression, and the broader autism phenotype. *American Journal of Medical Genetics Part A, 113*, 231–237.

Lambert, N., Strebel, P., Orenstein, W., Icenogle, J., & Poland, G. A. (2015). Rubella. *Lancet, 385*(9984), 2297–2307.

Landgren, M., Svensson, L., Strömland, K., Andersson Grönlund, M. (2010). Prenatal alcohol exposure and neurodevelopmental disorders in children adopted from eastern Europe. *Pediatrics, 125*(5), e1178–e1185.

Langen, M., Kas, M. J., Staal, W. G., van Engeland, H., & Durston, S. (2011). The neurobiology of repetitive behavior: Of mice… . *Neuroscience & Biobehavioral Reviews, 35*, 345–355.

Langen, M., Schnack, H. G., Nederveen, H., Bos, D., et al. (2009). Changes in the developmental trajectories of striatum in autism. *Biological Psychiatry, 66*, 327–333.

Laplane, D., Levasseur, M., Pillon, B., Dubois, B., et al. (1989). Obsessive-compulsive and other behavioral changes with bilateral basal ganglia lesions: A neuropsychological, magnetic resonance imaging and positron tomography study. *Brain, 112*, 699–725.

Lee, Y.-H., & Pratley, R. E. (2005). The evolving role of inflammation in obesity and the metabolic syndrome. *Current Diabetes Reports, 5*, 70–75.

Legler, J., & Brouwer, A. (2003). Are brominated flame retardants endocrine disruptors? *Environment International, 29*, 879–885.

Leitner, Y. (2014). The co-occurrence of autism and attention deficit hyperactivity disorder in children—what do we know? *Frontiers in Human Neuroscience, 8*, 268.

Lemoine, P., Harousseau, H., Borteyru, J. P., & Menuet, J. C. (1968). Les enfants des parents alcoholiques: Anomolies observes a propos de 127 cas. *Ouest-Medical, 8*, 476–482.

Leung, A. K., Sauve, R. S., & Davies, H. D. (2003). Congenital cytomegalovirus infection. *Journal of the National Medication Association, 95*, 213.

Leyfer, O. T., Folstein, S. E., Bacalman, S., Davis, N. O., et al. (2006). Comorbid psychiatric disorders in children with autism: Interview development and rates of disorders. *Journal of Autism and Developmental Disorders, 36*, 849–861.

Li, B. M., Liu, X. R., Yi, Y. H., Deng, Y. H., et al. (2011). Autism in Dravet syndrome: Prevalence, features, and relationship to the clinical characteristics of epilepsy and mental retardation. *Epilepsy & Behavior, 21*, 291–295.

Lichtenstein, P., Yip, B. H., Björk, C., Pawitan, Y., et al. (2009). Common genetic determinants of schizophrenia and bipolar disorder in Swedish families: A population-based study. *Lancet, 373*, 234–239.

Limperopoulos, C., Bassan, H., Sullivan, N. R., Soul, J. S., et al. (2008). Positive screening for autism in ex-preterm infants: Prevalence and risk factors. *Pediatrics, 121*, 758–765.

Lugnegård, T., Hallerbäck, M. U., & Gillberg, C. (2012). Personality disorders and autism spectrum disorders: What are the connections? *Comprehensive Psychiatry, 53*, 333–340.

Lutiger, B., Graham, K., Einarson, T. R., & Koren, G. (1991). Relationship between gestational cocaine use and pregnancy outcome: A meta-analysis. *Teratology, 44*(4), 405–414.

MacLean, P. D. (1990). *The Triune Brain in Evolution: Role in Paleocerebral Functions*. Berlin: Springer Science & Business Media.

Magiorkinis, E., Diamantis, A., Sidiropoulou, K., & Panteliadis, C. (2014). Highlights in the history of epilepsy: The last 200 years. *Epilepsy Research and Treatment*. Accessed on 17 July 2018 at www.hindawi.com/journals/ert/2014/582039/

Magoun, H. W., & Ranson, S. W. (1938). The behavior of cats following bilateral removal of the rostral portion of the cerebral hemispheres. *Journal of Neurophysiology, 1*, 39–44.

Mahmood, A., Bibat, G., Zhan, A. L., Izbudak, I., et al. (2010). White matter impairment in Rett syndrome: Diffusion tensor imaging study with clinical correlations. *American Journal of Neuroradiology, 31*, 295–299.

Malfait, F., Francomano, C., Byers, P., Belmont, J., et al. (2017). The 2017 international classification of the Ehlers-Danlos syndromes. *American Journal of Medical Genetics Part C: Seminars in Medical Genetics, 175*, 8–26.

Mansour, R., Dovi, A. T., Lane, D. M., Loveland, K. A., & Pearson, D. A. (2017). ADHD severity as it relates to comorbid psychiatric symptomatology in children with autism spectrum disorders (ASD). *Research in Developmental Disabilities, 60*, 52–64.

Manzo-Avalos, S., & Saavedra-Molina, A. (2010). Cellular and mitochondrial effects of alcohol consumption. *International Journal of Environmental Research and Public Health, 7*(12), 4281–4304.

March, W. A., Moore, V. M., Willson, K. J., Phillips, D. I., Norman, R. J., & Davies, M. J. (2009). The prevalence of polycystic ovary syndrome in a community sample assessed under contrasting diagnostic criteria. *Human Reproduction, 25*, 544–551.

Marino, L. (1998). A comparison of encephalization between odontocete cetacean and anthropoid primates. *Brain, Behavior and Evolution, 51*, 230–238.

Marino, M., Galluzzo, P., & Ascenzi, P. (2006). Estrogen signaling multiple pathways to impact gene transcription. *Current Genomics, 7*, 497–508.

Markram, H., Rinaldi, T., & Markram, K. (2007). The intense world syndrome—An alternative hypothesis for autism. *Frontiers in Neuroscience, 1*(1), 77–96.

Marques, F., Brito, M. J., Conde, M., Pinto, M., & Moreira, A. (2014). Autism spectrum disorder secondary to enterovirus encephalitis. *Journal of Child Neurology, 29*(5), 708–714.

Marriage, S., Wolverton, A., & Marriage, K. (2009). Autism spectrum disorder grown up: A chart review of adult functioning. *Journal of the Canadian Academy of Child and Adolescent Psychiatry, 18*, 322–328.

Marson, J., Meuris, S., Cooper, R., & Jouannet, P. (1991). Puberty in the male chimpanzee: Progressive maturation of semen characteristics. *Biology of Reproduction, 44*, 448–455.

Martindale, J. L., & Holbrook, N. J. (2002). Cellular response to oxidative stress: Signaling for suicide and survival. *Journal of Cellular Physiology, 192*, 1–15.

Matelski, L., & Van de Water, J. (2016). Risk factors in autism: Thinking outside the brain. *Journal of Autoimmunity, 67*, 1–7.

Mayes, L. C., Granger, R. H., Bornstein, M. H., & Zuckerman, B. (1992). The problem of prenatal cocaine exposure. A rush to judgment. *JAMA, 267*(3), 406–408.

Mayes, S. D., Calhoun, S. L., Murray, M. J., Ahuja, M., & Smith, L. A. (2011). Anxiety, depression, and irritability in children with autism relative to other neuropsychiatric disorders and typical development. *Research in Autism Spectrum Disorders, 5*, 474–485.

Mazefsky, C. A., Conner, C. M., & Oswald, D. P. (2010). Association between depression and anxiety in high-functioning children with autism spectrum disorders and maternal mood symptoms. *Autism Research, 3*, 120–127.

Mazefsky, C. A., Folstein, S. E., & Lainhart, J. E. (2008). Overrepresentation of mood and anxiety disorders in adults with autism and their first-degree relatives: What does it mean? *Autism Research, 1,* 193–197.

McCarthy, S. E., Gillis, J., Kramer, M., Lihm, J., et al. (2014). De novo mutations in schizophrenia implicate chromatin remodeling and support a genetic overlap with autism and intellectual disability. *Molecular Psychiatry, 19,* 652–658.

McCue, L. M., Flick, L. H., Twyman, K. A., Xian, H., & Conturo, T. E. (2016). Prevalence of non-febrile seizures in children with idiopathic autism spectrum disorder and their unaffected siblings: A retrospective cohort study. *BMC Neurology, 16,* 245.

McDonald, N. M., Varcin, K. J., Bhatt, R., Wu, J. Y., et al. (2017). Early autism symptoms in infants with tuberous sclerosis complex [Advance online publication]. *Autism Research.* doi:10.1002/aut.1846.

McHugh, J. C., & Delanty, N. (2008). Epidemiology and classification of epilepsy: Gender comparisons. *International Review of Neurobiology, 83,* 11–26.

McIntosh, A. M., McMahon, J., Dibbens, L. M., Iona, X., et al. (2010). Effects of vaccination on onset and outcome of Dravet syndrome: A retrospective study. *Lancet Neurology, 9*(6), 592–598.

McLean, C. Y., Reno, P. L., Pollen, A. A., Bassan, A. I., et al. (2011). Human-specific loss of regulatory DNA and the evolution of human specific traits. *Nature, 471,* 216–219.

McLean, M. J., & MacDonald, R. L. (1986). Sodium valproate, but not ethosuximide, produces use- and voltage-dependent limitation of high frequency repetitive firing of action potentials of mouse central neurons in cell culture. *Journal of Pharmacology and Experimental Therapeutics, 237*(3), 1001–1011.

McNamara, K. J. (2012). Heterochrony: The evolution of development. *Evolution: Education and Outreach, 5,* 203–218.

Merikangas, K. R., Akiskal, H. S., Angst, J., Greenberg, P. E., et al. (2007). Lifetime and 12-month prevalence of bipolar spectrum disorder in the National Comorbidity Survey Replication. *Archives of General Psychiatry, 64,* 543–552.

Messinger, D. S., Young, G. S., Webb, S. J., Ozonoff, S., et al. (2015). Early sex differences are not autism-specific: A Baby Siblings Research Consortium (BSRC) study. *Molecular Autism, 6,* 32.

Miller, D. T., Adam, M. P., Aradhya, S., Biesecker, L. G., et al. (2010). Consensus statement: Chromosomal microarray is a first-tier clinical diagnostic test for individuals with developmental disabilities or congenital anomalies. *American Journal of Human Genetics, 86,* 749–764.

Millichap, J. G. (2002). Patterns of regression in Rett syndrome. *Pediatric Neurology, Briefs, 16,* 76–77.

Milnerwood, A. J., & Raymond, L. A. (2010). Early synaptic pathophysiology in neurodegeneration: Insights from Huntington's disease. *Trends in Neurosciences, 33,* 513–523.

Ming, X., Brimacombe, M., & Wagner, G. C. (2007). Prevalence of motor impairment in autism spectrum disorders. *Brain and Development, 29,* 565–570.

Mione, M. C., Cavanagh, J. F., Harris, B., & Parnavelas, J. G. (1997). Cell fate specification and symmetrical/asymmetrical divisions in the developing cerebral cortex. *Journal of Neuroscience, 17,* 2018–2029.

Mnif, W., Hassine, A. I. H., Bouaziz, A., Bartegi, A., Thomas, O., & Roig, B. (2011). Effect of endocrine disruptor pesticides: A review. *International Journal of Environmental Research and Public Health, 8*, 2265–2302.

Molina, O., Anton, E., Vidal, F., & Blanco, J. (2011). Sperm rates of 7q11.23, 15q11q13 and 22q11.2 deletions and duplications: A FISH approach. *Human Genetics, 129*(1), 35–44.

Molloy, C. A., Morrow, A. L., Meinzen-Derr, J., Schleifer, K., et al. (2006). Elevated cytokine levels in children with autism spectrum disorder. *Journal of Neuroimmunology, 172*, 198–205.

Money, J., Bobrow, N. A., & Clarke, F. C. (1971). Autism and autoimmune disease: A family study. *Journal of Autism and Child Schizophrenia, 1*, 146–160.

Moore, S. J., Turnpenny, P., Quinn, A., Glover, S., et al. (2000). A clinical study of 57 children with fetal anticonvulsant syndromes. *Journal of Medical Genetics, 37*(7), 489–497.

Movsas, T. Z., Pinto-Martin, J. A., Whitaker, A. H., Feldman, J. F., et al. (2013). *Journal of Pediatrics, 163*, 73–78.

Mufson, E. J., Malek-Ahmadi, M., Perez, S. E., & Chen, K. (2016). Braak staging, plaque pathology, and APOE status in elderly persons without cognitive impairment. *Neurobiology of Aging, 37*, 147–153.

Munesue, T., Ono, Y., Mutoh, K., Shimoda, K., Nakatani, H., & Kikuchi, M. (2008). High prevalence of bipolar disorder comorbidity in adolescents and young adults with high-functioning autism spectrum disorder: A preliminary study of 44 patients. *Journal of Affective Disorders, 111*, 170–175.

Murakami, J. W., Courchesne, E., Haas, R. H., Press, G. A., & Yeung-Courchesne, R. (1992). Cerebellar and cerebral abnormalities in Rett syndrome: A quantitative MR analysis. *American Journal of Roentgenology, 159*, 177–183.

Murphy, M., Bolton, P. F., Pickles, A., Fombonne, E., Piven, J., & Rutter, M. (2000). Personality traits of the relatives of autistic probands. *Psychological Medicine, 30*, 1441–1424.

Myers, L., Anderlid, B. M., Nordgren, A., Willfors, C., et al. (2017). Minor physical anomalies in neurodevelopmental disorders: A twin study. *Child and Adolescent Psychiatry and Mental Health, 1*, 57.

Nader, A. M., Courchesne, V., Dawson, M., & Soulières, I. (2016). Does WISC-IV underestimate the intelligence of autistic children? *Journal of Autism and Developmental Disabilities, 46*(5), 1582–1589.

Nagae, L. M., Zarnow, D. M., Blaskey, L., Dell, J., et al. (2012). Elevated mean diffusivity in the left hemisphere superior longitudinal fasciculus in autism spectrum disorders increases with more profound language impairment. *American Journal of Neuroradiology, 33*, 1720–1725.

Nakaya, H. I., Wrammert, J., Lee, E. K., Racioppo, L., et al. (2011). Systems biology of vaccination for seasonal influenza in humans. *Nature Immunology, 12*(8), 786–795.

Nanson, J. L. (1992). Autism in fetal alcohol syndrome: A report of six cases. *Alcoholism, Clinical and Experimental Research, 16*(3), 558–565.

Napoli, E., Wong, S., & Giulivi, C. (2013). Evidence of reactive oxygen species-mediated damage to mitochondrial DNA in children with typical autism. *Molecular Autism, 4*, 2.

Nation, K., Clarke, P., Wright, B., & Williams, C. (2006). Patterns of reading ability in children with autism spectrum disorder. *Journal of Autism and Developmental Disorders, 36*, 911–919.

Nava, C., Dalle, C., Rastetter, A., Striano, P., et al. (2014). De novo mutations in HCN1 cause early infantile epileptic encephalopathy. *Nature Genetics, 46*(6), 640–645.

Nippold, M. A. (1993). Clinical forum: Adolescent language developmental markers in adolescent language: Syntax, semantics, and pragmatics. *Language, Speech, and Hearing Services in Schools, 24*, 21–28.

Niu, D.-K., & Yang, Y.-F. (2011). Why eukaryotic cells use introns to enhance gene expression: Splicing reduces transcription-associated mutagenesis by inhibiting topoisomerase I cutting activity. *Biology Direct, 6*, 24.

Nolan, T., McIntyre, P., Robertson, D., & Descamps, D. (2002). Reactogenicity and immunogenicity of a live attenuated tetravalent measles-mumps-rubella-varicella (MMRV) vaccine. *Vaccine, 21*, 281–289.

Nordsletten, A. E., Larsson, H., Crowley, J. J., Almqvist, C., Lichtenstein, P., & Mataix-Cols, D. (2016). Patterns of nonrandom mating within and across 11 major psychiatric disorders. *JAMA Psychiatry, 73*, 354–361.

Numis, A. L., Major, P., Montenegro, M. A., Muzkewicz, D. A., Pulsifer, M. B., Thiele, E. A. (2011). Identification of risk factors for autism spectrum disorders in tuberous sclerosis complex. *Neurology, 76*, 981–987.

Nydén, A., Hagberg, B., Goussé, V., & Rastam, M. (2011). A cognitive endophenotype of autism in families with multiple incidence. *Research in Autism Spectrum Disorders, 5*, 191–200.

O'Neil, E. (2011). *The discovery of fetal alcohol syndrome.* Embryo Project Encyclopedia. Accessed on 21 May 2018 at http://embryo.asu.edu/handle/10776/2100

Oberman, L. M., Enticott, P. G., Casanova, M. F., Rotenberg, A., Pascual-Leone, A., & McCracken, J. T. (2016). Transcranial magnetic stimulation in autism spectrum disorder: Challenges, promise, and roadmap for future research. *Autism Research, 9*, 184–203.

Oliveira, G., Diogo, L., Grazina, M., Garcia, P., et al. (2005). Mitochondrial dysfunction in autism spectrum disorders: A population-based study. *Developmental Medicine and Child Neurology, 47*, 185–189.

OMIM (Online Mendelian Inheritance in Man). (2014). *FG Syndrome.* Accessed on 13 December 2017 at www.omim.org/entry/300321?search=fg%20syndrome&highlight=syndromic%20syndrome%20fg

Oosterbaan, A. M., Steegers, E. A., & Ursem, N. T. (2012). The effects of homocysteine and folic acid on angiogenesis and VEGF expression during chicken vascular development. *Microvascular Research, 83*(2), 98–104.

Opitz, J. M., Smith, J. F., & Santoro, L. (2008). The FG Syndrome (Online Mendelian Inheritance in Man 305450): Perspective in 2008. *Advances in Pediatrics, 55*, 123–170.

Oslejsková, H. Dusek, L., Makovska, Z., Pejcochova, J., Autrata, R., & Slapak, I. (2008). Complicated relationship between autism with regression and epilepsy. *Neuroendocrinology Letters, 29*, 558–570.

Ozonoff, S., Williams, B. J., Rauch, A. M., & Opitz, J. O. (2000). Behavior phenotype of FG syndrome: Cognition, personality, and behavior in eleven affected boys. *American Journal of Medical Genetics, 97*, 112–118.

Ozonoff, S., Young, G. S., Belding, A., Hill, M., et al. (2015). The broader autism phenotype in infancy: When does it emerge? *Journal of the American Academy of Child & Adolescent Psychiatry, 53*, 398–407.

Ozonoff, S., Young, G. S., Carter, A., Messinger, D., et al. (2011). Recurrence risk for autism spectrum disorders: A baby siblings research consortium study. *Pediatrics, 128*, e448–e495.

Palop, J. J., & Mucke, L. (2009). Epilepsy and cognitive impairments in Alzheimer's disease. *Archives of Neurology, 66*, 435–440.

Paravar, T., & Lee, D. J. (2008). Thalidomide: Mechanisms of action. *International Reviews of Immunology, 27*(3), 111–135.

Park, S. Y., Kim, J. W., Kim, Y. M., Kim, J. M., et al. (2001). Frequencies of fetal chromosomal abnormalities at prenatal diagnosis: 10 years experiences in a single institution. *Journal of Korean Medical Science, 16*(3), 290–293.

Parr, J., & Le Couteur, A. S. (2013). Broader autism phenotype. *Encyclopedia of Autism Spectrum Disorders* (p. 478) New York, NY: Springer.

Paul, L. K., Van Lancker-Sidtis, D., Schieffer, B., Dietrich, R., & Brown, W. S. (2003). Communicative deficits in agenesis of the corpus callosum: Nonliteral language and affective prosody. *Brain and Language, 85*, 313–324.

Paula-Pérez, I. (2013). Differential diagnosis between obsessive compulsive disorder and restrictive and repetitive behavioural patterns, activities and interests in autism spectrum disorders. *Revista de Psiquiatría y Salud Mental, 6*, 178–186.

Pedersen, A. L., Pettygrover, S., Lu, Z., Andrews, J., et al. (2016). DSM criteria that best differentiate intellectual disability from autism spectrum disorder. *Child Psychiatry and Human Development, 48*, 537–545.

Pellegrino, L. (2013). Patterns in development and disability. In M. L. Batshaw, N. J. Roizen, & G. R. Lotrecchiano (Eds.), *Children with Disabilities* (7th edn). Baltimore, MD: Paul H. Brookes.

Phiel, C. J., Zhang, F., Huang, E. Y., Guenther, M. G., Lazar, M. A., & Klein, P. S. (2001). Histone deacetylase is a direct target of valproic acid, a potent anticonvulsant, mood stabilizer, and teratogen. *Journal of Biological Chemistry, 276*(39), 36734–36741.

Pinto, D., Pagnamenta, A. T., Klei, L., Anney, R., et al. (2010). Functional impact of global rare copy number variation in autism spectrum disorder. *Nature, 466*(7304), 368–372.

Piven, J., Chase, G. A., Landa, R., Wzorek, M., et al. (1991). Psychiatric disorders in the parents of autistic individuals. *Journal of the American Academy of Child and Adolescent Psychiatry, 30*, 471–478.

Piven, J., Palmer, P., Jacobi, D., Childress, D., & Arndt, S. (1997). Broader autism phenotype: Evidence from a family history study of multiple-incidence autism families. *American Journal of Psychiatry, 154*, 185–190.

Plomin, R., & Deary, I. J. (2015). Genetics and intelligence differences: Five special findings. *Molecular Psychiatry, 20*, 98–108.

Poduri, A., & Lowenstein, D. (2011). Epilepsy genetics: Past, present, and future. *Current Opinion in Genetic Development, 21*, 325–332.

Prabhakar, S., Noonan, J. P., Pääbo, S., & Rubin, E. M. (2006). Accelerated evolution of conserved noncoding sequences in humans. *Science, 314,* 786.

Prakash, Prabhu, L. V., Rai, R., Pai, M. M., et al. (2008). Teratogenic effects of the anticonvulsant gabapentin in mice. *Singapore Medical Journal, 49*(1), 47–53.

Puschel, A. W., & Betz, H. (1995). Neurexins are differentially expressed in the embryonic nervous system of mice. *Journal of Neuroscience, 15*(4), 2849–2856.

Rai, D., Lee, B. K., Dalman, C., Golding, J., Lewis, G., & Magnusson, C. (2013). Parental depression, maternal antidepressant use during pregnancy, and risk of autism spectrum disorders: Population based case-control study. *British Medical Journal, 346,* f2059.

Rai, D., Lewis, G., Lundberg, M., Araya, R., et al. (2012). Parental socioeconomic status and risk of offspring autism spectrum disorders in a Swedish population-based study. *Journal of the American Academy of Child & Adolescent Psychiatry, 51,* 467–476.

Rais-Bahrami, K., & Short, B. L. (2013). Premature and small-for-dates infants. In M. L. Batshaw, N. J. Roizen, & G. R. Lotrecchiano (Eds.), *Children with Disabilities* (7th edn, pp. 87–104). Baltimore, MD: Paul H. Brookes.

Rajagopalan, P., Jahanshad, N., Stein, J. L., Hua, X., et al. (2012). Common folate gene variant, *MTHFR* C677T, is associated with brain structure in two independent cohorts of people with mild cognitive impairment. *Neuroimage: Clinical, 1*(1), 179–187.

Rasalam, A. S., Hailey, H., Williams, J. H., Moore, S. J., et al. (2005). Characteristics of fetal anticonvulsant syndrome associated autistic disorder. *Developmental Medicine and Child Neurology, 47*(8), 551–555.

Reiter, R. J. (1996). Antioxidant actions of melatonin. *Advances in Pharmacology, 38,* 103–117.

Rhodes, G., Jeffrey, L., Taylor, L., & Ewing, L. (2013). Autistic traits are linked to reduced adaptive coding of face identity and selectively poorer face recognition in men but not women. *Neuropsychologia, 51,* 2702–2708.

Rimland, B. (1964). *Infantile Autism: The Syndrome and Its Implications for a Neural Theory of Behavior.* New York, NY: Appleton-Century-Crofts.

Rimland, B. (1978). Inside the mind of the autistic savant. *Psychology Today,* August, pp. 69–80.

Rimland, B. (1990). Rain Man and the savant's secrets. *Autism Research Review International, 2,* 3.

Rimland, B., & Hill, A. L. (1984). Idiot savants. In *Mental Retardation and Developmental Disabilities* (pp. 155–169). Springer: Boston.

Roberts, E. M., English, P. B., Grether, J. K., Windham, G. C., Somberg, L., & Wolff, C. (2007). Maternal residence near agricultural pesticide applications and autism spectrum disorders among children in the California central valley. *Environmental Health Perspectives, 115,* 1482–1489.

Robinson, E. B., Lichtenstein, P., Anckarsäter, H., Happé, F., & Ronald, A. (2013). Examining and interpreting the female protective effect against autistic behavior. *Proceedings of the National Academy of Sciences USA, 110,* 5258–5262.

Robinson, E. B., Samocha, K. E., Kosmicki, J. A., McGrath, L., et al. (2014). Autism spectrum disorder severity reflects the average contribution of de novo and familial influences. *Proceedings of the National Academy of Sciences, 111*, 15161–15165.

Robison, J. E. (2016). *Switched On: A Memoir of Brain Change and Emotional Awakening.* New York, NY: Spiegel & Grau.

Rodier, P. M., Ingram, J. L., Tisdale, B., Nelson, S., & Romano, J. (1996). Embryological origin for autism: Developmental anomalies of the cranial nerve motor nuclei. *Journal of Comparative Neurology, 370*, 247–261.

Roelfsema, M. T., Hoekstra, R. A., Allison, C., Wheelwright, S., et al. (2012). Are autism spectrum conditions more prevalent in an information-technology region? A school-based study of three regions in the Netherlands. *Journal of Autism and Developmental Disorders, 42*, 734–739.

Rogers, S. J. (2004). Developmental regression in autism spectrum disorders. *Mental Retardation and Developmental Disabilities Research Reviews, 10*(2), 139–143.

Rojas, D. C., Teale, P. D., Maharajh, K., Kronberg, E., et al. (2011). Transient and steady-state auditory gamma-band responses in first-degree relatives of people with autism spectrum disorder. *Molecular Autism, 2*, 11.

Rojko, J. L., & Price-Schiavi, S. (2008). Physiologic IgG biodistribution, transport, and clearance: Implications for monoclonal antibody products. In J. A. Cavagnaro (Ed.), *Preclinical Safety Evaluation of Biopharmaceuticals* (pp. 241–276). New York, NY: Wiley.

Ronald, A., Pennell, C. E., & Whitehouse, A. J. O. (2010). Prenatal maternal stress associated with ADHD and autistic traits in early childhood. *Frontiers in Psychology, 1*, 223.

Ross, L. E., Grigoriadis, S., Mamisashvili, L., VonderPorten, E. H., et al. (2013). Selected pregnancy and delivery outcomes after exposure to antidepressant medication: A systematic review and meta-analysis. *JAMA Psychiatry, 70*, 436–443.

Rossi, P. G., Posar, A., & Parmeggiani, A. (2000). Epilepsy in adolescents and young adults with autistic disorder. *Brain and Development, 22*, 102–106.

Roth, G., & Dicke, U. (2005). Evolution of the brain and intelligence. *Trends in Cognitive Sciences, 9*, 250–257.

Rubenstein, J. L. R., & Merzenich, M. M. (2003). Model of autism: Increased ratio of excitation/inhibition in key neural systems. *Genes, Brain and Behavior, 2*, 255–267.

Russell, G., Steer, C., & Golding, J. (2011). Social and demographic factors that influence the diagnosis of autistic spectrum disorders. *Social Psychiatry and Psychiatric Epidemiology, 46*, 1283–1293.

Rutter, M. (2000). Genetic studies of autism: From the 1970s into the millennium. *Journal of Abnormal Child Psychology, 28*, 3–14.

Ryan, L., Ehrlich, S., & Finnegan, L. (1987). Cocaine abuse in pregnancy: Effects on the fetus and newborn. *Neurotoxicology and Teratology, 9*(4), 295–299.

Ryan, N. P., Catroppa, C., Beare, R., Coleman, L., et al. (2015). Predictors of longitudinal outcome and recovery of pragmatic language and its relation to externalizing behaviour after pediatric traumatic brain injury. *Brain and Language, 142*, 86–95.

Safe, S. (2003). Cadmium's disguise dupes the estrogen receptor. *Nature Medicine, 9,* 1000–1001.

Sakai, T., Mikami, A., Tomonaga, M., Matsui, M., Suzuki, J., Hamada, Y., et al. (2011). Differential prefrontal white matter development in chimpanzees and humans. *Current Biology, 21,* 1397–1402.

Sakamoto, A., Moriuchi, H., Matsuzaki, J., Motoyama, K., & Moriuchi, M. (2015). Retrospective diagnosis of congenital cytomegalovirus infection in children with autism spectrum disorder but no other major neurologic deficit. *Brain and Development, 37*(2), 200–205.

Saks, E. R. (2007). *The Center Cannot Hold: My Journey through Madness.* Hachette Books: New York.

Salzano, S., Checconi, P., Hanschmann, E. M., Lillig, C. H., et al. (2014). Linkage of inflammation and oxidative stress via release of glutathionylated peroxiredoxin-2, which acts as a danger signal. *Proceedings of the National Academy of Sciences, 111,* 12157–12162.

Samoilova, E. B., Horton, J. L., Hilliard, B., Liu, T. S., & Chen, Y. (1998). IL-6-deficient mice are resistant to experimental autoimmune encephalomyelitis: Roles of IL-6 in the activation and differentiation of autoreactive T cells. *Journal of Immunology, 161,* 6480–6486.

Sanders, S. J., He, X., Willsey, A. J., Ercan-Sencicek, A. G., et al. (2015). Insights into autism spectrum disorder genomic architecture and biology from 71 risk loci. *Neuron, 87*(6), 1215–1233.

Sarazin, M., Pillon, B., Giannakopoulos, P., Rancurel, G., Samson, Y., & Dubois, B. (1998). Clinicometabolic dissociation of cognitive functions and social behavior in frontal lobe lesions. *Neurology, 51,* 142–148.

Sarnat, H. B., & Flores-Sarnat, L. (2015). Infantile tauopathies: Hemimegalencephaly; tuberous sclerosis complex; focal cortical dysplasia 2; gangiolglioma. *Brain and Development, 37,* 553–562.

Schmidt, G. L., Kimel, L. K., Winterrowd, E., Pennington, B. F., Hepburn S. L., & Rojas, D. C. (2008). Impairments in phonological processing and nonverbal intellectual function in parents of children with autism. *Journal of Clinical and Experimental Neuropsychology, 30,* 557–567.

Schmidt, R. J., Hansen, R. L., Hartiala, J., Allayee, H., et al. (2015). Selected vitamin D metabolic gene variants and risk for autism spectrum disorder in the CHARGE study. *Early Human Development, 91*(8), 483–489.

Schmidt, R. J., Tancredi, D. J., Krakowiak, P., Hansen, R. L., & Ozonoff, S. (2014). Maternal intake of supplemental iron and risk of autism spectrum disorder. *American Journal of Epidemiology, 180,* 890–900.

Schmidt, R. J., Tancredi, D. J., Ozonoff, S., Hansen, R. L., et al. (2012). Maternal periconceptional folic acid intake and risk of autism spectrum disorders and developmental delay in the CHARGE (CHildhood Autism Risks from Genetics and Environment) case-control study. *American Journal of Clinical Nutrition, 96*(1), 80–89.

Schneider, M., Debbané, M., Bassett, A. S., Chow, E. W., et al. (2014). Psychiatric disorders from childhood to adulthood in 22q11.2 deletion syndrome: Results from the International Consortium on Brain and Behavior in 22q11.2 Deletion Syndrome. *American Journal of Psychiatry, 171,* 627–639.

Schoenemann, P. T., Sheehan, M. J., & Glotzer, L. D. (2005). Prefrontal white matter volume is disproportionately larger in humans than in other primates. *Nature Neuroscience, 8*, 242–252.

Scholl, T. O., & Johnson, W. G. (2000). Folic acid: Influence on the outcome of pregnancy. *American Journal of Clinical Nutrition, 71*(5 Suppl), 1295S–1303S.

Scott, O., Richer, L., Forbes, K., Sonnenberg, L., et al. (2014). Anti-N-methyl-D-aspartate (NMDA) receptor encephalitis: an unusual cause of autistic regression in a toddler. *Journal of Child Neurology, 29*(5), 691–694.

Scott, O., Shi, D., Andriashek, D., Clark, B., & Goez, H. R. (2017). Clinical cues for autoimmunity and neuroinflammation in patients with autistic regression. *Developmental Medicine & Child Neurology, 59*, 947–951.

Seattle Children's Hospital Research Foundation. (2013). Autism and tic disorders. *The Autism Blog*, 23 September. Accessed on 22 May 2018 at http://theautismblog.seattlechildrens.org/autism-and-tic-disorders

Sebat, J., Lakshmi, B., Malhotra, D., Troge, J., et al. (2005). Strong association of de novo copy number mutations with autism. *Science, 316*(5823), 445–449.

Semendeferi, K., Armstrong, E., Schleicher, A., Zilles, K., & Van Hoesen, G. W. (2001). Prefrontal cortex in humans and apes: A comparative study of area 10. *American Journal of Physical Anthropology, 114*, 224–241.

Serdaroğlu, G., Alpman, A., Tosun, A., Pehlıvan, S., et al. (2009). Febrile seizures: Interleukin 1beta and interleukin-1 receptor antagonist polymorphisms. *Pediatric Neurology, 40*, 113–116.

Shackleton, D. P., Westendorp, R. G. J., Trenité, D. K. N., & Vandenbroucke, J. P. (1999). Mortality in patients with epilepsy: 40 years of follow up in a Dutch cohort study. *Journal of Neurology, Neurosurgery, & Psychiatry, 66*, 636–640.

Shashi, V., Muddasani, S., Santos, C. C., Berry, M. N., et al. (2004). Abnormalities of the corpus callosum in nonpsychotic children with chromosome 22q11 deletion syndrome. *Neuroimage, 21*, 1399–1406.

Shelton, J. F., Geraghty, E. M., Tancredi, D. J., Delwiche, L. D., et al. (2014). Neurodevelopmental disorders and prenatal residential proximity to agricultural pesticides: The CHARGE study. *Environmental Health Perspectives, 122*, 1103.

Shetreat-Klein, M., Shinnar, S., & Rapin, I. (2014). Abnormalities of joint mobility with autism spectrum disorders. *Brain Development, 36*, 91–96.

Shoffner, J., Hyams, L., Langley, G. N., Cossette, S., et al. (2010). Fever plus mitochondrial disease could be risk factors for autistic regression. *Journal of Child Neurology, 25*, 429–434.

Shorter, E. (2008). History of psychiatry. *Current Opinion in Psychiatry, 21*, 593.

Silberman, S. (2001). The geek syndrome. *WIRED*, 1 December 2001.

Simon, T. J., Ding, L., Bish, J. P., McDonald-McGinn, D. M., Zackai, E. H., & Gee, J. (2005). Volumetric, connective, and morphologic changes in the brains of children with chromosome 22q11.2 deletion syndrome: An integrative study. *Neuroimaging, 25*, 169–180.

Singer, H. S., Morris, C. M., Williams, P. N., Yoon, D. Y., Hong, J. J., & Zimmerman, A. W. (2006). Antibrain antibodies in children with autism and their unaffected siblings. *Journal of Neuroimmunology, 178*, 149–155.

Sisodiya, S. M., Fauser, S., Cross, J. H., & Thom, M. (2009). Focal cortical dysplasia type II: Biological features and clinical perspectives. *Lancet Neurology, 8*, 830–843.

Smalley, S. L. (1998). Autism and tuberous sclerosis. *Journal of Autism and Developmental Disorders, 28*, 407–414.

Smith, I. M., Nichols, S. L., Issekutz, K., & Blake, K. (2005). Behavioral profiles and symptoms of autism in CHARGE syndrome: Preliminary Canadian epidemiological data. *American Journal of Medical Genetics Part A, 133*, 248–256.

Snyder, A. (2004). Autism and creativity: Is there a link between autism and exceptional ability? [Book review]. *Nature, 428*, 470–471.

Sokhadze, E. M., Bartuh, J. M., Sears, L., Sokhadze, G. E., El-Baz, A. S., & Casanova, M. F. (2012). Prefrontal neuromodulation using rTMS improves error monitoring and correction function in autism. *Applied Psychophysiology and Biofeedback, 37*, 91–102.

Sokhadze, E. M., El-Baz, A. S., Baruth, J., Mathai, G., Sears, L., & Casanova, M. F. (2009). Effects of low frequency repetitive transcranial magnetic stimulation (rTMS) on gamma frequency oscillations and event-related potentials during processing of illusory figures in autism. *Journal of Autism and Developmental Disorders, 39*, 619–634.

Sokhadze, E. M., El-Baz, A. S., Sears, L. L., Opris, I., & Casanova, M. F. (2014a). rTMS neuromodulation improves electrocortical functional measures of information processing and behavioral responses in autism. *Frontiers in Systems Neuroscience, 8*, 134.

Sokhadze, E. M., El-Baz, A. S., Tasman, A., Sears, L. L., et al. (2014b). Neuromodulation integrating rTMS and neurofeedback for the treatment of autism spectrum disorder: An exploratory study. *Applied Psychophysiology and Biofeedback, 39*, 237–257.

Soorya, L., Kolevzon, A., Zweifach, J., Lim, T., et al. (2013). Prospective investigation of autism and genotype-phenotype correlations in 22q13 deletion syndrome and SHANK3 deficiency. *Molecular Autism, 4*(1), 18.

Soulières, I., Dawson, M., Gernsbacher, M. A., & Mottron, L. (2011). The level and nature of autistic intelligence II: What about Asperger syndrome? *PLoS One, 6*, e25372.

Soultanis, K. C., Payatakes, A. H., Chouliaras, V. T., Mandellos, G. C., et al. (2007). Rare causes of scoliosis and spine deformity: Experience and particular features. *Scoliosis, 2*, 15

Spence, S. J., & Schneider, M. T. (2009). The role of epilepsy and epileptiform EEGs in autism spectrum disorders. *Pediatric Research, 65*, 599–606.

Šponer, J., Burda, J. V., Sabat, M., Leszczynski, J., & Hobza, P. (1998). Interaction between the guanine- cytosine Watson-crick DNA base pair and hydrated Group IIa (Mg2+, Ca2+, Sr2+, Ba2+) and Group IIb (Zn2+, Cd2+, Hg2+) metal cations. *Journal of Physical Chemistry 1, 102*, 5951–5957.

Sporns, O., & Zwi, J. D. (2004). The small world of the cerebral cortex. *Neuroinformatics, 2*, 145–162.

Stafstrom, C. E. (2002). The incidence and prevalence of febrile seizures. In T. Z. Baram, & S. Shinnar (Eds.), *Febrile Seizures* (pp. 1–25). San Diego, CA: Academic Press.

Stahlberg, O., Soderstrom, H., Rastam, M., & Gillberg, C. (2004). Bipolar disorder, schizophrenia, and other psychotic disorders in adults with childhood onset AD/HD and/or autism spectrum disorders. *Journal of Neural Transmission, 111*, 891–902.

Stegmann, B. J., & Carey, J. C. (2002). TORCH infections. Toxoplasmosis, other (syphilis, varicella-zoster, parvovirus B19), rubella, cytomegalovirus (CMV), and herpes infections. *Current Women's Health Reports, 2*(4), 253–258.

Stevens, H. E., Su, T., Yanagawa, Y., & Vaccarino, F. M. (2013). Prenatal stress delays inhibitory neuron progenitor migration in the developing neocortex. *Psychoneuroendocrinology, 38*, 509–521.

Stiles, J. (2008). *The Fundamentals of Brain Development: Integrating Nature and Nurture.* Boston, MA: Harvard University Press.

Stouffer, M. A., Woods, C. A., Patel, J. C., Lee, C. R., et al. (2015). Insulin enhances striatal dopamine release by activating cholinergic interneurons and thereby signals reward. *Nature Communications, 6*, 8543.

Strauss, K. A., Puffenberger, E. G., Huentelman, M. J., Gottlieb, S., et al. (2006). Recessive symptomatic focal epilepsy and mutation contactin-associated protein-like 2. *New England Journal of Medicine, 354*(13), 1370–1377.

Strömland, K., Nordin, V., Miller, M., Akerström, B., & Gillberg, C. (1994). Autism in thalidomide embryopathy: A population study. *Developmental Medicine and Child Neurology, 36*(4), 351–356.

Stubbs, E. G. (1978). Autistic symptoms in a child with congenital cytomegalovirus infection. *Journal of Autism and Childhood Schizophrenia, 8*(1), 37–43.

Sucksmith, E., Roth, I., & Hoekstra, R. A. (2011). Autistic traits below the clinical threshold: Re-examining the broader autism phenotype in the 21st century. *Neuropsychology Review, 21*, 360–389.

Sugranyes, G., Kyriakopoulos, M., Corrigall, R., Taylor, E., & Frangou, S. (2011). Autism spectrum disorders and schizophrenia: Meta-analysis of the neural correlates of social cognition. *PLoS One, 6*, e25322.

Sujan, A. C., Rickert, M. E., Öberg, A. S., Quinn, P. D., et al. (2017). Associations of maternal antidepressant use during the first trimester of pregnancy with preterm birth, small for gestational age, autism spectrum disorders, and attention-deficit/ hyperactivity disorder in offspring. *Journal of the American Medical Association, 317*, 1553–1562.

Sullivan, L. H. (1896). The tall office building artistically considered. *Lippincott's Magazine*, March, pp. 403–409.

Sullivan, P. F., Magnusson, C., Reichenberg, A., Boman, M., et al. (2012). Family history of schizophrenia and bipolar disorder as risk factors for autism. *Archives of General Psychiatry, 69*, 1099–1103

Suskind, R. (2014). Reaching my autistic son through Disney. *The New York Times Magazine.* 7 March 2014. Accessed on 22 May 2018 at www.nytimes. com/2014/03/09/magazine/reaching-my-autistic-son-through-disney.html

Szatmari, P., Georgiades, S., Duku, E., Zwaigenbaum, L., & Goldberg, J. (2008). Alexithymia in parents of children with autism spectrum disorder. *Journal of Autism and Developmental Disorders, 38*, 1859–1865.

Taga, T., & Fukuda, S. (2005). Role of IL–6 in the neural stem cell differentiation. *Clinical Reviews in Allergy & Immunology, 28*, 249–256.

Takei, A., Mera, K., Sato, Y., & Haraoka, Y. (2011). High-functioning autistic disorder with Ehlers-Danlos syndrome. *Psychiatry and Clinical Neurosciences, 65*, 605–606.

Tallon-Baudry, C., & Bertrand, O. (1999). Oscillatory gamma activity in humans and its role in object representation. *Trends in Cognitive Sciences, 3*, 151–162.

Tammet, D. (2006). *Born on a Blue Day*. New York, NY: Free Press.

Tan, D. W., Gilani, S. Z., Maybery, M. T., Lian, A., et al. (2017). Hypermasculinized facial morphology in boys and girls with autism spectrum disorder and its association with symptomatology. *Scientific Reports, 7*, 9348.

Tan, G. M., Arnone, D., McIntosh, A. M., & Ebmeier, K. P. (2009). Meta-analysis of magnetic resonance imaging studies in chromosome 22q11.2 deletion syndrome (velocardiofacial syndrome). *Schizophrenia Research, 115*, 173–181.

Tarpley, R. J., & Ridgway, S. H. (1994). Corpus callosum size in delphinid cetaceans. *Brain, Behavior and Evolution, 44*, 156–165.

Taylor, L. J., Maybery, M. T., Wray, J., Ravine, D., Hunt, A., & Whitehouse, A. J. (2015). Are there differences in the behavioural phenotypes of autism spectrum disorder probands from simplex and multiplex families? *Research in Autism Spectrum Disorders, 11*, 56–62.

Temkin, O. (1945). *The Falling Sickness*. Baltimore, MD: Johns Hopkins University Press.

Temkin, S. (1994) *The Falling Sickness: A History of Epilepsy from the Greeks to the Beginnings of Modern Neurology* (Rev. edn). Johns Hopkins University Press: Baltimore, MD.

Thomas, C., Avidan, G., Humphreys, K., Jung, K. J., Gao, F., & Behrmann, M. (2009). Reduced structural connectivity in ventral visual cortex in congenital prosopagnosia. *Nature Neuroscience, 12*, 29–31.

Thomas, M. S., Davis, R., Karmiloff-Smith, A., Knowland, V. C., & Charman, T. (2016). The over-pruning hypothesis of autism. *Developmental Science, 19*, 284–305.

Thurm, A., Manwaring, S. S., Luckenbaugh, D. A., Lord, C., & Swedo, S. E. (2014). Patterns of skill attainment and loss in young children with autism. *Developmental Psychopathology, 26*(1), 203–214.

Tillonen, J. (2000). *Ethanol, Acetaldehyde and Gastrointestinal Flora: Regulatory Factors and Pathophysiological Consequences of Microbial Ethanol Oxidation and Acetaldehyde Production in the Digestive Tract*. Helsinki: University of Helsinki,.

Tomasello, M. (2009). *The Cultural Origins of Human Cognition*. Cambridge, MA: Harvard University Press.

Torrey, E. F. (2001). *Surviving Schizophrenia: A Manual for Families, Consumers, and Providers*. New York, NY: HarperPerennial.

Torrey, E. F., Miller, J., Rawlings, R., & Yolken, R. H. (1997). Seasonality of births in schizophrenia and bipolar disorder: A review of the literature. *Schizophrenia Research, 28*, 1–38.

Tran, P. V., Carlson, E. S., Fretham, S. J., & Georgieff, M. K. (2008). Early-life iron deficiency anemia alters neurotrophic factor expression and hippocampal neuron differentiation in male rats. *Journal of Nutrition, 138*, 2495–2501.

Treffert, D. A. (2004). Asperger's disorder and savant syndrome. *The New York Times*, 29 April.

Treffert, D. A. (2011). Hyperlexia III: Separating 'autistic-like' behaviors from autistic disorder: Assessing children who read early or speak late. *WMJ, 110*, 281–286.

Tuchman, R., Moshé, S. L., & Rapin, I. (2009). Convulsing toward the pathophysiology of autism. *Brain and Development, 31*, 95–103.

Turner, L. M., Stone, W. L., Pozdol, S. L., & Coonrod, E. E. (2006). Follow-up of children with autism spectrum disorders from age 2 to age 9. *Autism, 10*, 243–265.

U.S. Food and Drug Administration. (2011). *FDA drug safety communication: New warnings against use of terbutaline to treat preterm labor.* Accessed on 23 May 2018 at www.fda.gov/Drugs/DrugSafety/ucm243539.htm

Uban, K. A., Sliwowska, J. H., Lieblich, S., Ellis, L. A., et al. (2010). Prenatal alcohol exposure reduces the proportion of newly produced neurons and glia in the dentate gyrus of the hippocampus in female rats. *Hormones and Behavior, 58*(5), 835–843.

Uhari, M., Rantala, H., Vainionpää, L., & Kurttila, R. (1995). Effect of acetaminophen and of low intermittent doses of diazepam on prevention of recurrences of febrile seizures. *Journal of Pediatrics, 126*, 991–995.

Vajda, F. J., Graham, J. E., Hitchcock, A. A., O'Brien, T. J., Lander, C. M., & Eadie, M. J. (2010). Is lamotrigine a significant human teratogen? Observations from the Australian Pregnancy Register. *Seizure, 19*(9), 558–561.

Valente, K. D., Koiffmann, C. P., Fridman, C., Varella, M., et al. (2006). Epilepsy in patients with Angelman syndrome caused by deletion of the chromosome 15q11-q13. *Archives of Neurology, 63*(1), 122–128.

Vallières, L., Campbell, I. L., Gage, F. H., & Sawchenko, P. E. (2002). Reduced hippocampal neurogenesis in adult transgenic mice with chronic astrocytic production of interleurkin-6. *Journal of Neuroscience, 22*, 486–492.

Van der Jeugd, A., Hochgräfe, K., Ahmed, T., Decker, J. M., et al. (2012). Cognitive defects are reversible in inducible mice expressing pro-aggregant full-length human Tau. *Acta Neuropathologica, 123*, 787–805.

Van Meter, K. C., Christiansen, L. E., Delwiche, L. D., Azari, R., Carpenter, T. E., & Hertz-Picciotto, I. (2010). Geographic distribution of autism in California: A retrospective birth cohort. *Autism Research, 3*, 19–29.

Van Steensel, F. J., Bögels, S. M., & Perrin, S. (2011). Anxiety disorders in children and adolescents with autistic spectrum disorders: A meta-analysis. *Clinical Child and Family Psychology Review, 14*, 302–317.

Vauzelle, C., Beghin, D., Cournot, M.-P., & Elefant, E. (2013). Birth defects after exposure to misoprostol in the first trimester of pregnancy: Prospective follow-up study. *Reproductive Toxicology, 36*, 98–103.

Verity, C. M., Winstone, A., Stellitano, L., Krishnakumar, D., Will, R., & McFarland, R. (2009). The clinical presentation of mitochondrial diseases in children with progressive intellectual and neurological deterioration: A national, prospective, population-based study. *Developmental Medicine & Child Neurology, 52*, 434–440.

Vezzani, A., Maroso, M., Balosso, S., Sanchez, M. A., & Bartfai, T. (2011). IL-1 receptor/Toll-like receptor signaling in infection, inflammation, stress and neurodegeneration couples hyperexcitability and seizures. *Brain, Behavior, and Immunity, 25*(7), 1281–1289.

Vilidaite, G., Yu, M., & Baker, D. H. (2017). Internal noise estimates correlate with autistic traits. *Autism Research, 10*, 1384–1391.

Villemagne, P. M., Naidu, S., Villemagne, V. L., Yaster, M., et al. (2002). Brain glucose metabolism in Rett syndrome. *Pediatric Neurology, 27*, 117–122.

Vincent, A., & Crino, P. B. (2011). Systemic and neurologic autoimmune disorders associated with seizures or epilepsy. *Epilepsia, 52*, 12–17.

Volkmar, F. R., & Rutter, M. (1995). Childhood disintegrative disorder: Results of the DSM-IV autism field trial. *Journal of the American Academy of Child & Adolescent Psychiatry, 34*, 1092–1095.

Vorstman, J. A., Staal, W. G., van Daalen, E., van Engeland, H., Hochstenbach, P. F., & Franke, L. (2006). Identification of novel autism candidate regions through analysis of reported cytogenetic abnormalities associated with autism. *Molecular Psychiatry, 11*(1), 18–28.

Ward, P. (2006). *Out of Thin Air: Dinosaurs, Birds, and Earth's Ancient Atmosphere.* Washington, DC: National Academies Press.

Warren, R. P., Yonk, L. J., Burger, R. A., Cole, P., et al. (1990). Deficiency of suppressor-inducer (CD4+CD45RA+) T cells in autism. *Immunological Investigations, 19*, 245–251.

Waterhouse, L. (2013). *Rethinking Autism: Variation and Complexity.* San Diego, CA: Academic Press.

Watts, G. (2014). Lorna Wing. *The Lancet, 384*, 658.

Wegiel, J., Flory, M., Kaczmarski, W., Brown, W. T., et al. (2017). Partial agenesis and hypoplasia of the corpus callosum in idiopathic autism. *Journal of Neuropathology and Experimental Neurology, 7*, 225–237.

Wegiel, J., Kuchna, I., Nowicki, K., Imaki, H., et al. (2010). The neuropathology of autism: Defects of neurogenesis and neuronal migration, and dysplastic changes. *Acta Neuropathologica, 119*, 755–770.

Weissman, J. R., Kelley, R. I., Bauman, M. L., Cohen, B. H., et al. (2008). Mitochondrial disease in autism spectrum disorder patients: A cohort analysis. *PLoS One, 3*, e3815.

Werling, D. M., Parikshak, N. N., & Geschwind, D. H. (2016). Gene expression in human brain implicates sexually dimorphic pathways in autism spectrum disorders. *Nature Communications, 7*, 10717.

Werner, E., & Dawson, G. (2005). Validation of the phenomenon of autistic regression using home videotapes. *Archives of General Psychiatry, 62*, 889–895.

Whitehouse, A. J., Coon, H., Miller, J., Salisbury, B., & Bishop, D. V. (2010). Narrowing the broader autism phenotype: A study using the Communication Checklist – Adult Version (CC-A). *Autism, 14*, 559–574.

Williams, E. L., & Casanova, M. F. (2010). Autism and dyslexia: A spectrum of cognitive styles as defined by minicolumnar morphometry. *Medical Hypotheses, 74*, 59–62.

Willingham, E. (2014). Does regressive autism exist? *Forbes – Pharma & Healthcare*, 27 March 2014. Accessed 23 May 2018 at www.forbes.com/sites/emilywillingham/2014/03/27/does-regressive-autism-exist/#656fe5275520

Wills, S., Cabanlit, M., Bennett, J., Ashwood, P., Amaral, D., & Van De Water, J. (2007). Autoantibodies in autism spectrum disorders (ASD). *Annals of the New York Academy of Sciences, 1107*, 79–91.

Wilson, C. E., Freeman, P., Brock, J., Burton, A. M., & Palermo, R. (2010). Facial identity recognition in the broader autism phenotype. *PLoS One, 5*, e12876.

Wing, L. (1981). Asperger's syndrome: A clinical account. *Psychological Medicine, 11*, 115–129.

Wishart, T. M., Parson, S. H., & Gillingwater, T. H. (2006). Synaptic vulnerability in neurodegenerative disease. *Journal of Neuropathology & Experimental Neurology, 65*, 733–739.

Wolff, J. J., Gu, H., Gerig, G., Elison, J. T., et al. (2012). Differences in white matter fiber tract development present from 6 to 24 months in infants with autism. *American Journal of Psychiatry, 169*, 589–600.

Wolff, S., Narayan, S., & Moyes, B. (1988). Personality characteristics of parents of autistic children: A controlled study. *Journal of Child Psychology and Psychiatry, 29*, 143–153.

Wong, D., Maybery, M., Bishop, D. V. M., Maley, A., & Hallmayer, J. (2006). Profiles of executive function in parents and siblings of individuals with autism spectrum disorders. *Genes, Brain and Behavior, 5*, 561–576.

Woolfe, A., & Elgar, G. (2008). Organization of conserved elements near key developmental regulators in vertebrate genomes. *Advances in Genetics, 61*, 307–338.

WHO (World Health Organization). (2016). *Immunization, Vaccines and Biologicals: Rubella – the disease.* Accessed on 4 March 2016 at www.who.int/immunization/topics/rubella/en/index1.html

Worley, G., Crissman, B. G., Cadogan E., Milleson, C., Adkins, D. W., & Kishnani, P. S. (2015). Down syndrome disintegrative disorder: New-onset autistic regression, dementia, and insomnia in older children and adolescents with Down syndrome. *Journal of Child Neurology, 30*, 1147–1152.

Xu, G., Bowers, K., Liu, B., & Bao, W. (2015). Maternal diabetes and the risk of autism spectrum disorders in the offspring: A systematic review and meta-analysis. *Journal of Autism and Developmental Disorders, 44*, 766–775.

Xu, L. M., Li, J. R., Huang, Y., Zhao, M., Tang, X., & Wei, L. (2012). AutismKB: An evidence-based knowledgebase of autism genetics. *Nucleic Acids Research, 40*, D1016–D1022.

Yamashita, Y., Fujimoto, C., Nakajima, E., Isagai, T., & Matsuishi, T. (2003). Possible association between congenital cytomegalovirus infection and autistic disorder. *Journal of Autism and Developmental Disorders, 33*(4), 455–459.

Yan, G. M., Ni, B., Weller, M., Wood, K. A., & Paul, S. M. (1994). Depolarization or glutamate receptor activation blocks apoptotic cell death of cultured cerebellar granule neurons. *Brain Research, 656*, 43–51.

Yeh, C. C., Chen, T. L., Hu, C. J., Chiu, W. T., & Liao, C. C. (2013). Risk of epilepsy after traumatic brain injury: A retrospective population-based cohort study. *Journal of Neurology, Neurosurgery, and Psychiatry, 84*, 441–445.

Yirmiya, N., & Shaked, M. (2005). Psychiatric disorders in parents of children with autism: A meta-analysis. *Journal of Child Psychology and Psychiatry, 46*, 69–83.

Zaretsky, M., Alexander, J. M., Byrd, W., & Bawdon, R. E. (2004). Transfer of inflammatory cytokines across the placenta. *Obstetrics and Gynecology, 103*, 546–550.

Zeng, J., Konopka, G., Hunt, B. G., Preuss, T. M., Geschwind, D., & Yi, S. V. (2012). Divergent whole-genome methylation maps of human and chimpanzee brains reveal epigenetic basis of human regulatory evolution. *American Journal of Human Genetics, 91*, 455–465.

Zerbo, O., Leong, A., Barcellos, L., Bernal, P., Fireman, B., & Croen, L. A. (2015). Immune mediated conditions in autism spectrum disorders. *Brain, Behavior, and Immunity, 46*, 232–236.

Zhang, C., Milunsky, J. M., Newton, S., Ko, J., et al. (2009). A neuroligin-4 missense mutation associated with autism impairs neuroligin-4 folding and endoplasmic reticulum export. *Journal of Neuroscience, 29*(35), 10843–10854.

Zinkstok, J., & Amelsvoort, T. V. (2005). Neuropsychological profile and neuroimaging in patients with 22q11.2 deletion syndrome: A review. *Child Neuropsychology, 11*, 21–37.

Zoghbi, H. Y. (2003). Postnatal neurodevelopmental disorders: Meeting at the synapse? *Science, 302*(5646), 826–830.

Zwaigenbaum, P., Szatmari, P., Mahoney, W., Bryson, S., Bartolucci, G., & MacLean, J. (2000). Case report: High functioning autism and childhood disintegrative disorder in half brothers. *Journal of Autism and Developmental Disorders, 30*, 121–126.

Subject Index

Author Index